Reflective Practice in ⌐⌐

⌐URN

Reflective Practice in Educational Research
Developing Advanced Skills

Linda Evans

continuum
NEW YORK · LONDON

Continuum
The Tower Building
11 York Road
London SE1 7NX

370 Lexington Avenue
New York
NY 10017-6503

www.continuumbooks.com

First published 2002

British Library Cataloguing-in-Publication Data
A catalogue record for this book is available from the British Library.

ISBN 0-8264-5364-3 (hardback)
    0-8264-5363-5 (paperback)

Typeset by BookEns Ltd., Royston, Herts
Printed and bound in Great Britain by Biddles Ltd, Guildford and King's Lynn

Contents

List of tables

List of figures

Preface

Educational research has taken a knock in recent years. Its credibility has been undermined by criticism from several quarters; most notably in the UK from Professor David Hargreaves and from two reports with which everyone in the British educational research community will be all too familiar: the Hillage (Hillage *et al.*, 1998) and Tooley Reports (Tooley with Darby, 1998). Our American educational research colleagues, too, have been subjected to similar criticism. The message conveyed is clear enough: educational research is failing to come up to scratch.

When I first heard of the Hillage and Tooley Reports I recall being unsurprised at what were reported in the media as the key criticisms. I was not alone in responding in this way; colleagues shared my view that, for the most part, what were highlighted as the deficiencies, or weaknesses, or – to use the terminology of the Tooley Report (Tooley with Darby, 1998) – 'worrying tendencies' were, indeed, evident or even prevalent in educational research. When I later read the Reports I found myself nodding in concurrence as I turned the pages. The picture being presented rang true. On the whole, this criticism seemed justified.

This book is, in part, a response to the criticism. As I developed as an educational researcher I became increasingly aware of a general lack of rigour in much of the work with which I came into contact. It seemed that, whereas I was constantly striving to increase my competence and enhance my research skills, others working in the specific fields in which I was engaged were unaware of, or unconcerned to tackle, the problems and difficulties that, I felt, undermined rigour. I do not, by any means, claim to have reached standards of excellence; merely to have developed – to have improved. There were, of course, many researchers who – like me – clearly *did* adopt a developmental attitude to their work and many, too, whose work reflected the highest standards of excellence. But there seemed to be more for whom this was not the case. I was sent their research bids and their submitted articles to referee; I read their published work; I heard their conference paper presentations.

As I developed as an educational researcher I passed on to students the benefit of my knowledge and skills. In research methods courses I raised awareness of specific methodological problems and weaknesses and introduced my ideas for increasing rigour and developing analytical capacity, passing on techniques and tips based on what had worked for me. Student feedback was very positive. Not only did it seem that some of the ideas that I was passing on were unavailable elsewhere and went beyond the content of standard research methods manuals or textbooks, but I also appeared to be stretching students intellectually; one comment passed on to me at the end of a session, 'That's the hardest I've worked with my brain for a long time', was echoed by those who overheard it. This book is, in part, also a response to that feedback. Before long, students started asking me if I had written up my teaching material as a book, and eventually I decided that perhaps I ought to do so.

What this book offers is a collection of ideas and guidelines for developing more advanced skills in relation to specific selected qualitative research issues and, alongside these, discussion of these issues. 'Advanced', of course, is a relative term, and, using my teaching experience as a basis for my judgement, I apply it here to refer to skills that research students and, indeed, some academics often find difficult and challenging. This is not a comprehensive manual of advanced qualitative research skills; many important research themes and issues are omitted. I have confined myself to tackling only some of those issues in relation to which I feel I have something useful to say that others may find helpful. The ideas and guidelines that I pass on are based on successful teaching material – though it is not always easy to present as written material the kinds of activities that work well in interactive teaching and learning exchanges, and in some cases I feel that something has inevitably been lost in the translation.

This book is a guide to developing as an educational researcher. It is written for those who have been introduced to basic research methods and wish to extend their repertoire of skills and increase their knowledge, competence and expertise. The weaknesses of educational research that were exposed in the Tooley and Hillage

Reports reflect, I believe, a prevalent attitude within the educational research community that once one has learned the basic research skills one is then fully qualified and need learn nothing more. Part I of the book, 'The Need for Improvement', contains two chapters that examine the problems within educational research and the rationale for making improvements. Part II, 'Developing Advanced Research Skills', focuses on ways of making such improvements. It contains eight chapters that examine specific qualitative research issues and, in relation to each, present ideas and guidelines for developing skills. *Reflective Practice in Educational Research* reflects my concern that there is a real need to raise standards within educational research. The book represents a small contribution towards doing so.

Part I
THE NEED FOR IMPROVEMENT

—1—

Developing as an educational researcher

When I was a schoolteacher, some years ago, I became aware of a distinction among my colleagues. There were those who taught in certain ways because they had always taught in those ways and these seemed to work; and those whose practice was underpinned by a sound, incisive rationale. In a sense, these categories could be very loosely identified as the intuitive, experientially driven teachers, and the reflective, investigative and developmental teachers. They are, to a limited extent, illustrated through the comments – made during research interviews – of two primary school teachers who were each addressing the issue of coping with pupils' different ability levels and who articulated in characteristically distinct ways their quite different views on the subject. Firstly I present Amanda's[1] comments:

> I can tell you where anybody in my class is on a book ... But, I feel I *have* to be doing that because, otherwise, you can't have children working individually ... you've no *choice*, I don't think. You know ... to be effective you've *got* to meet individual needs – to meet individual needs you've got to be on-the-ball yourself and you've got to have a system which is so good ... er ... you know ... the sequence of how you're going to do things ... which schemes you're going to use for which particular needs, and so on ... And, also, not only is it a lot of work, but it means that you, yourself, have to keep very *au fait* with what's available, and, when something new is introduced into the school you've got to be able to appraise *that* and your supplementary material in the light of what's going to be mainstream ... So, I suppose, in a way, a lot of my satisfaction is

---

[1] Pseudonyms are used in all references to research samples.

not coming directly from teacher–child contact ... it's coming from, I suppose, in *my* way, being as organised as I can ... being as aware of what's available as I can ... reading as much as I can ... and finding out as much as I can about how to meet individual needs *for* children, and putting a lot of time and effort into organising my teaching activity to accommodate what I know is appropriate for those children ... (Amanda, Rockville County Primary School)

Contrasting sharply with Amanda's reasoned and considered views were the comments of her colleague, Joanne:

I think, in *our* school, in *our* particular situation, streaming works. And I think it ... it's the best solution to our problem ... because ... I mean, I've taught under both – I did it when we had non-streaming – and when you had non-streaming it was ... *extremely* difficult to deal with ... It was *awful*. (Joanne, Rockville County Primary School)

Of course, portraying teachers in this dichotomized way is inaccurate. The crude categorization that I apply is intended to convey only a general impression of the disparity that pervades the profession. Teachers do not fall into either of two categories; rather, they occupy a place somewhere along a continuum whose extremes are represented by the broad categories I identify above, and between which the profession is variously scattered.

What I am referring to, essentially, is a range of developmentalism that has given rise to descriptive labels, such as the 'extended professional', the 'restricted professional' (Hoyle, 1975), the 'reflective teacher' (Pollard and Tann, 1993), the 'teacher leader' (Rosenholtz, 1991), the 'enquiring teacher' (Nias and Groundwater-Smith, 1988) and the 'intuitive professional' (Atkinson and Claxton, 2000; Eraut, 2000), which convey the notion that the profession is heterogeneous in relation to professional-related epistemology, ideologies, values, attitudes, expectations and perceptions of roles and responsibilities. On a day-to-day level, this heterogeneity is parodied by images and caricatures portrayed in unambiguous, blunt terminology – by teachers described as 'on-the-ball', 'dynamic', 'a high flier', or as 'dead wood', 'a dinosaur', 'going nowhere'. Most recently, this disparity has been given official government recognition in the UK; the introduction in 2000 of a performance-related pay scheme to reward teachers who are able to demonstrate advanced skills (DfEE, 1998, para. 65; DfEE, 2000a; DfEE, 2000b;

Evans, 2001a) implies acceptance of a distinction on the basis of professional development level.

Educational researchers have always been quick to uncover and to draw attention to the differentiated nature of teacher development. Indeed, it was they who both coined the descriptive labels, presented above, and introduced the distinctive terminology that has become assimilated into the language of fields of study like teachers' lives and careers, schools and schooling, and professionalism and professionalization. It is they who, over the years, have highlighted the shortcomings of intransigent attitudes to professional development and the impact that these have on school effectiveness and school improvement, and on professional standards and status (Darling-Hammond, 1994; Day, 1999; Fullan, 1991; Fullan and Hargreaves, 1992; Hargreaves and Fullan, 1998; Mortimore *et al.*, 1986). It is they who have given great prominence to teacher development; they who established teacher development as a distinct field of study; they who emphasize its importance:

> Continuing, career-long professional development is necessary for all teachers in order to keep pace with change and review and renew their own knowledge, skills and vision for good teaching ... Successful school development is dependent upon successful teacher development ... Professional development, then, is a serious business. (Day, 1999, p. 2)

So serious a business to educational researchers is teacher development that it is enshrined as the basis of what several of them identify as in some cases an actual, and in other cases a prescribed, 'new professionalism' (Day, 1999; Hargreaves, 1994; Hargreaves and Fullan, 1998; Helsby, 1999; Robertson, 1996; Sachs, 1997), which, in some cases, is given a more specific identity, such as Whitty's (2001, p. 169) 'democratic professionalism'. Within the 'new professionalism' teachers are proactive rather than reactive in relation to change and innovation, taking control of the development of the profession and striving to move it forwards on their own terms and towards their own standards. Indeed, Hammersley (2000, p. 401) argues that one of today's most important educational issues is that of whether teachers are being de-professionalized or whether a new professionalism is evolving.

Yet, ironically, whilst they are so vociferous about, and manifestly keen to contribute to, the development of a profession to which most of them do not belong, when it comes to a consideration of their own profession, educational researchers generally seem less inclined towards their own development. Whilst there are certainly notable exceptions – including many of those researchers to whom I refer above – development within the educational research profession is surprisingly thin on the ground.

I expand on this observation later, having introduced it here simply to set the scene for the chapter, but it is the issue of developmentalism within educational research as an activity and as a profession that is the focus of this chapter. The chapter examines the issues related to, and presents a rationale for promoting, reflective practice and for developing advanced skills in educational research, which are the foci of this book. The first issue to examine – since I have claimed it is in short supply – is what I mean by 'development' in the context of the educational research profession.

EDUCATIONAL RESEARCHER DEVELOPMENT

When I refer to development in the context of the educational research profession I mean the professional development of educational researchers, or, put another way, educational researcher development. To explain precisely what I mean by this I draw upon what I consider to be a parallel concept: teacher development.

The disparity within the teaching profession, to which I refer at the beginning of this chapter, between reflective, 'on-the-ball', inquiring teachers and those who operate at a more intuitive, unquestioning level was highlighted in the 1970s by Eric Hoyle. In much of my work I have been influenced by Hoyle's (1975) identification of two distinct aspects of teachers' professional lives: professionalism and professionality. Hoyle does not offer stipulative definintions of these two terms, but he explains his distinction as being between status-related elements of teachers' work, which he categorizes as professionalism, and those elements of the job that constitute the knowledge, skills and procedures that teachers use in their work, and which he categorizes as professionality. Outside the community of academics whose work is in the field of teachers' professionalism and professional lives, professionality is neither a widely used nor a widely known term. It seldom appears in the work of authors from outside the UK and, even within the UK, I am frequently asked by fellow academics and teachers to explain the term and its distinction from professionalism. After extensive consideration and analysis, I have defined it as *an ideologically, attitudinally, intellectually and epistemologically based stance on the part of an individual, in relation to the practice of the profession to which s/he belongs, and which influences her/his professional practice.*

Hoyle formulated two models of teacher professionality: 'For the sake of discussion we can hypothesize two models of professionality: *restricted* and *extended*' (Hoyle, 1975, p. 318). The characteristics used to illustrate these two hypothetical models created what may effectively be seen as a continuum with, at one end, a model of the 'restricted' professional who is essentially reliant upon experience and intuition and is guided by a narrow, classroom-based perspective which values that which is related to the day-to-day practicalities of teaching. The characteristics of the model of 'extended' professionality, at the other end of the continuum, reflect a much wider vision of what education involves, valuing of the theory underpinning pedagogy, and the adoption of a generally intellectual and rationally based approach to the job. I use the term *professionality orientation* to refer to individuals' location on the 'extended–restricted' continuum.

It is easy to see how Hoyle's continuum matches the perception of disparity amongst teachers to which I refer. My perception is research based, since my own work and that of others (Evans, 1997a, 1998; Nias, 1985, 1989; Robertson, 1996; Sachs, 1999; Talbert and McLaughlin, 1996) has revealed professionality-related disparity amongst teachers, even though the terms 'restricted' and 'extended' professionals are not necessarily applied. It is also experientially based. When I first became a primary school teacher in the 1970s I was very much what Hoyle (1975) identifies as a 'restricted' professional. I was conscientious and hard-working, thoroughly enjoyed my work and had a high level of commitment to it. I was generally considered by colleagues to be an extremely competent practitioner, but, being a 'restricted' professional, I operated mainly at an intuitive level, with very little rationality underpinning my work. I lacked vision and an interest in developing my practice. I considered educational theory to be entirely irrelevant to classroom practice. I attended in-service courses – but only those of a practical nature – and I was not in the least bit interested in undertaking long, award-bearing courses, even though I had left college with only a teacher's certificate.

Fifteen years later I left teaching to become an academic. In the interim I had acquired, through part-time study, an advanced diploma in mathematical education, a BEd (Hons) degree, and a MA in education, and I was later to go on to attain a doctorate. In my final teaching post my practice had become so innovative that teachers from neighbouring schools came to see my classroom and watch me working (Evans, 1991; 1992a). I chose to become an academic so that I could continue, as part of my job, to do what I had enjoyed so much on my degree courses – research.

What, precisely, I had developed during the fifteen years that spanned my teaching career includes an increased capacity for reflection; a questioning approach to my own practice and the policy-making and decision-making within my school; a concern to underpin my teaching with rationality; an experimental, innovative approach to classroom organization and lesson planning and delivery; a new set of values and ideologies that embraced issues related to social justice; a broader vision and more enlightened outlook on educational and wider social issues. I had, gradually and imperceptibly, transposed myself from one end of Hoyle's (1975) professionality continuum to the other. I had travelled far.

My own story, then, is clearly one of professional development on an individual level – a story of teacher development. But the point is, stories like mine do not just happen to teachers; they can happen to anyone. Every profession, I believe, has its own professionality continuum, though I accept that, because of the nature of some professions, the expanse between the two extremes may be narrower than that in other professions. Educational researching – the name I give to the profession of doing educational research, to distinguish it from educational research as an activity and a product – has its 'extended' and its 'restricted' professionals. There are those who, as researchers, are considerably more developed than others.

Of course, the notion of educational researching being a profession is not universally accepted, as McIntyre (1997) points out. Indeed, he asks: 'To what extent … do we see ourselves as professional educational researchers …?' and poses the question: how helpful and how necessary is it 'for at least some of us to see ourselves' as such (p. 127) He evidently believes – as I do – that it is both helpful and necessary: 'to be a good educational researcher one needs extensive knowledge, wide-ranging expertise and creative intelligence, to an extent that is only likely to be achievable through the kind of disciplined commitment that is described as professionalism' (p. 129). He goes on to identify the features of what he refers to as the 'profession of educational research' (p. 133):

> For Lawrence Stenhouse educational research, as the above quotation [Stenhouse, in Rudduck and Hopkins] indicates, was

'systematic enquiry ... to provide a theory of educational practice ... made public'. For me, these are the key concepts in relation to *professional* educational research: the conduct and claims of the research need to be open to public scrutiny and criticism; the enquiry must be systematic, with all the complex requirements that that entails; the purpose must be to improve our theoretical understanding; and it should usefully inform the development of educational practice.

I share this view of educational research as a profession; that is, I believe this is the level of professionalism, or, perhaps, more accurately — after Hoyle (1975) — professionality, to which educational researchers should aspire and for which they should aim. Yet I believe many have neither reached this level nor aspire to do so.

My career as an educational researcher has followed the same path as my earlier teaching career. When I first started researching I kept to tried-and-trusted methodologies which I applied unvaryingly and unquestioningly from project to project. They were, I believed, methodologically sound and effective, so I saw no reason to deviate from them. The same basic pattern was regurgitated again and again and, since I had received excellent training in research methodology and had successfully applied this to real research, I considered myself a fully fledged educational researcher who knew more or less all that I needed to know in order to conduct the kind of research that I wanted to conduct. If anyone had asked me why I did the specific things that I did I would probably have replied that this was the correct and accepted way of doing them — the 'textbook' method. I was a 'restricted' educational researcher. My attitude probably reflected the 'taken-for-granted notions of researching' against which Loughran (1999, p. 5) warns us.

I do not, however, think I was unusual. Indeed, as a 'restricted' educational researcher, I believe I represented the norm. From my own experience of having worked for well over ten years as a member of the educational research community, of having interacted with other researchers and having read countless research papers, I suggest that the majority of researchers reflect the 'taken-for-granted' notion of research; incorporated within which is the assumption, against which Hammersley (1993, p. 6) warns, that 'research can answer any and all questions that we might wish to have answered'. It is very difficult to substantiate my suggestion that this is the case, since evidence of its being so is elusive. Researchers, like their teacher counterparts, are unlikely to identify themselves as 'restricted' professionals, either because they are unaware of, or because they do not wish to admit to, being so, and I have no research-based evidence of the professionality range amongst educational researchers. As McIntyre (1997, p. 129) points out: 'Much of our debate about what educational research in Britain is like, and what is or is not wrong with it, is conducted on the basis of very limited and inadequate information ... We have ... little information about educational researchers.' Yet I am evidently not alone in believing that a great many fall into what I have identified as the 'restricted' professional category. Pratt and Swann (1999, p. 10), for example, attribute the 'crisis of method in educational research' to 'many researchers', and, by implication, Pring's (2000b, p. 5) complaint that there is 'much so-called research of poor quality' leads to the conclusion that there are many researchers who carry out this inferior work. McIntyre (1997, p. 129) evidently believes there are many researchers who fail to comprehend the nature and the demands of good educational research:

> One thing I know from several decades of experience is that I find it very difficult to do educational research well. It requires rigorous thinking, perceptiveness, imagination, self-awareness, social skills and self-discipline in such demanding combinations that I am usually disappointed with the quality of my own work. To judge from the many papers that I have to referee for research journals, other researchers find it difficult to do well, and many seem to lack an understanding of the diverse basic disciplines required.

And Hammersley (1993, p. 6) writes of his own 'increasing preoccupation with methodological issues' from the perspective of one who considers himself to be identified by others as deviant:

> Common responses on the part of fellow ethnographers have been that I am applying too stringent standards (methodological perfectionism or purism) and/or the wrong standards (those of the quantitative paradigm and not those of ethnography). Others have questioned the relevance of methodology, suggesting that I am giving undue emphasis to it. For them, ethnography is a practical activity in relation to which theoretical, methodological or philosophical considerations have only rather limited significance. That this idea has been

widespread amongst ethnographers is indicated by the fact that until quite recently most anthropologists were distinctly reluctant to engage in explicitly methodological discussion, preferring to operate on the basis of apprenticeship and learning by doing.

Elsewhere, Hammersley (1998, p. 144) refers again to the preponderance of an over-simplistic epistemological view within the educational research community. He identifies 'an empiricism which continues to inform the thinking of many researchers, whereby knowledge is "found" in the field rather than produced through the collective work of research communities'.

As I did in my teaching career, though, I moved on as an educational researcher. I developed. I travelled far – and I still have far to go. In my conceptual and ontological examination of it, I have defined teacher development as *the process whereby teachers' professionality and/or professionalism may be considered to be enhanced* (Evans, 2002, p. 131). I apply the same definition to educational researcher development – with the obvious replacement of the word 'teachers' with 'educational researchers'. My 'moving on', then, as a researcher – my development – has been the process that has advanced me along the professionality continuum that relates to the educational research profession: the process that has transformed me from a 'restricted' into an 'extended' educational researcher. Explaining what that process involves, and, therefore, explaining my interpretation of educational researcher development, is dependent upon clarifying what I mean by 'restricted' and 'extended' professionality in relation to educational researching.

I have already given some indication of what I include as characteristics of the 'restricted' educational researcher in my description of my own 'restricted' professionality. The 'restricted' educational researcher, as I interpret the term, parallels the 'restricted' teacher in many respects, and the point is that teachers who may be categorized as 'restricted' professionals are by no means necessarily 'bad' or 'ineffective' practitioners. They typically lack vision – or, more precisely, their vision is narrow – they are generally accepting, rather than critical, of their own practice, which results in their often resisting change and innovation; they are uninterested in intellectualizing about their practice, and they are, for the most part, unconcerned about wider educational and social issues that lie outside the sphere of their own, classroom-bound perspectives and experience. Yet, despite this, they may often be — though some of them are not — very conscientious, caring, hard-working, committed, efficient in their organization and delivery of learning activities, meticulous in their planning, and successful in meeting targets and achieving learning objectives with their students. Joanne, the teacher whose comments I present earlier in this chapter, epitomizes my interpretation of a rather extreme example of a 'restricted' professional. She was respected for her competence as a teacher and was well organized, hard-working, conscientious and methodical. Yet — and it is this that really distinguished her as a 'restricted' professional — she was very rarely able to provide an incisive rationale for her behaviour and decision-making. When asked for her reasons for doing something she would typically reply that she, or the school, had 'always done it that way, and it seems to work'. Her practice was intuitively based, her thinking seemed rather shallow and simplistic, she did not appear to be innovative, experimental or intellectually curious, and she was out of her depth in many of the discussions of policy and educational issues in which Amanda (whose comments I present as a contrast to Joanne's) and some of her colleagues engaged. Nevertheless, as a teacher, Joanne 'delivered'.

So it is, I believe, with educational researchers whom I categorize as 'restricted' professionals. They may be very competent researchers whose knowledge of 'textbook' methodology is comprehensive. They may be effective at delivering what is generally considered high-quality research. They may be reflective, analytical and meticulously thorough in their execution of their studies, and they may yield findings that are informative and perhaps even transformational. They may make important contributions to theory. They may even, perhaps, be regarded as leading experts in their field of study and — because they deliver effectively — top-class researchers. They may be all this and still be 'restricted' professionals in relation to educational research, and the explanation for how this could occur is that these researchers would apply their intellect to substantive, rather than methodological, development of their work.

By the same token — although I have not presented this as an illustrative scenario — it is possible to be both a 'restricted' professional and an incompetent practitioner in relation to research. Nevertheless, the less extreme example of someone who is, by conventional standards, a competent researcher but who — for whatever reason — does not question, analyse or develop the research process that s/he habitually applies, is real and, I suggest, prevalent. Underlying this prevalence of what I categorize as 'restricted' professionality in educational research is an attitude identified by Hammersley (1998, pp. 144–5):

> an important distinction is often ignored between standards that are difficult, or even impossible, to satisfy, but which may be necessary; and standards that are more demanding than they need to be for us to establish the validity of conclusions with reasonable confidence. While methodological ideals should certainly be tempered with practical realism, we must not simply give in to expediency, treating what we currently do as all that can be done or as automatically satisfactory.

Of course, as I have already emphasized in relation to teachers, it is entirely inaccurate to present an image of the educational research profession as dichotomized between two extremes that may be identified as 'restricted' and 'extended' professionality. Since it is a continuum that bridges them, rather than a boundary line that divides them, there are degrees of either, and most researchers will lie somewhere between, rather than at one of, the two extremes. I have used the extreme of 'restricted' professionality simply to illustrate the issue upon which this chapter – and, indeed, the whole book – focuses. For the same purpose, and by the same token, let us now take a look at what the 'extended' researcher might look like.

Once again, it may be useful to start by examining characteristics of the 'extended' professional teacher. Elsewhere (Evans, 1998, pp. 74–84) I present profiles of three teachers amongst my research sample whom, to varying degrees, I categorize as 'extended' professionals. The most extreme example of 'extended' professionality was found in Amanda, whose comments I present at the beginning of this chapter, and whose 'extended' professionality characteristics were referred to by several of her colleagues during research interviews:

> She's everything that a teacher *should* be ... Amanda questions development and the intellectual side of things ... would consider content, children's needs, suitable assessment. (Hilary)

Their 'extended' professionality was also evident in comments made by the three 'extended' professional teachers themselves during research interviews:

> I believe passionately in ... good education, and having sound aims and objectives ... and, you know, having purpose to what

you're doing ... I don't mean to sound big-headed, but I do look for the rationale behind things and I do look at the theory and the philosophy. I like to read reports and documents. (Mark)

Every so often I get bored ... mentally, and I need to take on the next challenge — the next intellectual challenge. And it's important to me ... er ... my intelligence is important ... I do need some kind of intellectual stimulus, and so, having done my Open University degree ... the next thing was my MA. (Helen)

As the term itself implies, 'extended' professionality involves characteristics and qualities which exceed the norm. There is therefore a distinctiveness about teachers who are 'extended' professionals which allows them to be singled out either from their colleagues in school or from the rest of the profession. 'Extended' professionals stand out from the crowd.

Amanda consistently applied such a high level of reflection and analysis to all aspects of her work, and her apparent perspective on, and concept of, education was so incisive, that she was distinct even from other teachers whose professionality orientation veered towards the 'extended' extreme. She saw teaching as a career which incorporated continued personal and professional development, underpinned by constant self-appraisal and self-improvement. She examined processes and questioned the bases of conventional practices that other, more 'restricted', colleagues were keen to preserve because they had become custom within the school.

It is the examining of processes and questioning of the bases of established practice that also characterizes the 'extended' professional educational researcher. The 'extended' professional researcher is reflective and analytical, not just about the topic of her/his research, but about the research itself. S/he adopts a developmental approach to research, seeing her/himself as a professional who is constantly striving to improve her/his practice and who therefore is continually scrutinizing it for inadequacies and weaknesses which may be reduced or removed. S/he seeks to increase and extend her/his research knowledge and skills by keeping abreast of developments in methodology, or by contributing his/her own ideas for methodological development. At the very least, the 'extended' professional researcher is a career-long learner: someone who develops advanced research skills; at best, s/he is this and, in addition, a pioneer and innovator: a 'methodological scholar', who makes a significant contribution towards moving educational research forward. In the latter case, s/he is probably identified within the educational research community as a 'methodologist' and will have written books and papers on the subject of methodology and methodological development. Such a person is what I refer to as an 'analytical researcher', but I emphasize that the word 'analytical' applies to the treatment of the research process itself and is not confined to the treatment of research findings.

What I mean by 'educational researcher development', then, is the process whereby researchers become analytical researchers: the process whereby they move towards the 'extended' end of the professionality continuum. As I imply in my description of an analytical researcher, that process predominantly involves adopting an approach to undertaking research that has variously been described as 'reflective' (Alvesson and Sköldberg, 2000; Schön, 1995) or 'reflexive' (Luttrell, 2000).

REFLECTIVE PRACTICE IN EDUCATIONAL RESEARCH

Reflective practice, as I interpret it, is an approach that leads to the development of advanced research skills, the purpose of which is to undertake more effective research. Borrowing once again from my analysis of teacher development (Evans, 2002) and modifying the terminology to make it applicable to researchers, I identify two constituent elements of educational researcher development: attitudinal development, which I define as *the process whereby researchers' attitudes to their work are modified*, and functional development, which I define as *the process whereby individuals' research practice may be considered to be improved*. Both of these definitions are encompassed within my definition of researcher development, presented above. The 'reflective', or 'reflexive' approach to undertaking research has the potential to incorporate both attitudinal and functional development.

Strauss and Corbin (1990, p. 18) identify basic qualitative research skills: 'The requisite skills for doing qualitative research ... are these: to step back and critically analyze situations, to recognize and avoid bias, to obtain valid and reliable data, and to think abstractly.' Reflective practice in educational research goes beyond these basics in several different ways. It involves the creativity to which Bogdan and Taylor (1975, p. 101) refer: 'research is a craft. To be a successful researcher is to be something more than a technician. You must create technique rather than slavishly follow procedures.' To Hammersley (1993; 1998), reflective practice involves the quest for methodological perfection through a relentless struggle to eradicate what are identified as deficiencies and inadequacies in the research process – a quest that has identified him as a methodological purist.

With its flexible, compromising, 'good enough' yardstick of acceptability that she applies to measuring the success of methodology, Luttrell's (2000, p. 500) interpretation of 'researcher reflexivity' contrasts with Hammersley's pursuit of the 'holy grail' of methodological perfection:

> I want to make a case for what I call 'good enough' methods, whereby researchers view their fieldwork as a series of ongoing realizations that lead to complex choices and decisionmaking. By 'good enough' I mean thinking about research decisions in terms of what is lost and what is gained, rather than what might be ideal. Accounting for these good enough decisions is, in my view, the nitty-gritty of researcher reflexivity.

She elaborates on this view of 'the nitty-gritty of researcher reflexivity':

> Good enough researchers accept rather than defend against healthy tensions in fieldwork. And they accept the mistakes they make – errors often made because of their blind spots and the intensity of their social, emotional, and intellectual involvement in and with the subject(s) of their research. The many times that they will do it right can compensate for these mistakes ...
>
> Being reflexive is something to be learned in terms of degrees rather than absolutes (a good enough ethnography is more or less reflexive, not either-or in my view). I think of being reflexive as an exercise in sustaining multiple and sometimes opposing emotions, keeping alive contradictory ways of theorizing the world, and seeking compatibility, not necessarily consensus. Being reflexive means expanding rather than narrowing the psychic, social, cultural, and political fields of analysis. (Luttrell, 2000, p. 516)

Alvesson and Sköldberg's (2000, p. vii) interpretation of a 'reflective approach' seems to share many similarities with Luttrell's 'reflexivity'. There is a focus in both interpretations on width of vision and receptivity to new insights on the part of the researcher:

> By a 'reflective approach' we mean that due attention is paid to the interpretive, political and rhetorical nature of empirical

research. This in turn calls for an awareness among researchers of a broad range of insights: onto interpretive act, into the political, ideological and ethical issues of the social sciences, and into their own construction of the 'data' or empirical material about which they have something to say. It also means introducing these insights into their empirical work. Reflection (reflexivity) is thus above all a question of recognizing fully the notoriously ambivalent relation of a researcher's text to the realities studied. Reflection means interpreting one's own interpretations, looking at one's own perspectives from other perspectives, and turning a self-critical eye onto one's own authority as interpreter and author.

Alvesson and Sköldberg then offer a more detailed explanation of what a reflective approach involves:

Reflective research has two basic characteristics: careful interpretation and reflection. The first implies that all references – trivial and non-trivial – to empirical data are the *results of interpretation*. Thus the idea that measurements, observations, the statements of interview subjects, and the study of secondary data such as statistics or archival data have an *unequivocal* or unproblematic relationship to anything outside the empirical material is rejected on principle. Consideration of the fundamental importance of interpretation means that an assumption of a simple mirroring thesis of the relationship between 'reality' or 'empirical facts' and the research results (text) has to be rejected. Interpretation comes to the forefront of research work. This calls for the utmost awareness of the theoretical assumptions, the importance of language and pre-understanding, all of which constitute major determinants of the interpretation. The second element, reflection, turns attention 'onwards' towards the person of the researcher, the relevant research community, society as a whole, intellectual and cultural traditions, and the central importance, as well as problematic nature, of language and narrative (the form of presentation) in the research context. Systematic reflection on several different levels can endow the interpretation with a quality that makes empirical research of value. Reflection can, in the context of empirical research, be defined as the *interpretation of interpretation* and the launching of critical self-exploration of one's own interpretations of empirical material (including its construction). Reflection can mean that we consistently consider various basic dimensions behind and in the work of interpretation, by means of which this can be qualified. (Alvesson and Sköldberg, 2000, pp. 5–6)

Here they seem to place as much importance on the analytical processes that the researcher applies to the products of research – the things that emanate from or are generated by it: raw data, ideas, theoretical insights etc. – as on analysis of the research process. In practice it is difficult to separate these two strands. Since the distinction between what counts as research process and what counts as research products is blurred to the extent of its being imperceptible in places, there is a fine line separating analysis of the one from analysis of the other. More often than not it is through analysis of what would be categorized as a research product that analysis of the process through which the product occurred is prompted. Indeed, I suggest that initial identification of the need for analysis of any specific methodological issue will always stem from the contextualized illustration of that issue supplied by a specific research product. In my own research, for example, I first became aware of the need to examine the issue of conceptual clarity and its impact on construct validity (discussed in detail in Chapter 3) when I became aware of problems with my data on teacher morale, job satisfaction and motivation that stemmed from underdeveloped conceptualization.

So reflective practice in educational research – depending on whose interpretation of the term is used – may well be as much about reaching a deep level of analysis *within* the research process as it is about analysis *of* the research process. The 'guru' of reflective practice, Donald Schön, offers an interpretation that is sufficiently generic to present reflectivity as a multi-purpose improvement tool, rather than as a tool specifically designed to improve process or product, for example:

> A practitioner's reflection can serve as a corrective to over-learning. Through reflection, he [sic] can surface and criticize the tacit understandings that have grown up around the repetitive experiences of a specialized practice, and can make new sense of the situations of uncertainty or uniqueness which he may allow himself to experience. (Schön, 1995, p. 61)

It highlights the emancipatory capacity of reflection as a vehicle for breaking away from intuitive, unquestioning practice, from preconceived notions and from habits that reflect conventional, rather than reasoned, wisdom.

My own interpretation of reflective practice in relation to educational research lies close to Hammersley's (1993; 1998). To me, reflective practice is about what I have already referred to as the constant striving for improvement by a process involving evaluative reflection to identify areas for improvement and creative reflection to identify remedial practice. In relation to educational research this is achieved by a cycle whereby researchers analyse what they do, evaluate their output, seek a better way of doing things where they feel one is needed, and then apply to their research practice as much of that better way of doing things as circumstances permit. This is the approach of what I have identified as the analytical researcher. It is an approach that leads to the development of advanced research skills. It is an approach that constitutes educational researcher development.

A RATIONALE FOR EDUCATIONAL RESEARCHER DEVELOPMENT

As with teacher development, which I have used as a parallel throughout this chapter, the fundamental rationale for educational researcher development is to raise standards by improving, firstly, practice and, ultimately, the service provided. Raising standards is about identifying and tackling what is wrong: working towards putting it right. The rationale that I present for educational researcher development has three strands. These relate to the issues of *methodological rigour, educational research as an academic pursuit* and *researcher fulfilment*.

Methodological Rigour
By developing reflective practice and, through this, advanced research skills, educational researchers make an important contribution towards injecting increased rigour into methodology. In Part II of this book I examine several specific methodological issues and discuss ways in which researchers may apply more rigour to their work in relation to these issues and, by doing so, develop specific advanced research skills. In research terms, rigour is the key to effectiveness and the quality of research should be judged in relation to it. Methodological rigour provides a significant justification for educational researcher development since it is one of its the main by-products.

Methodological rigour, then, is a worthwhile goal in its own right – one that ought to be pursued in any circumstances. It is a particularly important goal in the current climate, however, in which it has been identified as a specific inadequacy within a more widespread, general, attack on educational research in the UK. Indeed, Pratt and Swann (1999, p.10) identify what they call a 'crisis of method', which they attribute to the issue of rigour:

> We ... do not approve of ... all that passes for educational research. We believe that educational researchers should adopt rigorous methods and standards of analysis. Pursuit of these standards requires an understanding of the nature of knowledge and the way it is generated. We believe that the crisis of method in educational research has arisen because many researchers (and those who fund their work) have failed to address these issues.

The nature and the extent of this criticism are examined in more detail in the next chapter.

Educational Research as an Academic Pursuit

The 'restricted' professional view of educational research is that it is a tool for finding things out: perhaps even a tool for academic study – a vehicle for epistemological and theoretical development. I take a much wider view. I see educational research as a field of study in its own right; one that has an accumulated knowledge base. The analytical researcher is therefore a student of this field of study, as Scott (2000, p. 2) points out: 'Educational research is itself educational. The researcher is as much a learner as those who form the subject matter of the research.'

As with any other field of study, in order to avoid stagnation, those working in it ought to aim to contribute towards increasing, rather than simply to utilize, the knowledge base. This has occurred to a limited extent through the work of methodologists or methodological analysts, but, in general, reflecting what I suggest to be the predominant 'restricted' professional view, the educational research community has adopted a utilitarian, rather than a developmental, attitude towards doing research. There is a need for much more methodological development, as the UK's Education and Social Research Council (ESRC) working party on educational research recognizes: 'In the areas of methodological improvement ... there is more room for debate about the current contribution. There is growing awareness, for instance, of the need to improve the major methodologies being employed' (Gray, 1998, p. 23).

Mortimore (2000, p. 19) reiterates this point: 'We can seek to expand our repertoire of empirical methodologies – experiments,

case studies, surveys, action research – or, as the Americans call it ...
practitioner research' and he emphasizes the need to adopt a
learning attitude towards research (p. 19): 'we also need to invest
more in our own learning. BERA [the British Educational Research
Association] currently has a training programme aimed at new
researchers but I suggest that we need to think about updating this
for researchers at all career stages'; 'My own view is that BERA
must become a better learning organisation – we still have much to
learn about new developments in our own field as well as about
working in a *political* context' (p. 22).

It is not only through methodological development that
educational research as a field of study may be enhanced. There is
also a need to study, to analyse and to update the substance of all
issues relating to educational research. Scott and Usher (1999, p. 10)
make the point that educational research is much more than a
technology:

> The contemporary situation is such that we now need to think
> loudly and publicly, not just about methods, outcomes and
> applications, but about the research process itself; and to think
> in this way not after the event but during it.
>
> What is it, then, that we silently think when it comes to
> research? Obviously, this is a question which does not readily
> lend itself to a single answer. One possible answer is to do with
> the tendency to assume that doing research is simply a matter of
> following the right procedures or methods. This assumption,
> however, needs to be questioned because it misleadingly
> portrays research as mechanistic and algorithmic. If we
> uncritically accept this portrayal we forget that research is a
> social practice and that it is therefore both embedded and
> embodied. Thus one thing we can do in terms of becoming
> more aware of what we silently think is to recognize that
> research is not a technology but a practice, that it is not
> individualistic but social and that there are no universal methods
> to be applied invariantly.

The danger in perceiving research as a technology, as a set of
procedures from which we make a selection before applying them to
the pursuit of a separate field of study, is that we see no real need to
explore issues such as those relating to the bases, the nature and the
enhancement of these procedures. In this way the status of
educational research as an academic discipline is undermined; its
knowledge base remains underdeveloped and, therefore, deficient,

and the practice which emanates from it is, in turn, less effective than it potentially could be. Educational researcher development may be justified because it provides the mechanism for counteracting this effect.

The credibility and status of educational research as an academic pursuit – particularly in the light of recent criticism directed towards it in the UK and the USA – depend upon its being well led and its knowledge base being continually developed. This needs to be done from within the educational research profession itself. It is for this reason that the growth of 'extended' professionality amongst researchers needs to occur. 'Restricted' professionals may often be competent practitioners, but they are not competent leaders, pioneers and innovators. I draw once again on the schoolteacher parallel to make my point: I have known many 'restricted' professionals whom I would have been perfectly happy to see teaching my own children – but I would not have been happy to send my children to schools led by 'restricted' professionals. The competence of 'restricted' professionals is dependent, to a large extent, upon their being well led and directed by others – others who are 'extended' professionals. It is when 'restricted' professionals are placed in leadership and management roles that stagnation and underdevelopment prevail. If educational research as an academic pursuit and as an area of study and educational researching as a profession are to develop to their full potential, then analytical researchers, who represent the 'extended' branch of the profession, need to be given the reins. Analytical researchers have been the pioneers of the development of research methodology as we know it today, and they have the capacity to take it even further. Educational researcher development is needed not only so that individuals may develop, but so that they may, in turn, contribute towards developing the profession as a whole and the work that it does. A developmental knock-on effect is needed.

Researcher Fulfilment
Although educational researcher development is needed in order to reach more widely into, and to regenerate, the profession, it is important not to lose sight of the benefits afforded the individual researcher. Elsewhere (Evans, 1998; 1999; Evans and Abbott, 1998) I present and explain in detail a research-based model of what I identify as the eight-stage process whereby individuals experience job fulfilment. This draws upon, and refines, theories of job satisfaction and motivation such as those of Maslow (1954) and

Herzberg (1968), and identifies as a significant influence upon job fulfilment the individual feeling a sense of achievement in relation to what s/he perceives to be a valued, worthwhile activity.

One of the most fulfilling experiences of my career was the work that I did (described in Chapter 3), spanning several years, on reconceptualizing job satisfaction and applying the insight that this gave me to the development of my research methodology. The analytical researcher whose practice is reflective, who strives to develop methodology and to learn from, as well as to make a contribution towards the advancement of, educational research as an academic pursuit and field of study in its own right, has much to gain personally and professionally. Activities such as these allow the researcher to make a creative input into the research process and the study of educational research, rather than adopt a more passive role as the utilizer of knowledge in the form of technical procedures and established methods. Such activities present intellectual challenges since developing research practice – particularly developing advanced research skills – is predominantly an intellectual activity. Such challenges are the pathway to fulfilment.

REGENERATING THE EDUCATIONAL RESEARCH PROFESSION

The notion of a new professionalism has emerged as a recognized (Day, 1999; Hargreaves, 1994; Helsby and McCulloch, 1996) – or, in some cases, disputed (Bottery and Wright, 1996; Troman, 1996) – post-reform feature of the teaching profession in the developed world (Hargreaves and Goodson, 1996; Helsby, 1999; Robertson, 1996). 'The teaching profession', Hargreaves and Fullan (1998, p. 110) observe, '... is not yet come of age.' Recognizing the window of opportunity provided by the period of change that education reforms precipitated, they predict (p. 111): 'The next few years, we believe, will be a defining era for the teaching profession.'

Whether or not the teaching profession fulfils Hargreaves and Fullan's prediction remains to be seen, but a similar window of opportunity for regeneration has now presented itself to the educational research profession. Resonating with Hargreaves and Fullan's observation about the teaching profession, above, is Levin and O'Donnell's (1999, p. 178) suggestion that 'educational research is at the crossroads'. The window of opportunity has occurred through recent criticism directed at educational research in the UK (Hargreaves, 1996; Hillage *et al.*, 1998; Tooley with Darby, 1998;

Blunkett, 2000) and in the USA (see Boyd, 2000; Kirst, 2000). Responding to this criticism has been a preoccupation of many educational researchers. Many have taken a defensive line; fewer have added their voices to those of the critics and acknowledged a 'fair cop'. The point is, though, that being called to account for the quality of the service that it provides gives the educational research profession the impetus that it perhaps needs to look inwards and consider how it wants to shape its professional culture. McIntyre (1997, p. 134) reminds us:

> We do ... need to consider very coolly the validity of the specific criticisms being made at educational research and the suggestions for its improvement, because the best way for us to serve the interests of both educational research and professional educational researchers is to act effectively, and to be seen to act effectively, to improve the quality of the research that is done.

Perhaps, like the teaching profession, the educational research profession has 'not yet come of age' (Hargreaves and Fullan, 1998, p.110), or perhaps it has already done so, but needs rejuvenating because it has not kept up-to-date with the changing culture of the world of education, with which it needs to interact. This may be the time to sketch out a 'new professionalism' for educational research; one that reflects 'extended' professionality; one that is conducive to the development of the analytical researcher. If this is so, then educational researcher development is timely and essential.

What's wrong with educational research?

'It is time to move forward' is the recommendation of one of the most publicized recent reports on educational research in the UK (Hillage *et al.*, 1998, p. 60); 'To produce a more effective research system requires change by all parties.' Perhaps the change required in order to take educational research forward is that of the formulation and development of a 'new professionalism', suggested at the end of Chapter 1: a professionalism in which the 'extended' professional analytical researcher develops a more effective research system by taking on board and tackling the inadequacies that have been highlighted by the profession's most vociferous critics.

Irrespective of whether or not we will see the emergence of a 'new professionalism', it is important that the issue of the criticism of educational research should be addressed. Anyone who considers her/himself to be, or who wishes to develop into, an 'extended' professional cannot ignore the attacks on educational research, nor simply dismiss them as unfounded or exaggerated. Their substance needs to be examined, analysed and evaluated before the nature of response may be determined. Moreover, consistent with the focus within reflective practice on continually looking for better ways of doing things, the analytical researcher ought to go beyond the specific inadequacies identified by critics and, on the basis of her/his own judgement, examine the quality of educational research, in order to develop improvements.

Professional development at either a profession-wide or an individual level will not be effective without incorporating consideration of what have been identified as deficiencies. This chapter continues with the theme of whether or not educational research(ing) is in need of improvement. It examines in outline what I, and others, consider to be important deficiencies.

THE DEFICIENCIES

'[D]isturbing' is the word suggested by Tooley and Darby (1998, p. 6) to describe evidence of the state of 'general health' of the educational research community in the UK. Pring (2000b, p. 495) refers to 'the disdain for educational research'. Sylva (2000, p. 293) writes: 'The battle lines are drawn. There are some who see educational research at the turn of the century as failing to achieve its mission.' Boyd (2000, p. 347) points out that 'on both sides of the Atlantic, the quality of educational research is under attack ... attacks on educational research in the United States now involve not only academics and journalists but politicians and government policy'. Beveridge (1998, p. 95) questions the 'overall quality of educational research' and 'its value for money'. Pratt and Swann (1999, p. 3) are unequivocal: 'There is a crisis in educational research', and Levin and O'Donnell (1999) refer to educational research's 'credibility gaps' and predict in the USA a 'credibility crisis' and a 'great educational research depression' (p. 177). Clearly, there are deficiencies in educational research or there are lots of people who think there are. Either way, the profession has serious problems.

Listing the deficiencies, though, is not easy, as Hargreaves (1998, p. 117) recognizes: 'Determining weaknesses in educational research is ... a matter of judgment, not evidence. Each critic of educational research tends to adduce a different set of weaknesses, depending on his or her stance on a number of issues.' After examining a range of different lists of weaknesses I find it impossible to conflate them into one set that represents a consensual view. Pring (2000b, p. 2) attempts to do this:

> The criticisms of educational research might be summarised as follows.
>
> First, research does not provide the answers to the questions which policy makers ask in deciding between alternative policies.
>
> Second, research does not help professional practice (for example, in how to teach).
>
> Third, research is fragmented – lots of bits and pieces which, though often addressing similar questions, start from different positions or use different samples, not creating a coherent and reliable basis for practice or policy.
>
> Fourth, research is often tendentious and politically motivated – and exclusive of those who do not share the ideological underpinnings of the research programme.

Yet he appears to have overlooked consideration of several of those criticisms relating to methodological rigour, such as the issues of sampling bias and lack of triangulation, uncovered by Tooley and Darby (1998, pp. 42–4); Hammersley's (1998) general dissatisfaction with standards of rigour and his specific criticism that few researchers pursue or develop theory; and those criticisms presented by Scott (2000, p. 1) in the form of his own list of specific 'common fallacies in educational research', all of which, I suggest, essentially relate broadly to rigour.

My own examination of the main recognized weaknesses, or deficiencies, leads me to identify three broad themes: *the fragmentation of research; lack of rigour;* and *insufficient relevance and usefulness to policy and practice.*

The Fragmentation of Research

Fragmentation is one of the four specific criticisms listed and explained by Pring, above. Elsewhere (2000c, p. 496) he elaborates:

> despite the amount of research (and the theses, journal articles and books are witness to there being a lot), it by and large remains fragmented and piecemeal. It is difficult to put it all together and to construct the big picture. There is little synthesis (albeit many literature reviews) of this fragmented mosaic of case studies, ethnographic enquiries, small scale investigations.

It is, I believe, the fragmentation issue to which two of Hargreaves's (1998, p. 117) six main weaknesses of educational research belong: '5) The non-cumulative character of much educational research; 6) The lack of large centres of educational research', and to which Gipps (1998, p. 75), McIntyre (1997, p. 138) and Keeves and McKenzie (1997, p. 236) refer in their observations that educational researchers need to build much more than they currently do on existing knowledge, not only in the field of educational research but in allied disciplines, in order to develop a more coherent knowledge base. Ranson (1998, p. 48), too, asks: 'Is education research neglecting the theoretical knowledge and discoveries occurring in the various academic disciplines?' and Beveridge (1998) argues for closer ties with social science and other disciplines. The Hillage Report (Hillage *et al.*, 1998, p. 26, para. 3.4.1) refers to the fragmentation issue as 'non-cumulative work':

Most of the researchers with whom we have had contact felt

that while there was some duplication, there was a lack of replication and accumulation of knowledge. For example:

> *'Much research work is wasted, due to a general failure to replicate and to work cumulatively.'*
> *'All too frequently, researchers find themselves re-discovering the wheel, especially in relation to other disciplines'*
> *'Yes, there is repetition. Researchers should use earlier work and look for (and test) alternative explanations.'*

The Tooley Report (Tooley with Darby, 1998, p. 67) also identifies this issue as a weakness in educational research: 'In our sub-sample of 41 articles there were no replications of earlier research of any description, and, indeed, this was also true with the larger sample of 264 articles. Researchers clearly did not feel that it was part of their brief to be engaged in this way.'

The problem seems to be that, because they find conducting original research more intellectually satisfying than replication or research synthesis, researchers invariably prefer to work within the cocooned world of a study that they have thought up and designed themselves. Drawing on the earlier, similar work of others represents, in many cases, a token gesture because it is an accepted facet of research. Seldom is other research given the scrutiny that it ought to be given if it is to be incorporated meaningfully into the rationale for and the design of the research. Seldom is other research used as a springboard for a study.

This problem is, I feel, exacerbated by the profusion of very specific areas of study into which educational studies is sub-divided. These create unhelpful and, in some cases, artificial, barriers between researchers – often keeping out those who may have useful and important contributions to make to the knowledge base but whose work is not labelled in such a way that associates it with the area. They seem to have been created for the wrong reasons, in some cases; to provide an environment of small ponds that allow elite groups of 'big fish' academics the opportunity to distinguish themselves. I do not suggest that there should be no sub-divisions in education as an area of study, merely that there are far too many identifiable and narrow specialisms and that, with each of these, a small group of recognized experts has come to be identified, and that these groups tend to be permitted to 'call the shots' in relation to the direction in which their area develops in a way that is too introspective and self-centred in focus to constitute the kind of stewardship of disciplines to which Page (2000) refers. The quality of the work of the academics in these controlling groups is seldom questioned; recognition is accorded them simply on the basis of their clearly labelling their work to ensure that it is categorized into the sub-division in which they exert control – often, in fact, they will have used this labelling as a means of pioneering and establishing a new area of study, in which they will have expected the academic privileges that come with the recognition that is accorded founding 'fathers' – or mothers. The general picture – and I emphasize that there are exceptions to this – is one in which the fragmentary nature of educational research seems to stem too much from egocentric interests on the part of academics. It reflects competitiveness, rather than collegiality.

Lack of Rigour

Rigour refers to the quality of the research process, as measured by the appropriateness, and the care and level of expertise applied to the execution, of its procedures. Rigour relates, too, to the theoretical basis of research: the soundness of the reasoning, or the philosophical stance, underpinning the process. The Hillage Report (Hillage *et al.*, 1998, p. 30, para. 3.4.4) refers to 'the concerns of a number of respondents over the methodological rigour of much educational research' and quotes a researcher respondent: 'Having been on the editorial board of a prestigious educational research journal, it is quite clear that the quality of research papers submitted is often low.' This concern is mirrored across the Atlantic. Levin and O'Donnell (1999) refer to 'consternation' about the quality of educational research, to 'concerns about research methods, the quality of educational research, and the preparation of the next generation of educational researchers' (p. 178), and to 'the lack of focus on rigorous research approaches' (p. 180).

More specific issues relating to rigour are identified by Scott (2000, p. 2), who presents his own specific list of 'common fallacies in educational research':

1 *The epistemic fallacy* – Ontology and epistemology are conflated so that it is not possible to understand how transitive methods may be used to examine relatively intransitive structures.
2 *The fallacy of homogeneity* – The characteristics given to a group of people are assumed to apply to individuals within that group.
3 *The causal fallacy* – Observed patterns of behaviour are construed as causal configurations.

4 *The essentialist fallacy* – Appearances are frequently conflated with essences and understood as all there is.
5 *The fallacy of value-free knowledge* – Knowledge of educational institutions and systems is thought of as value-free. Educational researchers therefore ignore the value-rich dimension of their activities.
6 *The prospective fallacy* – Retrospective viewpoints are frequently conflated with prospective viewpoints. Educational researchers may be able to explain what has happened, but this does not mean that they know what will happen.
7 *The reductive fallacy* – Human characteristics and attributes are reduced to variables which cannot be further reduced and which when combined capture the essence of either that human being or the educational activities they are engaged in. This acts to trivialise and distort descriptions of those activities.
8 *The deterministic fallacy* – Frequently educational researchers neglect human intention and creativity in their descriptions of educational activities.
9 *The fallacy of pragmatism* – Educational researchers understand research as a practical activity which can be carried on without reference to epistemological and ontological concerns.

Scott's 'fallacies' are philosophical, yet, since he presents them as factors that potentially undermine research quality and, more specifically, authenticity, they are nevertheless related to issues of rigour even though they do not fall into the category of what might be labelled 'research process technique', which is more generally associated with rigour.

Of the four themes 'worthy of reporting', the Tooley Report highlighted three related to rigour: the partisan researcher; problems of methodology; and non-empirical educational research (Tooley with Darby, 1998, p. 5; p. 28). More specifically, the notion of 'good practice' in educational research is introduced and criteria for assessing the extent to which research conforms with the notion of 'good practice' are identified in the form of questions:

> For *empirical* research, we would expect the following questions to be answered in the affirmative concerning the *conduct* of the research:
>
> > Does the research involve triangulation in order to establish its trustworthiness?

> Does the research avoid sampling bias?
>
> Does the research use primary sources in the literature review?
>
> Does the research avoid partisanship in the way it is carried out, and in the interpretation of the data? (Tooley with Darby, 1998, p. 11)

Moreover, it is not just in the conduct of the research itself that criteria of 'good practice' must be satisfied, but also in the *presentation* of the research ... the following questions need to be answered in the affirmative:

> Is the presentation of the research such as to enable the above questions to be adequately explored?
>
> Does the presentation of the research avoid partisanship? (Tooley with Darby, 1998, p. 12)

For *non-empirical* research, the distinction between the *conduct* and *presentation* of the research is clearly more difficult to work with ... Hence ... we focus on what we call the *argument* of the research ... At a minimum, we would expect the following questions to be answered in the affirmative to satisfy the criteria for good practice:

> Is the argument coherent and lucidly expressed?
>
> Do the conclusions follow from the premises and argument?
>
> Are unfamiliar terms adequately defined and assumptions clearly set out?
>
> Are concepts used consistently?
>
> Are primary sources used?
>
> If empirical propositions are introduced, are references given for these?
>
> If controversial empirical and non-empirical propositions are introduced, is their controversy acknowledged?
>
> Is the relevant literature adequately surveyed?
>
> Is the argument free of partisanship? (Tooley with Darby, 1998, p. 12)

Against these criteria Tooley and Darby judged the quality of educational research as represented by a sample of articles published in specific 'high ranking' UK academic journals. Their findings revealed several areas of deficiency: 'One of the most striking themes which emerged ... was how partisan much of educational research seemed to be' (Tooley with Darby, 1998, p. 28). In relation to qualitative methodology, Tooley with Darby (1998, p. 43) report that 'many of the articles examined gave rise to serious concern' on account of the subjectivity of the research and, in particular, 'the lack of triangulation and the problem of sampling bias'. Moreover, in relation to lack of rigour in the presentation of research, they report (p. 46) many cases of authors' failure to provide adequate information on sample size and selection procedures:

> This does mean that readers are at a complete loss in many cases to make their own judgements about the conduct of the research, and to build on it in terms of critique and replication. This is a very disappointing finding, and reflects badly on the quality of the research in general. It was even more unusual for the researchers to reflect upon limitations of their sampling.

I share the concern that there is a general lack of rigour in educational research, though I have difficulty understanding the rationale behind some of the distinctions that Tooley and Darby make between the specific forms of rigour associated with empirical and non-empirical research. I believe the questions that they list as relating to non-empirical research are equally relevant to empirical research. In particular, as I argue in Chapter 3 and have argued elsewhere (Evans, 1997b; 1998), the general lack of conceptual clarity in empirical, as well as non-empirical, research is a manifestation of a serious form of lack of rigour since it has a knock-on effect on methodology; in particular, it undermines construct validity.

Lack of rigour in research usually relates to issues of validity and reliability and, as LeCompte and Goetz (1982, p. 31) point out, qualitative research is much criticized on the grounds that, generally, 'it fails to adhere to canons of reliability and validity'. Yet I interpret rigour as involving more than this; I believe it relates also to the depth and quality of data analysis. A rigorous approach to analysis involves reaching to the depths – going beyond simply presenting research findings, even going beyond identifying implications for policy and practice – and striving to develop theory. I agree with Hammersley (1998), to whom I referred earlier in this chapter, that in this respect, too, educational research is lacking; too few researchers contribute to and generate theory – real theory, as I interpret it in Chapter 9, not just superficial ideas – from their findings. This view is clearly shared by others within the educational research community. Gray (1998, p. 23), for example, makes the observation:

There have been times in recent years when the development of theory has either been seen as unfashionable or been pushed off many researchers' agendas by the pressures of short-term, narrowly focused studies. Researchers in education need to keep abreast of developments elsewhere if they are to sustain the theoretical vigour of their enquiries and to impact, more generally, on the collective social science endeavour. As with all forms of science, if this aspect of the research process is neglected, empirical findings (no matter how important in themselves) will remain unconnected.

Ranson (1998, p. 50) makes a similar – though more explicitly articulated – point: 'Although disputed by some, it is increasingly acknowledged that educational studies has become too isolated from the key theoretical debates of the period. This neglect of theory has impoverished its research', and Bridges's (1998, p. 85) comment follows the same line: 'In my observation the theory that comes out of empirical research in education rarely represents much of an advance on the theory that went into it.'

Lack of rigour, then, clearly extends to lack of theory generated from educational research, perpetuating an image of a second-rate discipline and of an intellectually second-rate profession. This is a serious deficiency.

Insufficient Relevance and Usefulness to Policy and Practice
A recurring specific criticism on both sides of the Atlantic has been the failure of educational research to influence and inform policy and practice. The Hillage Report, for example (Hillage *et al.*, 1998), concluded: 'the actions and decisions of policy-makers and practitioners are insufficiently informed by research' (p. 46), while the then Secretary of State for Education in the UK exhorted 'social scientists to tell us what works and why and what types of policy initiatives are likely to be most effective' (Blunkett, 2000). Kirst (2000, p. 379) outlines a parallel situation in the USA: 'There has been a pervasive feeling among policymakers and researchers alike that policy research either does not reach or is not used by educational policymakers.' However, it is worth pointing out that it is not only educational research but other social science research that is currently having its direction and impact questioned and its apparent over-emphasis on theory questioned (Crace, 2001).

Some of the important issues stemming from these charges of inadequacy have already been thoroughly discussed within the educational research community, particularly, in the UK, in the immediate aftermath of the publication of the Tooley and Hillage Reports (Tooley with Darby, 1998; Hillage *et al.*, 1998). The extent to which claims that research has little or no impact upon policy and practice are justified has been examined by several analysts (e.g. Edwards, 2000; Hammersley, 2000; Sylva, 2000; Pring, 2000b), and from those who recognize a need for them, remedial strategies – or, perhaps more precisely, in some cases, ideas for improvement – have been suggested (e.g. Hargreaves, 1998; McIntyre, 1997, 1998; Salmons, 2000; Weinert, 1997). To examine in more detail the nature and the extent of what has been identified as the deficiency of educational research's failure to impact upon policy and practice, it is necessary to identify what kind of knowledge and information policy-makers and practitioners seek.

WHAT DO POLICY-MAKERS AND PRACTITIONERS WANT TO KNOW?
If teachers and policy-makers were to set the agenda for educational research, what items would they include on it? There is very little evidence available of what these people specifically want to know. Of course, at a general level, it is reasonable to assume that they are likely to want to know how to increase their own effectiveness, and this may include wanting to know how better to meet any competences and standards of performance required of them. Examining published lists of such competences and standards will therefore provide a general, broad indication of the kinds of research-based knowledge and understanding that teachers and educational leaders and managers would potentially be interested in acquiring. For an indication of the more specific information that might be considered a useful contribution to teachers' and policy-makers' decision-making, however, we are reliant upon the scant research evidence available, combined with conjecture and assumption.

The research evidence falls into two categories: evidence of what teachers choose to research themselves, and evidence of their evaluations of what others research. Foster's (1999) methodological assessment of research carried out by teachers in the UK provides an indication of the kinds of topics selected for study by practitioners who, for the most part, were inexperienced at research and were participating in a Teacher Training Agency (TTA) research funding initiative for teachers. The majority of these studies had a strong practical focus and were 'concerned with the improvement of teaching, learning or educational achievement, rather than the production of knowledge'; many of them constituted accounts or descriptions of teachers' own practice and experiences (Foster, 1999, p. 383). The specific topics included: students' understanding of graphs; one school's remedial reading practice; parental involvement in a centre for under fives; one school's staff appraisal/mentoring scheme; a comparison of handwriting teaching in England and France; children's language development in a nursery school; the teaching of Shakespeare in one school; the effectiveness of a 'Stern approach' to teaching relational number understanding; and pupils' motivation.

Corroborating Foster's (1999) findings that teachers' research interests lie in the area of practical-focused knowledge acquisition is Evans, Lomax and Morgan's (2000) account of the Denbigh Action Research Group, a group of teachers who 'came together voluntarily to improve their own practice'. These teachers used their own work-related concerns as the bases for research activity (Evans, Lomax and Morgan, 2000, p. 407). One member of this group, for example, investigated what motivated and demotivated sixth form students[1] in their studies.

Loughran (1999) refers to two Australian projects that have involved teachers in researching issues related to their work, PEEL (Project for the Enhancement of Effective Learning) and PAVOT (Perspective and Voice of the Teacher). His list of some of the key features of these projects provides an indication of the nature of the information that teachers seek through research:

> teachers begin with comprehensive 'big picture' aspirations as they begin to study their classrooms ... They are reluctant to focus on more narrowly defined areas as they become aware of the complexity and uniqueness of their classrooms and the way many factors interact in these settings ...
>
> Teachers focus on their classroom issues and are conscious that this limits generalizability to other situations ...
>
> Teachers have shown little interest in merely studying a problem to clarify it, or prove its existence ... they want to do something about it.
>
> This means that their research almost always includes designing and implementing new approaches – classroom interventions that are intended to achieve change ...
>
> For most teachers, the primary purpose in studying their

[1] Aged 16–18; representing the post-compulsory, and usually pre-higher-education, sector

teaching is to teach more effectively in their own classroom settings. This is a very personal purpose and is one that is usually not part of the research agenda for an academic researcher who is researching other people's classrooms and wider contexts. (Loughran, 1999, p. 4)

Yet using information about what teachers choose to research themselves as an indicator of the kinds of research information they might consider relevant and useful to their practice may represent over-simplistic reasoning. Teachers undertaking research – particularly if they are inexperienced at it – may be influenced in their choice of topic by factors other than their interest in it. If they are participating in a scheme that offers funding, as were Foster's (1999) sample, they may be constrained by regulations or guidelines in their choice of topic. If they lack confidence, knowledge or resources, they may choose a study to match their capabilities. Their choice of a topic that relates closely to what they do in their own classrooms may be based upon convenience, rather than curiosity, and may reflect their difficulty in securing time away from work to investigate wider issues. They may seem 'classroom-bound' in their interests simply because, as inexperienced researchers, they are epistemologically underdeveloped and, as such, are unlikely to be familiar with the range of issues and problems for investigation that fascinate those who habitually delve deeper and deeper in their analyses, and that may just as easily fascinate teachers, if they are introduced to them. Teachers embarking for the first time on research have to start somewhere, and that may not necessarily be where their strongest interests lie. Moreover, it is over-simplistic to assume that their interests in relation to new knowledge will be confined to those issues and concerns with which they are already familiar. Certainly, the topics that teachers choose to research provide an *indication* of the kinds of issues that they consider relevant and useful, but I do not believe they give us the full picture.

On the other hand, what little evidence there is of teachers' responses to educational research bears out the suggestion of a gap between researchers and practitioners (Page, Samson and Crockett, 1998). In an aticle (Freeman, 1986) that begins as a complaint about teachers being unrepresented amongst the authors contributing papers to the *British Educational Research Journal*, a teacher refers first (p. 199) to Cane and Schroeder's asking: 'the major project questions 1. What research would teachers like to see done?', and then (p. 199) to McCutcheon's point that one reason for the lack of credibility of educational research within the professional community is that '[o]utsiders often investigate questions of little concern to teachers'. He then contends: 'Research ... should bring us into greater contact with the realities of teaching' (Freeman, 1986, p. 202). However, the most specific indication of the kinds of topics that this teacher considers relevant and useful comes not directly from his evaluation of what he refers to as 'outsider' research but from his report of what his teacher colleagues choose to research:

> In the school in which I teach staff are always working on one problem or another – a small group is at present investigating the behaviour of a particularly troublesome class. This is involving teachers sitting in on each other's lessons, investigating techniques of recording behaviour and drawing up programmes to overcome problems that might be termed 'socially remedial'. This is not world-shattering stuff but it involves professionalism of a high degree. (Freeman, 1986, p. 204)

Kennedy's (1999) study of American teachers' preferences for specific genres and features of research reveals similar findings:

> The studies that teachers found to be most persuasive, most relevant, and most influential to their thinking were all studies that addressed the relationship between teaching and learning. Those that they perceived to be the least persuasive, least relevant, and least influential addressed only one aspect of teaching – only the subject matter, for instance, or only student learning – without speaking to the relationship to teaching practice itself ...
>
> It was clear ... that teachers forged analogies between the studies they read and their own situations or practices. (pp. 536–7).

The picture emerging is that the teaching profession values practical applicability in educational research. Evidence shows this to be the case even at pre-service level. A study of trainee teachers in the UK who were following a one-year postgraduate certificate of education (PGCE) history course reveals research that 'was of immediate *practical* use' to have been particularly valued by the trainees in relation to their own development as teachers. Examples of more specific questionnaire responses indicate more precisely the nature of the kind of research that these trainees valued: 'it helped me devise classroom strategies, it was informative and helpful'; 'it was helpful about how to implement something'; 'it gave me ideas for teaching' (Pendry and Husbands, 2000, p. 328).

It is not only teachers themselves, of course, who contribute ideas for more practically focused questions to be included in research agendas on the grounds that these address what teachers want to know. Educational researchers and teacher educators, for example, have criticized research into the teaching and learning of reading in the USA (Hoffman, 1999; Pressley and Allington, 1999). Researchers Pressley and Allington (1999, pp. 25–6) suggest:

> What we need is more research that meshes well with the world of early childhood – that is, research on what can work in families and playschools. We also need more research that focuses on teaching in primary classrooms the many tasks and skills that are beginning literacy, rather than more studies of tutoring primary students on word recognition ... There also needs to be more work on how to make reading as motivating as possible, for the instruction of the day is only turning off students to reading across the school years.

In relation to policy-makers, the most useful evidence available of the kind of research they value is provided by Carol Weiss, one of the key analysts in the field of research utilization by policy-makers. From a study in the USA requiring decision-makers to rate the usefulness of a selection of studies presented to them, Weiss (1995, p. 143) identified five dimensions: relevance to the decision-maker's own work; conformity with prior knowledge; research quality; an orientation to action – 'decision makers prefer a study that gives them direction for tangible action'; and, challenge to current policy.

How justified, then, are claims that educational research is failing to deliver the relevance and usefulness that critics consider so essential? This question can be addressed, in part, by examining evidence of the extent to which policy-makers and practitioners appear to be getting what they want from educational research.

EXAMINING THE RELEVANCE AND USEFULNESS OF EDUCATIONAL RESEARCH

There is a strong body of opinion – mainly, it appears, representing the research community – that refutes these charges and contends that educational research does have an impact upon policy and practice. A commonly accepted explanation of the process whereby this occurs is what is variously referred to as the 'percolation', the 'knowledge creep' or the 'enlightenment' effect (De Landsheere, 1997; Edwards, 2000; Gipps, 1998; Husén, 1997; Nisbet, 1997; Weiss, 1995); what Edwards (2000, p. 301) refers to as 'a process of gradual accretion', and which is summed up by Trow (1997, p. 205): 'research somehow (and just how is of greatest interest) influences policy indirectly, by entering into the consciousness of the actors and shaping the terms of their discussion about policy alternatives'. Nisbet (1997, p. 216) outlines the process involved:

> Academic status tends to be accorded to those who make contributions to theory. In the social sciences, their ideas and new concepts are gradually absorbed into popular thought and discussion until they become a new climate of opinion ... Administrators and politicians respond to the 'resonance' of research findings.

Some of those who refute the irrelevance charge directed at educational research (and most of whom are supporters of the notion of a 'percolation' or 'enlightenment' process) draw upon rather more specific evidence to support their argument. The degree of specificity applied varies. Mortimore (2000, pp. 12–14) catalogues a collection of specific areas of study which he identifies as examples of 'successes of educational research' in so far as they have been successful in influencing policy and practice in the UK and, in some cases, beyond. Similarly, Sylva (2000, p. 295) commends the work of Halsey and Floud in the 1950s and 1960s as a specific example of the political arithmetic tradition of educational research which 'had a considerable influence upon our understanding of the links between social class, educational achievement and selection for schools and universities', and Gipps (1998, p. 73) writes: 'The APU [Assessment of Performance Unit] is a good example of how money spent on research *does* impact on teachers' practice, although in a far from simplistic route'. Pring (2000b, pp. 3–4), too, provides 'but five' specific examples of research that has had an impact upon policy and practice in the UK work on: Educational Priority Areas (EPAs); parental support for schools; the Humanities Curriculum Project; the APU; and selection; and Kirst (2000) provides the specific example of the case of the 'think tank', *Policy Analysis for California Education*. Sometimes, too, examples of research that has impacted upon policy and practice are identified by its detractors. In their attack on researchers of reading instruction who promote the 'skills approach', Pressley and Allington (1999, p. 2) argue: 'It is important to address this issue because of the impact some of these researchers seem to have in shaping educational and research funding policies.'

Alongside these are more general assertions of the relevance and usefulness of educational research, many of which incorporate outline explanations of the processes involved. Glaser and Strauss (1967, p. 30), for example, suggest that researchers make a useful contribution by developing theory and introducing different perspectives through the provision of theoretical guides for practitioners' use. More recently, in 1993, *Frameworks and Priorities for Research in Education: Towards a Strategy for the ESRC*, the report of the UK's Economic and Sociological Research Council's (ESRC) working party on educational research, chaired by Professor John Gray, highlighted relevance and usefulness:

> The practical significance of much research in education is considerable; indeed, at the current time, this may well be the field's particular strength. Ideas drawn from research have, for example, informed much curriculum development and some aspects of assessment. (As reported in Gray, 1998, p. 23)

And elsewhere the Report identifies the development of research networks as a significant component of the link between research policy and practice.

There, is, however, an 'other side of the coin' perspective. Not everyone acknowledges that educational research has an impact upon policy and practice. A teacher writing in the *British Educational Research Journal* over fifteen years ago, to whom I refer in the preceding section, presented a gloomy picture: 'I would suggest that most outsider-research is either ignored or ridiculed by practising teachers' (Freeman, 1986, p. 199) and the evidence provided more recently by the highly publicized attacks on educational research, referred to in the introduction to this chapter, suggest that Freeman's suggestion is as accurate today as it presumably was when he made it.

Freeman's is one of the few published criticisms of educational research to appear from a teacher. This is hardly surprising since publishing articles in journals is not a mode of communication that teachers typically practise. It is, therefore, from within the academic community that the bulk of published criticism has emanated. In the UK one of the most vociferous critics has been David Hargreaves (1998, p. 119):

> Relatively little educational research leads to applied outcomes

in either the policy or practice in education ... There are understandable reasons why direct influence on policy-making is unusual: politicians decide policy on the basis of values alone rather than in association with relevant evidence, unless the evidence is consonant with their values; they usually work to very short timescales and will not risk putting their policies to trial; and in recent years much educational work on policy has been highly critical of right-wing governments. It is, however, much less easy to defend the low levels of application by practitioners, especially school teachers.

The most common response is to explain the record of the application of educational research as a consequence of poor dissemination. Some blame researchers, some blame funders, some even blame teachers.

Whether or not Beveridge (1998, pp. 94–5) may justifiably be included as one of those who blames teachers is unclear from his comments, but he nevertheless implies a view that the onus of responsibility for utilizing research lies with the potential users:

> there is little chance of relevant and important knowledge finding its way into education unless the outcomes of research are actively sought out by practitioners. Users of research need to be able to understand it, evaluate it, reject it when it is contextually inappropriate and think out its implications for their own practice.

Those who are sceptical about whether educational research influences policy and practice – or, in some cases, adamant that it does not – seldom present their views without offering some explanation for why they believe this occurs. Beveridges's (1998) point about users needing to understand findings represents a recurring theme running through criticism of educational research – the comprehensibility issue, which is underpinned by the communication issue. Riddell (1989, p. 95) relates this issue to her own specific area of research: 'If the object of feminist research is to help to understand and to change the position of women in society, it is difficult to see how this can be achieved if only a small group of the initiated can understand what has been written.' Salmons (2000) makes a similar point. From her study of a sample of fifty-six academic journal papers, intended to ascertain the extent to which they are 'actually or potentially relevant to educational policy and practice' (p. 230), Salmons concludes that any teachers reading the articles 'would on occasions need to cross a formidable language and terminology barrier to gain access to the academic thought present in the research' (p. 239). Her findings revealed a trend for papers to have potential, rather than actual, implications for policy and practice, and she identified only seven of the fifty-six articles that clearly applied research to the school context.

The crux of the matter here, it seems, relates to Nisbet's (1997) point, presented above, that academic status is acquired through contributions to theory, and is succinctly explained by Back (2001):

> Scholarly writing has become self-referential and full of convoluted argot. It seems that we are writing too much to impress our peers. This produces a kind of surfeit of meta-language that passes largely unread from the desktop to the university library. But in order to be published in the right places, work has to conform to conventions that value academic technique over accessible prose.

At this point it is worth raising for consideration several issues relating to the points made above. The first is that the 'percolation' or 'enlightenment' process, by which so many researchers seem to set great store, is applied only to policy-makers and not to practitioners. There do not appear to be any claims of research-based knowledge gradually and imperceptibly filtering into teachers' repertoire of professional skills. The 'percolation' idea may therefore be considered to be only a partial vindication of the value of researchers' work in relation to relevance and usefulness. If, through 'percolation', research findings reach the classroom they do so through the intervention of policy-makers; second-hand, as it were, and having followed a circuitous route. There does not seem to be much evidence of a direct link between researcher and teacher, cutting out the middle 'man' – or woman. It is this issue that concerns David Hargreaves, and others, who want to see a more direct impact.

The second point is that some of those who acknowledge the 'percolation' or 'enlightenment' process do not, on the basis of it, rest easy or secure in the knowledge that the impact of research on policy is satisfactory. Rather, these analysts seem to see it, in a sense, as an imperfect and unreliable process, but all they have to work with for the present. Considered in this light, those who do not question the process as a means of linking research to policy and practice could perhaps be accused of complacency. Weiss (1995, p. 141) is one of those who acknowledges the imperfections of the process:

Enlightenment is all well and good, but it is a chancy business. Officials hear about some research conclusions but not others. Sometimes they hear distorted versions of the findings, or they hear about findings that are obsolete. Enlightenment can turn out to be endarkenment.

As a result of her dissatisfaction with the 'enlightenment' process, Weiss (1995) has continued to work on discovering better ways of getting research to make an impact on policy and practice, leading to her identifying characteristics of research that improve usefulness and modes of communication that increase use.

The third issue is the claim of some researchers supporting the principle of research percolation that research has been ultimately responsible for bringing about changes of attitudes and societal norms that have, in turn, been fed into policy and practice to bring about change and advancement. This cause-and-effect claim is contentious; it is impossible to substantiate, but it is equally impossible to disprove. It has parallels with the 'chicken–egg' conundrum: which came first? Is it more likely that research has uncovered issues that then, gradually, become the focus of awareness-raising, or, rather, that researchers chose to investigate issues and questions that had become topical through society's questioning of conventional wisdom and established modes of behaviour? Are the changes that have occurred in schools over the last few decades in relation to gender issues, for example, attributable to research in that field, or were they simply responses to the growing awareness within Western society of the problems of sexual discrimination and differentiation that was sparked off by the resurgence of activity from the women's movement? Would such changes in schools have occurred anyway, irrespective of research carried out, and reflecting the political climate at the time? Would they have occurred within the same timescale in which they did occur? Of course, we will never know the answers to these questions. But the fact that we cannot answer these questions undermines, just as much as it supports, the credibility of claims that, through the 'enlightenment' process, research has influenced policy and practice. Research that relies on the 'percolation' process of utilization cannot, because the process is so nebulous, be proved to have relevance and usefulness.

The final issue that I want to raise relates back to my point about the danger in assuming that teachers will be interested only in findings from research that are similar in scope and nature to that which they choose to carry out themselves. The key issue here is that what teachers *value* in terms of research-based knowledge does not necessarily equate to what they *seek*. Research findings may achieve relevance and usefulness to practitioners by raising their awareness, introducing them to a wider sphere of knowledge than they might otherwise never have sought. (In Chapter 10 I identify awareness-raising as one of four criteria for relevance and usefulness in relation to educational research.) Indeed, as Nisbet (1997, p. 216) points out, there is a danger of stagnation if research is used only in a reactive, confirmatory, capacity, rather than as a tool for development and innovation:

> The danger ... is that if research is too closely tied to existing educational provision and practice, where the concept of 'relevance' implies implementation without radical change, the effects may be only marginal and may even be an obstacle to reform.

I do not dispute that, through some means or other, research may indeed 'percolate' through to policy and, from there, to practice. However, as I have already argued, we can never be sure that this is actually happening and, if it is, to what extent. I believe the educational research community now needs to turn its attention to considering how it may improve upon the 'percolation' process.

ADDRESSING THE DEFICIENCIES

Educational research, then, is deficient in several areas; the critics do not appear to have got it wrong. It is, indeed, time to move forward, as the Hillage Report (Hillage *et al.*, 1998) recommends.

The way forward is through raising standards. Too many educational researchers produce second-rate work and there are, for the most part, too few checks against this occurring. The system as a whole – the educational research community en masse – is in danger of allowing low standards to prevail by failing to take on board seriously the need to tackle the deficiencies that have been identified. There is much that needs to be done collectively to remedy the problems. The quality of research papers submitted for publication needs to be more carefully monitored and editorial boards need to apply mechanisms for ensuring this, including monitoring the standard of refereeing – a system that is notoriously erratic; there are some excellent referees but there are also at large many who are simply inadequate for the job. The quality of papers submitted for presentation at conferences also needs to be assessed more carefully. Furthermore, the academic community needs to recognize more clearly those who represent the 'extended' professionals – the analytical researchers and the scholars – and it is these people who should be promoted to the highest levels, so that they may use their influence to ensure that a 'new professionalism' may flourish. Many who hold senior academic posts in the field of education do, indeed, fall into this category – but there are too many who do not: too many professors of education whose work lacks rigour and fails to incorporate the development of theory, as I interpret it in Chapter 9 of this book. Perhaps this reflects what Brown (1998, p. 126) identifies as one specific problem in educational research – 'Shortage of people with appropriate experience and qualifications in some specialisms to be appointable to chairs in education' – but the solution should not lie in a dilution of standards through the appointments of people who do not represent the 'extended' professionals among the research community.

As individuals, educational researchers can play their part in raising standards by developing advanced research skills, under-taking reflective practice and developing into analytical researchers. Learning to do educational research should not be like learning to drive a car or ride a bicycle, at which one considers oneself sufficiently proficient once one has passed a test or mastered the techniques and skills involved. Doing educational research should be seen as an intellectual activity – one that involves continued learning and improvement in the interests of developing oneself as well as the research itself. Part II of this book examines specific ways in which this may be achieved.

Part II
DEVELOPING ADVANCED RESEARCH SKILLS

3

Taking conceptualization seriously

There is an old joke that used to be popular when I was a child: *What's the difference between an elephant and a postbox?* When the inevitable reply, 'I don't know', was made, the response followed: *Well, I must remember not to send you to post my letters.*

I will return later in the chapter to the significance for educational research of elephants and postboxes, and of remarks made by characters in children's fiction: 'There's glory for you', said Humpty Dumpty in Lewis Carroll's *Through the Looking Glass.*

> 'I don't know what you mean by "glory",' Alice said.
>
> Humpty Dumpty smiled contemptuously. 'Of course you don't – till I tell you. I meant "there's a nice knock-down argument for you".'
>
> 'But "glory" doesn't mean "a nice knock-down argument",' Alice objected.
>
> 'When *I* use a word,' Humpty Dumpty said in a rather scornful tone, 'it means just what I choose it to mean – neither more or less.'

The underlying issue is that of words and their meanings: of concepts and conceptualization.

It was when I began researching teacher morale, many years ago, that I first became aware of the importance of understanding precisely what I meant when I referred to certain key terms. Equally important, I discovered, was communicating to others precisely what I meant. The implications of failing to do either were that my research lacked rigour and, as a result, its quality was impoverished.

The words that we use in our research and the meanings attached to those words determine the degree of conceptual clarity that pervades our work. Conceptual clarity is an essential methodological tool – essential, that is, if research is to be rigorous. Yet it is a tool that many researchers do not use. Evidently they are unaware of its existence or they have failed to master its use. It is not the easiest of tools to use, but it is worth taking the time and effort to get to grips with because, when it is properly used, it opens up many avenues into advanced research practice.

This chapter is about conceptual clarity in research. It highlights the importance of taking conceptualization seriously by illustrating the kinds of methodological problems that occur when researchers fail to incorporate conceptual clarity into their work, and it provides guidance on developing specific research skills related to conceptualization.

THE IMPORTANCE OF CONCEPTUAL CLARITY

When, as a graduate student, I began researching teacher morale I recall being told by my supervisor, 'You need to explain what you mean by "morale".' So I set off along the path of searching through all the literature that I could lay my hands on to try to find an acceptable definition of 'morale'. This was enlightening. Until then it had simply never occurred to me that how I conceptualized the key term used in my research would be important. After all, I reasoned, everyone understands the term 'morale': it's fairly unambiguous. What I discovered, though, was that other people had taken the issue very seriously. I uncovered a collection of research papers and sections in books that offered what ranged from discussions to conceptual analyses of morale. I discovered that the concept is far from simple and straightforward. Those who take conceptual analysis and definition seriously accept that morale is a very nebulous, ill-defined concept, whose meaning is generally in-adequately explored (Baehr and Renck, 1959; Williams and Lane, 1975; Redefer, 1959; Williams 1986). It was being examined at least as early as the 1950s, mainly in the USA. Guion (1958) refers to the 'definitional limb' on which writers about morale find themselves, and Smith (1976) points out that some writers avoid using the term in order to eliminate the problems of defining it. Concepts and conceptualization, then, seemed to play an important part in the research process.

From examining morale I moved on to the concept of job satisfaction, and it was at this point that I really became aware of the enormous significance on research of conceptual clarity. The aim of my research was to uncover the factors that influence teachers' job satisfaction, and my main method of data collection was semi-structured interviews with a sample of teachers, although I supplemented this with a form of participant observation over the course of a year and with follow-up questionnaires. Several teachers were interviewed more than once, involving at least two batches of interviews (further details of the research design are provided in Chapters 4 and 5 and full details in Evans, 1998).

My literature review had led me to one of the key studies in the field: that of Herzberg (1968). His research was not focused on teachers: it involved research into the job satisfaction of engineers and accountants in Pittsburgh. Below I go into some detail in describing Herzberg's work in order to explain the origins of my realization of the significance of conceptual clarity.

From analysis of his research findings Herzberg formulated what he calls his Motivation-Hygiene Theory or, as it is also called, the Two-Factor Theory. Herzberg's research findings revealed two distinct sets of factors – one set which motivates, or satisfies, employees, and one set which may demotivate or create dissatisfaction. This theory has been applied to, and tested in, education contexts (see, for example, Farrugia, 1986; Nias, 1981; Young and Davis, 1983). According to Herzberg there are five features of work which motivate people, or which are capable of providing job satisfaction: achievement; recognition (for achievement); the work itself; responsibility; and advancement. Herzberg refers to these as motivation factors, and they all share the distinction of being factors that are intrinsic to the work. Those features that Herzberg identifies as capable of demotivating, or creating dissatisfaction, are labelled hygiene factors and are all extrinsic to the work. These are listed as: salary; supervision; interpersonal relations; policy and administration; and working conditions.

One educational researcher who has tested Herzberg's theory in education settings is Jennifer Nias (1981; 1989). From her research she identifies (1989, pp. 88–9) as 'satisfiers' factors which may be considered to be intrinsic to the job, which are concerned with the work itself and with opportunities for personal achievement, recognition and growth. These findings, she suggests, corroborate Herzberg's findings. She then presents findings which, she suggests, are inconsistent with Herzberg's theory because they reveal teachers to derive satisfaction from extrinsic factors (Nias, 1989, p. 89).

This discrepancy puzzled and intrigued me and I turned my attention to examining the reason why there should be such apparent inconsistency between Herzberg's findings and those of Nias. My own findings, interestingly, had revealed what was a combination of corroboration of Herzberg's and Nias's findings. In the first batch of interviews, in which I asked teachers to identify those aspects of their work which were sources of satisfaction, some responses focused exclusively on the kinds of factors which fall into Herzberg's (1968) 'intrinsic' category. Some teachers, though, like those in Nias's sample, also included references to 'hygiene' (Herzberg, 1968) factors.

I was not satisfied with leaving my data analysis at the level of simply concluding that individuals differ: that what satisfies some people does not satisfy others. I delved deeper, and that delving deeper led me from examining differences between the teacher interviewees to examining job satisfaction as a concept. This was a process that took several months — perhaps even years; it is difficult to quantify the time spent on it because it is inevitably applied in a sporadic manner and the developments that it effects are often imperceptible throughout various stages in the process.

My lengthy, in-depth analysis of the concept of job satisfaction led me to re-conceptualize it. This involved bifurcating it. I reasoned that the concept of satisfaction in its simplest sense, rather than its application to work contexts, involves two quite different meanings — two separate dimensions, or even, perhaps, 'sub-concepts' — which are easiest to explain in the first instance if they are presented in adjectival form: satisfactory and satisfying. These are both classified under the umbrella term *satisfaction*, yet they equate, respectively, to being satisfied *with* and being satisfied *by* something. For illustration of this we have only to compare the quite distinct meanings attached to customer satisfaction and the satisfaction of conquering Everest. The first involves being satisfied *with* something; finding something satisfactory. The second is all about being satisfied *by* something; finding something satisfying, or fulfilling. The word 'satisfaction' is potentially confusing, I reasoned, because the concept is ambiguous and, by extension, the term 'job satisfaction' is likely to be equally confusing. If people are asked to identify those factors that are sources of job satisfaction then what follows is the possibility that some of them may interpret the term to refer only to what is satisfying about their work, but others may hold a different, wider, interpretation which may also incorporate what is satisfactory.

Herzberg does not define job satisfaction, nor does he distinguish it from motivation; indeed, he appears to use the two terms interchangeably. My analysis therefore led me to consider the possibility that some of his research subjects may have held different interpretations of job satisfaction from him. When asked to identify job satisfaction-influencing factors, some may have restricted themselves to factors that influenced the extent to which they were satisfied *by* their work – that is, the extent to which the work was satisfying – and others may have adopted a wider interpretation, including factors that contributed to how satisfactory the job was. What this represents is a potential threat to the research's construct validity.

Construct Validity
Construct validity involves consensual acceptance and under-standing of specific terms. It is threatened when researchers and subjects do not share the same interpretation and understanding of key constructs such as, in this context, job satisfaction. Referring back to the joke at the beginning of this chapter, the potential confusion arising from this is illustrated at a basic, and exaggerated, level by the hypothetical difficulty of sending someone to post a letter who is unable to distinguish between the two concepts: postbox and elephant. The important point is that, unless researchers clarify key terms, they cannot be sure that they and their research subjects are on the same wavelength; they could be communicating at cross-purposes in much the same way that Alice and Humpty Dumpty would have done if he had not explained his definition of 'glory'. The danger of this is that the whole process of data collection, analysis and dissemination is flawed.

While examining Nias's (1981; 1989) application of Herzberg's theory to education settings I became aware that, although she has made an invaluable contribution to work on teachers' attitudes to their jobs, her research is flawed in this way. Nias (1989, p. 84) reports how, through interviews, she sought information from teachers about their job satisfaction:

> In the first [set of interviews] I simply enquired: What do you like about your job? What plans do you have for the future, and why? In the second, I used these questions, but also asked those who said they liked their jobs to tell me half a dozen things they enjoyed doing and to give their reasons.

Threats to construct validity arise out of the inconsistency between how Nias defines job satisfaction (1989, p. 83) and how she asks interviewees about their job satisfaction. Each involves different terminology. Her definition focuses on the 'rewards of teaching'. Indeed, she interprets teachers' self-reports of personally rewarding aspects of their work as being synonymous with chief sources of job satisfaction (1989, p. 83). Her interview questions, however, focus on 'enjoyable' and 'likeable' aspects of teaching and the implication of her own report of her interviewing is that she did not use the terms 'rewards' or 'rewarding'. Yet Nias's interviewees may not have shared her interpretation that 'likeable' or 'enjoyable' are synonymous with 'rewarding'. Her claim (1989, p. 84) that the questions used in her interviews were consistent with what she identifies as her 'loose definition' of job satisfaction is highly questionable.

Nias's (1981; 1989) reports of the findings of her application of Herzberg's (1968) Two-Factor Theory to her own research provide a further illustration of the problems arising out of the lack of recognition of the ambiguity of the term 'job satisfaction'. What she reports as only partial corroboration of Herzberg's findings is, I suggest, essentially an issue of conceptual clarity. What is the likely cause of Nias's findings failing to corroborate Herzberg's is that her and Herzberg's interpretations of the concept of job satisfaction differ, and that those of Nias's teachers who reported deriving satisfaction from extrinsic factors were actually satisfied *with* them, rather than *by* them.

Since Herzberg fails to make explicit his interpretation of job satisfaction, it is possible only to make assumptions. Based on evidence from his writing I suggest that he interprets it narrowly, confining job satisfaction to involving satisfying elements of work. His exclusion of extrinsic factors, such as salary and working conditions, as satisfiers is consistent with this assumption. Those specific extrinsic factors which Nias (1989, p. 89) identifies as satisfiers would have been excluded by Herzberg because they fall outside of the parameters of what, to him, job satisfaction is all about. They may be satisfactory (or unsatisfactory) to teachers but it is unlikely that they are considered satisfying. The interpretation of job satisfaction that Nias appears to have applied to her data collection and analysis is evidently wider, though, and incorporates both satisfactory and satisfying elements. The extrinsic factors which she identifies as satisfiers lie within the parameters of her interpretation of the concept. Thus, what are interpreted as, and presented by, one researcher as research findings which fail to corroborate those of another researcher, may, in fact, be nothing of the sort. Herzberg's theory is challenged and its applicability to education settings questioned when, all the time, the lack of agreement is much more likely to be conceptual. If this is, indeed, the case, then the misconception has its origins firstly in the failure (on Herzberg's part) to define the key concept under study and, secondly, in failure to recognize the ambiguity associated with the concept. Pring's (2000a, p. 9) observation is applicable here:

> Disagreement between people is often a disagreement over the meaning of the words being used. Once they have been clarified, then often the source of disagreement disappears. Ambiguity is to be avoided.

TESTING THE AMBIGUITY ISSUE

So far, all I had done in my attempt to apply in-depth analysis to my research findings in comparison with those of others was speculate on the reasons why there was discrepancy between them. A lot of my reasoning was based on nothing more than conjecture and assumption. If there were any mileage in my idea that lack of conceptual clarity was the main reason for the discrepancy and that this was all tied up with what I had uncovered as the ambiguity of the concept of job satisfaction, then, as an analytical researcher, I needed to test it. I did this through my own research, incorporating the testing of 'the ambiguity issue' into my follow-up research interviews.

The findings from my first batch of interviews are outlined above. By the time of the second batch of interviews, over a year later, I had analysed the first set of data, given extensive consideration to the possible reasons why some of my findings were inconsistent with those of Herzberg (1968), and was in a position to be able to test what had emerged and is outlined above as a possible explanation for the discrepancy, not only between Herzberg's findings and mine, but between those of other researchers. In order to test the ambiguity issue I altered the key terminology used in my questioning from that used in the first batch of interviews when I had used the term 'job satisfaction' and asked interviewees to identify influences on it. In the second batch I asked interviewees two separate questions relating to satisfaction. I firstly asked them to identify sources of fulfilment and, secondly, to identify aspects of their work which could not be categorized as fulfilling, but which were satisfactory. I summed up this second question by saying: 'Tell me about the things that you are satisfied *with* but not satisfied *by*.' Finally, I asked teachers to focus on unfulfilling and unsatisfactory aspects of their work. Without exception, this resulted in the identification of two separate, distinct categories of factors, broadly consistent with Herzberg's (1968) two factors, but which some teachers in the first batch of interviews had indiscriminately identified as sources of satisfaction.

The second batch of interviews used a different sample from that upon which the first interviews focused. However, of greater significance with respect to the implications of the ambiguity issue are data collected during a third batch of interviews, and which was with the same sample of teachers as was the first batch of interviews. The third batch therefore constituted follow-up interviews, and it incorporated the revised form of questioning. This resulted in specific teachers distinguishing between factors which they identified as fulfilling and those which they identified as satisfactory but which, in their initial interviews, had all been reported indiscriminately as sources of satisfaction. The idea of the ambiguity issue, then, appeared to hold water. Moreover, it has since been tested repeatedly through seminars in which, in order to drive home the message that conceptual clarity is important, I ask graduate students to read through samples of research interview transcripts and use them as evidence to identify teachers' sources of job satisfaction and morale. This exercise invariably reveals discrepancy in relation to what students identify as factors influencing job satisfaction and morale, and the source of discrepancy is consistently revealed to be different interpretations of these concepts.

THE NEED FOR CONSTRUCT VALIDITY

Construct validity is a very specific form of validity and, like all forms of validity, it is a quality control feature. It is a mechanism aimed at ensuring that researchers are actually researching what they think – and what they report – they are researching. It is about talking the same language: putting people on the same wavelength and avoiding confusion resulting from misunderstanding, misinterpretation and vagueness.

As Wilson and Wilson (1998, p. 365) observe: 'we have to agree, otherwise each of us will be talking about different things under the same title-heading'. Those who need to talk the same language and share understanding are the researcher(s) and research subjects – or, in the case of non-empirical research involving documentary evidence, the researcher(s) and the authors of the documentary material – and the researcher(s) and those to whom the research is disseminated. These include other researchers as well as policy-makers and practitioners. Strauss and Corbin (1990) explain the need for this:

> Usually, when anyone sees words he or she will assign meanings to them, derived from common usage or experience. We often believe that because we would act and feel in a particular manner, that this, of course, is what the respondent means by these words. That belief is not necessarily accurate. Take a word – any word – and ask people what it means to them. The word 'red' is a good example. One person may say: 'bulls, lipstick and blood.' Another might respond: 'passion.' Perhaps for you it means a favorite dress, a rose, a glamorous sports car, or none of the above. (p. 81)

> Unless we validate possible meanings during interaction with the speakers, or train ourselves to ask what meanings the variously analytically salient terms have for our respondents, we limit the potential development of our theory. (pp. 83–4)

Without commonality of understanding of key concepts, the research may often be difficult to make sense of and, in some cases, depending on the level of ambiguity inherent in the key concepts, this may result in diminution of the value of the research as a contribution to knowledge, theory and practical application.

This diminution of value and usefulness is particularly applicable to research into job satisfaction and morale. Elsewhere (Evans 1998; Evans and Abbott, 1998) I have identified five levels of elucidation within the literature in the field, ranging from that representing commonsense reasoning and conventional wisdom and reflecting shallow analysis to that which identifies factors such as the fulfilment of individuals' needs and which illustrates these through contextual specificity. The width of this range means that it is not a simple and straightforward task to draw upon published evidence of what influences job satisfaction and morale. The main source of difficulty lies in the lack of rigour in relation to conceptual clarity which is applied to many studies and which reduces construct validity to the extent of limiting the research's usefulness and value to other researchers. Work representing the first three levels of elucidation generally neglects consideration of how key concepts may be defined, and seldom incorporates discussion of what is meant by 'job satisfaction' or 'morale'. Oshagbemi (1996), for example, reporting the findings of his survey of the job satisfaction of UK academics, writes:

> teaching contributes more to the university teachers' satisfaction than research, which, in turn, contributes more to overall satisfaction than administration and management. (pp. 365–6)

> In contrast with teaching and research, where they generally expressed a high level of satisfaction, the university teachers were dissatisfied with their administrative activities. (p. 396)

> We found from our survey that, on the whole, university teachers were generally fairly satisfied with their job. They were particularly satisfied with teaching and, to a lesser extent, research. Another area where they also derived great satisfaction was the interaction with colleagues. (p. 398)

Yet his failure to provide any definition or interpretation of job satisfaction impoverishes his work. Not only is it impossible to ascertain from the information provided whether Oshagbemi's references to 'satisfaction' or 'satisfied with' equate to job satisfaction in the sense of the work's being satisfactory or in the sense of its being satisfying, but it is also unclear what conceptions of job satisfaction are held by the survey respondents. It is important to know whether the sample was, for example, indicating greater satisfaction with the organizational-related facets of teaching than with those of research, or whether its responses indicate more positive self-assessments of individuals' own progress and success in teaching than in research, or whether teaching was a greater source of fulfilment than was research. The important distinction between being more satisfied *with* teaching than research, and being more satisfied *by* teaching than research is entirely overlooked and the information provided in the article conveys very little about the nature of academics' job satisfaction. More questions are raised than are answered by it.

The trend of neglecting conceptual clarity seems to be endemic among present-day educational researchers. Yet it has not always been so. I have already referred to the extensive examination of the concept of morale that was prevalent amongst researchers working in the field of occupational psychology during the middle decades of the twentieth century. The concept of job satisfaction received similar treatment during roughly the same period. Locke (1969), for example, estimates that, as of 1955, over two thousand articles on the subject of job satisfaction had been published and that, by 1969, the total may have exceeded four thousand. Many of these incorporated conceptual examination and analyses, one of the best examples being provided by Locke himself (1969): 'What is job satisfaction?' Certainly, within work carried out at this time there were claims that the concept was inadequately examined, and those researching this area identified problems arising from a general lack of conceptual clarity. There has been no real consensus about what job satisfaction is, and relatively few definitions are available. Mumford (1972, p. 4), for example, describes job satisfaction as 'a nebulous concept'. She writes:

> Two points emerge clearly from the work that has been done up to date. One is the elusiveness of the concept of job satisfaction. What does it mean? ... The second is the complexity of the whole subject. (Mumford, 1972, p. 67)

Thirty years after Mumford made this observation there has been little change. Indeed, a general neglect of concern for conceptual clarity seems to have pervaded more recent work in this field, prompting Nias, in the course of her work on teachers' job satisfaction, to comment in 1989:

> I encountered several difficulties ... The first was a conceptual one. As a topic for enquiry, teachers' job satisfaction has been largely ignored. Partly in consequence, it lacks clarity of definition. (Nias, 1989, p. 83)

Yet at least, despite the lack of it, conceptual clarity as an issue seems to have been addressed by previous generations of researchers and its significance on research has evidently been recognized. No such awareness is evident – apart from in a few exceptional cases – amongst the current generation. Seldom does work in the field draw upon earlier conceptual examinations, nor does it incorporate researchers' original ones. Conceptual clarity, for the most part, seems to be being disdainfully relegated to the status of outmoded pedantry: an attention to detail that is now considered irrelevant. The current generation of educational researchers – for the most part – does not appear to want to be bothered with defining the key terms used in its work, nor with carrying out extensive examination and analysis of concepts.

This trend is not confined to work in the field of job-related attitudes. It is prevalent in all of the fields of study in which I am or have been engaged: teacher development; educational leadership and management; teachers' professional lives and professionalism; initial teacher training; and teaching and learning in higher education. It is reasonable to assume that my observations are indicative of a general trend across educational research. Indeed, Donnelly (2000, p. 134), for example, identifies problems within the study of school ethos that emanate from their being 'relatively few conceptualisations or theoretical discussions of it [ethos]'. Moreover, this trend is evident beyond the confines of educational research and within other areas of social science research. Writing about his field of study – professionalism and professionalization in a broad sociological context – Freidson (1994, p. 15) makes similar criticisms of the lack of conceptual clarity, focusing on the implications not only for validity but also for the development of theory, an issue which I examine in Chapter 9:

> Because we seem to be no nearer consensus than we were in 1915, and because usage varies substantively, logically, and conceptually ... , some analysts have given the impression of condemning the very practice of seeking a definition. But surely such condemnation is inappropriate. In order to think clearly and systematically about anything, one must delimit the subject-matter to be addressed by empirical and intellectual analysis. We cannot develop theory if we are not certain what we are talking about ...
>
> To speak about the process of professionalization requires one to define the direction of the process, and the end-state of professionalism toward which an occupation may be moving. Without *some* definition of profession the concept of professionalization is virtually meaningless, as is the intention to study process rather than structure. One cannot study process without a definition guiding one's focus any more fruitfully than one can study structure without a definition.

Similarly, Thomas (1997, pp. 75–6) highlights the conceptual difficulties underpinning the development of educational theory:

> My thesis is that lack of definition has resulted in 'theory' coming loosely to denote, simply, intellectual endeavor. Many kinds of thinking and heuristics have come to be called theory. But why should they be entitled to this guise? It is like wanting to call a pig a cat. A cat certainly is a more elegant animal than a pig, but this is no reason to call one's pig a cat.

For the most part, clarifying what one means seems to be a thing of the past – though I reiterate that this is a general trend and that there are exceptions. Yet, reflective practice in educational research demands such rigour. The analytical researcher needs to undertake whatever measures are necessary to incorporate conceptual clarity into her/his work in order to provide a sound basis for the development of theory and to maximize the chances of ensuring construct validity. The next section presents guidelines for pursuing construct validity.

PURSUING CONSTRUCT VALIDITY

Validity of any form in research is elusive; we can never be sure of having achieved it. Since the most we can do is undertake measures to maximize our chances of achieving it, I refer to 'pursuing', rather than 'ensuring' construct validity.

I identify four elements of the process needed to develop your capacity for pursuing construct validity in your research. These are: *the identification of key concepts for clarification; conceptualization and construct clarification; communicating and matching constructs;* and *conceptual clarity and dissemination.*

Identification of Key Concepts for Clarification
Conceptualization, as I interpret it, is the process and the product of forming concepts. Pring (2000a) explains concepts as being how experience is organized. LeCompte and Preissle (1993, p. 119) elaborate on this:

> at the simplest level [concepts] are the classes of phenomena and their characteristics which humans use to organize their world. Essentially, they are names, or labels with definitions, which we attach to things which are salient to our own culture. They may be concrete – milk, go, dog, mother – or abstract – food, activity, animals, family. They also may have abstract referents – ethics, faith, government, alienation, love.

Conceptualization, then, is the process whereby we develop concepts – concepts of, for example: 'milk', 'go', 'dog', 'mother', 'ethics', 'faith', 'government', 'alienation' or 'love' – or, referring back to the introduction of this chapter, of 'elephant', 'postbox', or 'glory'. It is the process of attaching meaning to each of these words – the formulation of that meaning. It is also the product of this – the formulated meaning: one's conceptualization of 'milk', for example, is the meaning of milk that one has formulated. The clarification of a concept, or of one's conceptualization – the way, for example, that one might explain it to others, or even clarify it to oneself – is an interpretation or a definition of a concept.

In pursuing construct validity, the first thing you need to do is identify what you consider to be the key constructs within your research focus that need clarifying: the key concepts that need defining or explaining. I am sure that one of the reasons why conceptual clarity has been eschewed in recent years is that it does not sit easily with the postmodernism trend that has taken a strong hold of much educational research and which has led to a backlash against methodology that incorporates too much rigidity of structure and seemingly unnecessary and pointless procedures. Bailey (1999, p. 30), in fact, reminds us: 'Clarity of expression is not a quality immediately associated with postmodern theorizing.' Indeed, conceptual clarity may very easily get out of hand; it can be taken to extremes that leave it wide open to justifiable criticism and ridicule. What I mean by this is that it is, of course, possible to go on clarifying concept after concept as the definition of one introduces at least one other that needs defining or explaining, and so on, *ad infinitum*.

What you need to do, then, is consider which of the main concepts within your research focus are potentially ambiguous or susceptible to being interpreted differently by different people. The more nebulous the concept the more likely it is to need clarifying. Whilst we cannot, of course, be sure that any concept is construed similarly by different people, in order to avoid taking conceptual clarity to silly extremes it is reasonable to assume that concepts of tangible objects are less susceptible to multiple interpretation than are intangible concepts such as those of attitudes, states of transition and processes. If your research is to focus on student disaffection, for example, the concept of disaffection is much more nebulous and therefore more important to clarify than that of student. Nevertheless, it is important to clarify your interpretation of what you consider to be *all* of the key concepts within your research focus, however straightforward they appear to be at first glance. Often this will simply involve identifying the parameters of categorization – what you are including in and excluding from your use of a specific term. This may sometimes be achieved simply by identifying the population that you intend your research sample to represent.

Conceptualization and Construct Clarification
Having made an initial selection of the key concepts, the next stage is to clarify how you construe them; that is, to determine your definition or interpretation of them. This involves asking yourself,

'What precisely do I mean by ... ?' This is a process of conceptualization. Although it is a useful first step, simply 'knowing' in your own mind what you mean by something is insufficient if you are unable to explain it to others. The purpose of conceptual clarity in research is to allow you to communicate with others. Therefore, reasoning that you know yourself what you are talking about, or what you mean, but that you cannot explain it very well, is not good enough. You need to be able to present a definition or, at the very least, an interpretation, of the key concepts within your research focus if you are to have any hope of achieving construct validity or if you wish to develop your conceptualization into contributions to theory that are to be shared with others.

CONCEPTUAL INTERPRETATIONS AND DEFINITIONS

If you want to read an excellent, clear explanation of what definitions are and of why they are important in educational research you are unlikely to find a better one than that provided by Pring (2000a, pp. 9–12). He points out that definitions may be *stipulative* – involving the stipulation, 'in precise and unambiguous terms', of 'what you mean when you use a particular word' (pp. 9–10) – or they may be *ostensive* – 'where a word is defined by pointing to the objects to which it exclusively refers. Thus, in defining 'education' one might point to particular activities or to what goes on in particular schools' (p. 10). Pring then identifies two more forms of definitions. One of these involves explaining the meaning of a word by 'close examination of its *usage* – the complex logical interconnections entailed by its use in different contexts':

> Therefore, we think hard about what is implied in our description of someone as 'educated' or in calling an activity or experience 'educational'. What logically follows from such a description? What kind of evidence would make one withdraw one's judgement? Would it make sense, for example, to call the process of learning *educational* where there is clear evidence of indoctrination? (pp. 10–11)

The other form involves thinking 'of the different ways of understanding which are brought together under this one label':

> That requires the patient unravelling of these understandings. For example, there is criticism of 'child-centred education'. 'It' has been blamed for poor standards in schools, and some research claims to have demonstrated as much ... But there is no

stable usage of this term. It points to different sorts of practice. A useful philosophical job, therefore, is to trace the different traditions associated with this description. (Pring, 2000a, p. 11)

Professor Pring's philosophical expertise renders him much better qualified than I to interpret the term 'definition'. Nevertheless, I interpret it rather more narrowly than he does: as a precise, unambiguous explanation that stipulates what something is and that is exclusive in applicability. I accept Pring's point (2000a, p. 10) that the process of formulating stipulative definitions of this kind is flawed. However, some of the different forms of what Pring identifies as definitions are what I would call 'interpretations'. I use this term, rather than 'definition', to apply to clarifications of meanings that do not offer all of the stipulative criteria that I identify above.

To illustrate my distinction between what I refer to as 'definitions' and 'interpretations' I present a little exercise. Consider which of the following is a definition – as I interpret it – of a chair:

1 A chair is a piece of furniture intended for sitting on.
2 A chair is a seat.
3 A chair has four legs, a seat and a back and is sometimes padded. It is usually made of wood or plastic but other materials can be used.
4 A chair is intended to seat people.
5 A chair is a piece of furniture that people may sit on.

Remember that the definition should explain precisely what the thing being defined is, and it should be so precise and unambiguous that it excludes applicability to anything else.

Now take each of the five statements above and, in relation to each, ask yourself:

Does the statement stipulate what a chair *is* – what category of phenomena it lies within; that is, whether a chair is, for example, an article of clothing, an animal, an item of food, etc.?

Could the statement be applicable to anything other than a chair? In other words, could the word 'chair' in the statement be replaced with anything else and the statement still make sense?

According to my interpretation, the statement is not, strictly speaking, a definition unless, when each of these two questions is applied to it, the answer to the first is *yes*, and the answer to the second is *no*. All five of the statements above could be applied to specific items of furniture other than chairs. Depending on the statement, 'settee', 'stool', or 'bench', for example, could replace the word 'chair'. Pring (2000a, p. 10) makes this point in his explanation of ostensive definitions:

> Examples of good practice, pointed to by politicians or inspectors, are used to *show* what education is – and means. But this is unacceptable because one wants to know by what characteristics these different activities are picked out as examples of 'education'. What does this label signify that 'indoctrination' or 'training' does not?

Moreover, of the five statements above, 3 and 4 do not explain precisely what a chair is. They are distinct from the other three statements – which do stipulate what a chair is – because they do not begin with 'A chair is *a* ... '.

The difference between what I refer to as a conceptual interpretation and a definition is illustrated by what Day (1999, p. 4) presents as his definition of professional development:

> Professional development consists of all natural learning experiences and those conscious and planned activities which are intended to be of direct or indirect benefit to the individual, group or school and which contribute, through these, to the quality of education in the classroom. It is the process by which, alone and with others, teachers review, renew and extend their commitment as change agents to the moral purposes of teaching; and by which they acquire and develop critically the knowledge, skills, planning and practice with children, young people and colleagues through each phase of their teaching lives.

The first sentence is what I consider to be an interpretation of professional development – indeed, the entire paragraph is an interpretation since a definition, as I interpret it, is a specific form of, and is therefore subsumed within a, conceptual interpretation. Only the second sentence, though, constitutes what I interpret as a definition. It stipulates precisely what professional development *is*, rather than describe what it may sometimes look like, and it seems to be exclusive in applicability. The first sentence could just as easily be applied to 'teaching' as to 'professional development'. It provides information that is supplementary to stipulating precisely what professional development is. It is descriptive, rather than definitive. It tells us what professional development looks like; what it *consists of*, rather than what it *is*. This sentence would have been better following rather than preceding the second one since it elaborates on it. In a sense, the first sentence is illustrative of the second, though it is an example of what Pring (2000a) refers to as an ostensive definition.

The distinction between stipulative definitions and conceptual interpretations may be further illustrated by my own work. My current definition of morale is *a state of mind encompassing all of the feelings determined by the individual's anticipation of the extent of satisfaction of those needs which s/he perceives as significantly affecting her/his total work situation*. A conceptual interpretation of morale, on the other hand, would lack the precision of a definition, may be quite lengthy, and may incorporate much information that helps to elucidate the concept. It might be something like *morale has levels; it ranges from high to low and these levels may fluctuate as circumstances and situations affect them. Morale in a work context is about how people feel about their work. Morale is future-oriented, so it relates to people's feeling about their work in the future – whether they anticipate being happy or unhappy at work* ... and so on.

I want to make it clear that I consider it very important that researchers incorporate conceptual clarity into their work but that whether they do so by using conceptual interpretations or stipulative definitions is relatively unimportant. The point is that they should make every effort to communicate to others the meanings that they attach to key terms used in their research. Definitions are more precise and therefore less susceptible to being misunderstood or misinterpreted than are conceptual interpretations, but there is such a generally widespread disregard for conceptual clarity of any form in educational research that any attempts to counteract this are to be welcomed as a step in the right direction. I do not, by any means, eschew conceptual interpretations; I just think stipulative definitions – if they are well-formulated – are preferable because their precision provides so much more clarity. Moreover, because they are difficult to formulate and are therefore challenging they contribute much to the development of the researcher.

FORMULATING DEFINITIONS AND CONCEPTUAL INTERPRETATIONS
Achieving conceptual clarity does not necessarily require you to formulate your own definitions or interpretations of concepts. There

is no point in re-inventing the wheel, and your search through the literature may result in your finding a definition that you are happy to adopt or to adapt. If this does not happen, though, you will need to formulate your own conceptual interpretations or definitions.

Formulating definitions is not easy; in the context of research it is an advanced research skill. It takes time and, until you become experienced at it, involves repeated revision. My own definition of morale, for example, took several months to develop to the stage at which I was happy to publish it. I have since refined it and expect to do so again. Such is the nature of reflective research practice. The analytical researcher is continually seeking improvements to his/her work.

In this section I present guidelines for formulating definitions. I emphasize that these guidelines are developed from my own experience as an educational researcher; they are based upon what I have discovered through trial and error and what I have found useful to my own research as well as what has been useful to graduate students with whom I have shared it. I draw upon my scant knowledge of philosophy and recognize that since my background is not in philosophy those whose expertise is in this area may find it easy to pick holes in my suggestions.

I have found it a useful starting point to spend some time identifying the necessary conditions of the concept that I wish to define. Usually, these will be necessary conditions that we identify ourselves, but to illustrate I use the concept of punishment and I draw upon the necessary conditions of punishment identified by the philosopher Flew (1954). According to Flew, punishment must be

- unpleasant
- for an offence or a supposed offence
- of an offender or of a supposed offender
- carried out intentionally
- carried out by those in authority to do so.

A list of necessary conditions such as these, without adding anything more, constitutes one form of conceptual interpretation. If we wish to formulate a definition − as I interpret it − we need to develop the list further.

Try formulating a stipulative definition of punishment based upon acceptance of these necessary conditions. Remember, though, that it is necessary to stipulate precisely what punishment is; that is, what category of phenomena it falls within. This is often a difficult stage in formulating definitions. In some cases it is complicated because it involves a choice between different levels of category of phenomena: categories have sub-categories and you need to decide which level you consider most appropriate to use in your definition. In other cases it is complicated by the need to ascertain precisely what you consider something to be; decisions often have to be made, for example, about whether something is a process or a product, or whether it is to be defined as an action or as a form of behaviour, or whether it should be called an ideology or a belief. I recall, for instance, spending much time deciding whether I should define motivation as a *predisposition* or as an *inclination* towards activity.

I suggest that punishment may be defined as an action – an action that incorporates the necessary conditions identified by Flew (1954), though some people may prefer to define it as something other than an action, such as a process. Punishment, then, may be defined as *a deliberate action carried out by someone in authority to carry it out on, and causing unpleasantness to, an offender or a supposed offender for an offence or a supposed offence.*

Now, following the same procedure of first identifying necessary conditions, try to formulate a definition of a chair. Look back at the five statements about chairs, presented above, and at the reasons why none of them constitutes a stipulative definition, so that you may consider ways of improving on them.

The best definition of a chair that I have, so far, been able to formulate is *a chair is a piece of furniture with a back and is designed to seat one person at a time.* It is important to choose every single word in a definition with great care, and my revisions to my definitions have invariably involved my eventually rejecting one or more words in favour of another that I feel better conveys the meaning that I intend. In my definition of a chair the use of the words 'designed to' are deliberately chosen to incorporate recognition that although more than one person may simultaneously sit on a chair this is not consistent with one of the key design features of a chair – that it is *intended* to seat only one person at a time. Had I used the word 'seats' instead of 'is designed to seat' my definition would have been flawed. In definitions, choices between words such as 'does', 'may', 'could', and so on need to be made with great care. The way in which verbs are used – the tense and any qualifying terms that are used – is particularly important: whether, for example, you write 'seats', 'may seat', 'could seat', 'is intended to seat' or 'may be considered to seat' needs careful consideration if your definition is to match the precise meaning that you intend to convey.

.t is to specify the category of phenomena into which whatever
ı are defining falls, then your definition will be likely to begin *a* X
ɔ *a/an/the* ... , or perhaps *is one of the* ... If you find that your
definition begins *a* X followed by a verb other than *is* then you
should look at it again; it is more likely to be describing, rather than
defining the concept. Make your definition as concise as possible.
Avoid superfluous words. Examine every key word very carefully —
particularly adjectives and adverbs — and ask yourself, in relation to
each: Is this word necessary? What does it contribute to the
definition? Is there a better alternative?

Finally, test your definition by asking the same two questions
presented on p. 64, above.

Communicating and Matching Constructs

Achieving construct validity involves your ideally knowing what
your research subjects mean when they use the key words or terms
within your research focus. It also involves their ideally understanding what you mean when you use these key words or terms.
Construct validity will be threatened and undermined if, for
example, like Alice and Humpty Dumpty, you use the word 'glory'
to mean one thing and those with whom you are communicating
interpret the word quite differently. If, as the initial stages of
achieving conceptual clarity, you have taken the trouble to clarify in
your own mind precisely what you mean by certain key terms then
communicating clearly and unambiguously with research subjects
may be more problematic than you might think. The reason for this
is that you are likely to have moved on, conceptually, and they have
not; they will have had no need to do so. As a researcher you may
have devoted much exploratory thinking to the process of
conceptualizing key terms, and this will undoubtedly have been
based upon extensive knowledge of work in the relevant field. Your
research subjects, on the other hand, will be reliant upon more
everyday, less specialized, interpretations and usages of terminology. They will be less likely to share your commitment to rigorous
conceptual analysis and, in the time available to have concepts and
definitions explained to them, may be unable to grasp the intricacies
and subtle distinctions which you have uncovered over a much
greater timespan and through a process of fully immersing yourself
in the literature. Matching your constructs with those of your
research subjects, then, is not as easy as may be imagined.

I have found that trying to overcome the problem of construct
mismatch by explaining my own definition or interpretation of key

concepts does not work. Essentially, research subjects simply do not wish to bother trying to take on board an alternative, more complex, construct and are reluctant to relinquish their familiar conceptualization, which is perfectly adequate for their needs. Trying to 're-educate' them is likely to bore or alienate them. Moreover, Wilson and Wilson (1998, p. 361) suggest that researchers' grasp of concepts needs to exceed that of their research subjects:

> they [researchers] will themselves have to be *more* clear than their subjects or respondents about the concepts with which they deal ... otherwise they will not be able to come up with any truths that we do not already know, anything above the level of common sense.

The answer, I suggest, is to build into the data collection a mechanism for incorporating inclusion of what you consider to be the distinct dimensions of key concepts. Your method of data collection therefore acts as a filter that facilitates conceptual categorization. Interviewees need not necessarily be introduced to specialized terminology which you intend to use in your written reports of the work, but your interpretation of this terminology should be reflected in the questions that you put to them and the conversations that you have with them. Above I outline how my reconceptualization of job satisfaction led to my bifurcating the concept and distinguishing between being satisfied *with* and being satisfied *by*. Elsewhere I explain how I refer to these two dimensions of job satisfaction as *job comfort* and *job fulfilment* (Evans, 1997b; 1998). Yet, when I tested what I refer to as the ambiguity issue in job satisfaction in a further stage of data collection I did not try to explain to my interviewees the reconceptualization and bifurcation process that I undertook, nor did I introduce the terms *job comfort* and *job fulfilment*. Instead, I phrased my interview questions in such a way as to distinguish between job comfort and job fulfilment factors but using terminology that was comprehensible to my interviewees. I asked interviewees not to identify factors which affected their job comfort but to identify aspects of their jobs which they were satisfied *with*, but not satisfied *by*. In this way it appeared that understanding was shared, even though terminology was not. Bogdan and Taylor (1975, p. 34) offer sound advice: 'Leave your esoteric social science vocabulary at home.'

However, it is not always possible to incorporate conceptual constituents into data collection in this way since construct development need not necessarily precede data collection; it may arise out of the data analysis. My own constructs of job satisfaction and of morale (see Evans, 1992b; 1998) each developed out of a cyclical elucidatory process of data analysis, questioning inconsistencies, formulating concept-related hypotheses, and re-analysis: a process that should be part and parcel of the work of the analytical researcher. My constructs were continually developing throughout the entire research process – and, indeed, have continued to develop since. In such cases, where construct development continues well into the later stages of analysis, research subjects may need to be recontacted for the purpose of providing verification, or further data collection may be required. In addition, measures of coder-reliability (see, for example, Atkins, 1984; Miles and Huberman, 1994) should be established in order to indicate the degree of consensual interpretation of concepts upon which data analysis is based.

It is at the data analysis, rather than the data collection, stage that the real construct matching occurs. Here, relying much less on the terminology employed by your research subjects than on your interpretation of what they mean – based on the context in which the specific elements of data are provided – you classify the data according to how they fit into your own conceptualizations. If, for example, one of my interviewees had referred to 'job satisfaction' or had responded to my questions about influences on her job satisfaction by talking in such a way as to suggest that what she was really referring to, according to my interpretation of it, was morale, rather than job satisfaction, then I would categorize her comments as morale-related. Put more simply, and drawing once again on the postbox joke: if, in the course of researching people's experiences of using the postal service, I have a conversation with someone who, although he uses the word 'elephant', is clearly – from the evidence of the context of what he is saying – referring to a postbox, then I make meaning of his conversation on the basis of what I infer to be his construct of, rather than his use of the word for, a postbox. The issue is one of construct matching, rather than vocabulary matching; if there were clear evidence that his construct matched mine then I would categorize his comments as data on people's experiences of posting letters, rather than experiences of feeding elephants. However, my presentation of findings would incorporate reference to the discrepancy and explain the basis of and the process of my dealing with it.

Conceptual Clarity and Dissemination

To safeguard against problems of external reliability, such as those which I have identified as arising out of Nias's (1981) testing of Herzberg's (1968) theory, it is essential that you make explicit in publications and other forms of dissemination of your work your interpretations and/or definitions of key concepts and, where appropriate, the key wording or phraseology used in your interview questions or questionnaire items; indeed, in any of your communications with research subjects. Without this, not only will other researchers be unable to evaluate your work meaningfully but its capacity to contribute towards the development of theory by the cumulative process of researchers building on other researchers' findings will be limited.

THE ANALYTICAL RESEARCHER AND CONCEPTUAL CLARITY

The pursuit of conceptual clarity, then, should permeate the work of the analytical researcher. It is an essential ingredient of methodological rigour and of the development of theory; indeed, LeCompte and Preissle (1993, p. 119) identify clarification of the understanding and interpretation of the meaning of constructs as one specific kind of theory. Conceptual clarity is one of the hallmarks of high-quality research.

But, as an advanced research skill, conceptualization requires in-depth analysis and the application of precision. It is difficult to do and it takes time; you will not become expert at it overnight. Yet, like so many of the advanced research skills examined in this book, the intellectual challenges that conceptualization poses are a great source of intellectual reward.

Research that disregards the need for conceptual clarity risks being second-rate research. This is not simply because key terms may remain unclear and potentially ambiguous, but because so much of the substance of research quality hangs on conceptual clarity. The 'extended' professionals within the educational research community recognize this. Unfortunately, though, the 'extended' professionals represent a minority. Herein lies the essential problem underpinning what some analysts have identified as the 'crisis' within educational research (see Chapter 2). What is needed is a new generation of 'extended' professionals who will join the educational research community and influence it from within, initiating change for the better, brought about by a heightened awareness of the need for a more rigorous approach. A new wave of conceptual precision is needed as the basis of this change. Your own development as an analytical researcher who takes conceptualization seriously will contribute to these changes.

4

Comparative analysis: trying to see the big picture

As I point out in Chapter 3, one of the reasons why conceptual clarity is so important is to enable research findings to be made as intelligible and meaningful as possible to other researchers. All researchers are aware of their roles in the grand scheme of knowledge and theory development: some of them will have bit parts, some of them leading roles, and some – at least for a time – will hog centre stage in the cumulative production of research-generated information. Dissemination is a key element in the process of trying to see the 'big picture' of research findings that informs epistemological development. Researchers realize this, and so they publish their findings for the consumption of anyone who is interested in them. Letting others know what they have done and what they have discovered is not a problem amongst educational researchers; finding out and building on what others have done and have discovered is.

Gipps (1998, p. 75) suggests that educational researchers pay insufficient attention to using other researchers' work as a basis for their own work:

> We need as researchers to read more and write less. This is not a flippant observation; it is a serious comment on how little time we as academic researchers have to address properly other people's writing ... We need regular reviews of research findings, along the lines of those being commissioned by OFSTED at the moment, and also more academic reviews of recent research such as those produced by the American Educational Research Association.

Davies (2000, p. 365) also addresses the issue that is the basis of Gipps's point: the 'non-cumulative nature of its [educational research's] findings', while Keeves (1997b, p. 1) similarly points out: 'Failure to view the products of educational research as a coherent body of knowledge would seem to misunderstand the nature of the research enterprise.'

The issue upon which this chapter focuses is that of the need for educational researchers to work towards building up composite knowledge. As I point out in Chapter 2, the fragmented, incoherent nature of much educational research has prompted criticism. There is, for the most part, too much 'splendid isolationism' within the educational research profession. Although, as always, I emphasize that there are exceptions to this generalization, too often researchers are content to see their own studies as single entities rather than as pieces in a jigsaw puzzle which, when completed, reveals a much bigger picture of the nature of the phenomena being studied. This chapter focuses on a specific aspect of this issue. It examines the part played by comparative analyses in contributing towards a more coherent, cumulative approach to knowledge generation.

WHAT IS COMPARATIVE ANALYSIS?

Comparative analysis is a term that means different things to different researchers, as Glaser and Strauss (1967, p. 21) observe: 'The term *comparative analysis* – often used in sociology and anthropology – has grown to encompass several different meanings and thereby to carry several different burdens.' They provide pointers of their own interpretation of it: 'we must ... be clear at the outset as to our own use for comparative analysis – the generation of theory', within which they identify five purposes: *accurate evidence, empirical generalizations, specifying a concept, verifying a theory* and *generating theory*.

Some researchers use alternative terms. Miles and Huberman (1994, p. 173) refer to 'cross-case analysis' whose function is 'to enhance *generalizability*', and 'to deepen *understanding* and *explanation*', and LeCompte and Preissle (1993, p. 119) explain what amounts to comparative analysis without specifying a term:

> Theories which explain individual cases do not generalize; they cannot be used to predict the cause of a different kind of case ... However, they can be used in comparative fashion to alert researchers to themes or events which might be common to similar phenomena under different conditions.

Reeve and Walberg (1997, p. 439) use the term 'secondary analysis', which they define as: 'the reanalysis of data by the original or, more often, other investigators for similar or different purposes for which the data were collected'. Davies (2000, p. 366) refers to 'research synthesis or research integration' as the pursuit of understanding why similar studies have yielded either different or similar patterns in their findings.

What I mean by comparative analysis has similarities with some of these. I use the term to refer to analysis of data from two or more studies that are sufficiently similar in relation to one or more aspects of research design to merit their being considered comparable and whose findings are in some respect either contradictory or corroboratory for reasons that are not entirely apparent without further comparative analysis.

It is important to emphasize that I do not refer to replication when I use the term 'comparative analysis', nor to synthesis or meta-analysis, all of which serve useful purposes in so far as they are directed towards building up composite knowledge. It is the analysis of data that is the key component of comparative analysis, as I interpret the term, rather than simple comparison of reported findings. Access to raw data is therefore essential. Nias's (1981; 1989) testing of Herzberg's Motivation-Hygiene Theory on her own research subjects (to which I refer in Chapter 3) was not an example of what I consider to be comparative analysis since Nias did not have access to Herzberg's raw research data. As I interpret it, comparative analysis involves a process of re-analysis of the data from two or more studies in order to elucidate an issue that has emerged as puzzling in some respect when the sets of findings from each study are compared. Comparative analysis may be undertaken by a researcher on studies that were not conducted by her/him, but since access to the raw data is needed it is more likely to involve researchers' re-visiting their own studies. Nevertheless, this still tackles the issue of fragmentation in educational research since it encourages researchers to avoid seeing each of their studies as finite and discrete. It is the specific form of reflective practice manifested by a concern to re-visit and re-think that distinguishes the analytical researcher.

ILLUSTRATING COMPARATIVE ANALYSIS

From a recent comparative analysis of data from two of my own studies, my thinking about the relationship between morale, job satisfaction and motivation and leadership developed significantly. If I had been asked before my comparative analysis what I considered to be the most potent influence on teacher morale, job satisfaction and motivation I would have replied, 'leadership'. Indeed, I have made it quite clear in my published work that I considered this to be the case:

> the most strikingly common factor to emerge as influential on teachers' morale, job satisfaction and motivation is school leadership. Whether it was the extent to which it enabled or constrained teachers, created and fostered school professional climates that were compatible with teachers' ideals, or engaged their commitment and enthusiasm, the leadership effected by their headteachers was clearly a key determinant of how teachers felt about their jobs. (Evans, 1998, p. 118)

> My research findings revealed, categorically, that the greatest influences on teacher morale, job satisfaction and motivation are school leadership and management. (Evans, 1999, p. 17)

Now, my response would be a little less categorical. My comparative analysis led me to delve deeper and to uncover more, and I currently find myself in the position of believing that the relationship between educational leadership and teachers' attitudes to their work is less simple and straightforward than I previously considered it to be.

Much of my research has focused on identifying and explaining the factors that affect job-related attitudes in schoolteachers (Evans, 1997c; 1998) and in academics (Evans and Abbott, 1998) and has revealed the complexity and intricacies of three specific job-related attitudes: morale, job satisfaction and motivation. My findings pointed to factors that are considerably more influential on these attitudes than those generally identified by assumption and commonsense reasoning. In order to illustrate the nature and the benefits of comparative analysis, I pick up the 'story so far' of what – up to the point of undertaking my comparative analysis – my research-informed analyses led me to attribute as factors influencing morale, job satisfaction and motivation; identifying leadership as a key factor.

The 'Story so far': a Fifth Stage of Elucidation
Elsewhere (Evans, 1997c; 1998) I have identified what may be considered to be four levels of understanding, or stages of elucidation, represented by work in the field of job-related attitudes. These range from a first level of understanding that has as its basis

conventional wisdom and common sense, but over-simplistic, reasoning. This level is exemplified by arguments that are typically promulgated by the media, such as those which equate job satisfaction with centrally initiated policy and conditions of service, including pay. At the other end of the range is the fourth level: one of in-depth analysis and recognition of the need for conceptual clarity and precision. This level of understanding, recognizing the inaccuracies associated with crude generalization which ignores individualism, focuses upon the lowest common factor in relation to determinants of job satisfaction amongst individuals. Analysis at this fourth level seeks commonalities and generalization, but it seeks commonalities and generalization which are accurate, because they are free from contextual specificity. This level has contributed much to elucidation not only of what job satisfaction and morale are, but of what, fundamentally, are their determinants. Suggested determinants of job satisfaction are, typically, the fulfilment of individuals' needs, fulfilment of expectations or congruence of values.

To these, based on my research analyses, I added a fifth stage of elucidation since, for practical purposes, despite its analytical and conceptual sophistication, the elucidation provided by level four has, on its own, limited value. If we accept that the rationale for undertaking any piece of research must not simply be to develop theory, but also, as I point out in Chapter 10, to apply that developed theory to policy and practice, then information that, for example, teachers' or academics' job satisfaction is dependent upon their job-related needs or expectations being met is useful, but needs supplementing if it is to be applied meaningfully. The fifth level which I have contributed applies the lowest common factor analysis of level four to context-specific exemplars. In the case of my research into schoolteachers' job-related attitudes these are teaching-specific exemplars, and with the academics whom I studied the exemplars are specific to their work.

Representing this fifth level, described in detail elsewhere (Evans 1997c; 1998), my research findings revealed schoolteacher morale, job satisfaction and motivation to be influenced much less by externally initiated factors such as salary, educational policy and reforms, and conditions of service, than by factors emanating from the more immediate context within which teachers work: school-specific or, more precisely, job-specific factors. As a result, leadership emerged as a key attitudes-influencing factor. Underpinning this, three factors were highlighted as being influential upon morale, job satisfaction and motivation: realistic expectations, relative perspective and professionality orientation. Relative perspective is the individual's perspective on her/his situation in relation to comparable situations. In the context of work situations, for example, relative perspectives may incorporate consideration of previous posts — in whole or in part — or of other institutions, or of colleagues' situations. The current job-related situation is perceived and evaluated in relation to other jobs or occupations; former jobs; knowledge of the situations of colleagues in other institutions or departments. Relative perspective also includes consideration of the work-related situation in relation to the rest of one's life. This consideration includes the relative prioritization of work and personal life.

Realistic expectations are influenced by relative perspective. They do not necessarily reflect individuals' ideals; rather, they reflect what the individual *realistically* expects from her/his work-related situation.

Through an iterative process, professionality orientation both influences and is influenced by realistic expectations and relative perspective. Professionality is explained in Chapter 1.

I have highlighted intra-institutional disparity as one of the key findings of my research into schoolteachers' attitudes to their work (Evans, 1997c; 1998), arguing that it reflects a complex combination of individuals' professionality orientations, realistic expectations and relative perspectives. Essentially, my research findings led me to the interpretation that it is perceived proximity to their conception of their job-related ideal that underpins individuals' job-related attitudes. This ideal may not necessarily have been conceptualized as such, but its dimensions begin to take shape through individuals' conceptions of their preferences and priorities. It is also dynamic; being liable to fluctuation and modification. Job-related ideals — or, put another way, ideal jobs — reflect individuals' current values, needs and expectations. These are influenced by relative perspective, and they underpin professionality orientation and realistic expectations. Since these vary from individual to individual, even within one professional group, what satisfies one teacher may not necessarily satisfy another, and the school that suits one may not suit another.

This, in brief, is the point to which analyses of my research findings relating to schoolteachers' job-related attitudes had taken me before I undertook the comparative analysis described in this chapter. This comparative analysis encompassed the findings from my study of academics and my study of schoolteachers, in order to provide an even clearer understanding of morale, job satisfaction and motivation and of the nature of the impact upon them of leadership.

When the lowest common factor analysis, to which I refer above, was applied to teaching-specific exemplars, leadership emerged as a key attitudes-influencing factor since it shaped teachers' work contexts and had the capacity, through policy and decision-making, to enable people to do their work or to constrain their doing it, and to determine individuals' proximity to their ideal jobs. Leaders, I have argued (Evans, 1999), are capable of firing teachers with enthusiasm or making them dread going to work every morning; more significantly, they may exacerbate the problems created by the imposition of centrally initiated policy or they may buffer teachers against them. My samples of schoolteachers reported diverse and wide-ranging levels of morale, job satisfaction and motivation which could, for the most part, be attributed to the influence that leadership imposed on individuals' working lives. My sample of academics, on the other hand, reported generally more uniform and, compared with the schoolteachers, considerably higher levels of morale, job satisfaction and motivation.

The Research
My comparative analysis was of data from two separate studies: a composite study of morale and job satisfaction amongst primary school teachers in the UK, and a study of the effectiveness of teaching and learning in higher education.

COMPOSITE STUDY OF TEACHER MORALE AND JOB SATISFACTION
This comprised four studies, carried out in the UK from 1988 to 1992, each having a different focus within the broad, overall, remit of identifying and examining factors which influence teacher morale and job satisfaction. The four studies are summarized in Table 4.1. A more detailed description of the research design of this study, including samples of core interview questions and details of the questionnaire used, as well as sample details, is provided in Evans (1997 b; 1998). (See also Chapter 5.)

Table 4.1: Outline details of the research design of the composite study

Study	Focus of enquiry	Dates	Sample		Method(s) of data collection
			No. of schools	No. of teachers	
(i) Rockville	Investigation of the morale level at Rockville County Primary School and of the factors influencing it	1988–9	1	12	(i) Observation (ii) Semi-structured interview (iii) Questionnaire
(ii) school climate	Investigation of the effects on teachers' attitudes to their jobs of the combination of school climate and teachers' professionality	1989–90	2	6	(i) Observation (ii) Semi-structured interview
(iii) 'extended' professionality case studies	Investigation of factors affecting the job-related attitudes of 'extended' professionals	1990–2	4	6	Semi-structured interview
(iv) post-ERA follow-up	Investigation of the comparative effects on teachers' attitudes to their jobs of school-specific and centrally imposed factors	1992–3	1	8	Semi-structured interview

THE EFFECTIVENESS OF TEACHING AND LEARNING IN HIGHER EDUCATION

The main aim of this study was to acquire greater understanding of how teaching in higher education may be effective in meeting what both students and tutors perceived as their needs. Data were collected through semi-structured interviews with twenty tutors and thirty-six students from an English university which is recognized for its strong research focus. The sample of tutors and students represented four different degree courses. The tutor sample breakdown is shown in Table 4.2. Interviews with tutors

Table 4.2: Tutor sample breakdown

	Female			Male		
	Lect.	Snr lect.	Prof.	Lect.	Snr lect.	Prof.
English and American studies		1		2		
Physics	1			1	2	
Law	1		1	2	1	
Education	4	1		2		1

incorporated discussion of what they perceived to be their job-related ideals and needs, as well as issues influencing morale, job satisfaction and motivation. A more detailed description of the research design of this study, including interview schedules and processes of analysis, is provided in Evans and Abbott (1998), pp. 19–27.

Continuing the Story: Applying a Comparative Analysis
It was the disparity between the two different samples, school-teachers and academics, in relation to reported levels of morale, job satisfaction and motivation, that prompted me to want to delve deeper into analysing influences on these job-related attitudes. The schoolteacher sample reported diverse and wide-ranging levels, which were generally attributable to leadership, whilst the academics, who seemed unaffected by leadership, had, for the most part, comparatively higher levels of morale, job satisfaction and motivation. This disparity puzzled me. I wanted to delve deeper to try to shed some light on the issue of the influence of leadership on job-related attitudes.

Since I have presented the findings of each of my two studies elsewhere in detail (see Evans, 1998, for the fullest presentation of the findings of my research into schoolteachers' morale, job satisfaction and motivation, and Evans and Abbott, 1998, pp. 81–143, for findings relating to academics' job-related attitudes), I outline them only here. The purpose of this section of the chapter is to illustrate how I developed out of a comparative analysis of the two sets of research data a more complete understanding of morale, job satisfaction and motivation – and the influence upon them of leadership – amongst education professionals than I had previously achieved. An outline of the research findings from both studies is presented in Table 4.3, which is self-explanatory. General trends, rather than uniformity, are represented by these data.

Table 4.3: Outline of general trends, within each of the two samples, emerging from the research findings relating to schoolteachers' and academics' job-related attitudes

	Schoolteachers	Academics
Morale, job satisfaction and motivation levels	• diverse	• generally uniform
Description of levels	• wide-ranging: from very high to very low	• narrow in range: from high to very high
Key factors influencing diversity of levels within sample	• professionality orientation • prioritization of job	• length of service at the university
Key factors influencing morale, job satisfaction and motivation levels	• institutional leadership • institutional organization • institutional policy and practice • collegial relations	• compatibility with institutional ethos • link between teaching and research
General sources of positive job-related attitudes	• teaching • decisional participation • collegiality • interpersonal relations	• research • teaching • collegiality
General sources of negative job-related attitudes	• institutional policy • management decisions • interpersonal relations	• teaching • institutional policy • departmental policy
Specific sources of positive job-related attitudes	• passing on skills/knowledge • personal efficiency • leading INSET • collegial camaraderie • involvement in institutional policy-/decision-making • recognition from respected colleagues	• academic freedom • recognition from the academic community • contributing to advancing knowledge/understanding • passing on skills/knowledge • mentoring colleagues
Specific sources of negative job-related attitudes	• poor management • ineffective leadership • incompatibility with institutional professional climate	• 'low level' administrative responsibilities • teaching 'low calibre' students • teaching loads • responsibility for teaching general courses unrelated to own research

The starting point in trying to understand better the nature of, and the influences on, morale, job satisfaction and motivation amongst education professionals was to examine what accounts for commonalities and differences between and within the two samples.

Here the comparative analysis began. A reasonable assumption, based upon the information about my findings that I have presented so far, would be that, since the schoolteachers represented four different institutions, and the academics only one, the distinction between the two samples in relation to the range of levels of job-related attitudes was institutional. This was not the case, however. Whilst it could be claimed that, if my sample of tutors is representative, the university in question was one that fostered positive job-related attitudes amongst its academic staff, it was certainly not the case that the four institutions represented by my schoolteacher sample each sustained staff morale, job satisfaction and motivation levels that were sufficiently uniform to warrant its being categorized as a 'high morale' or a 'low morale' school. Within each of the four primary schools morale, job satisfaction and motivation levels varied; in some cases dramatically, and in other cases less significantly.

My interpretation that proximity to an 'ideal job' determines job satisfaction, morale and motivation levels was borne out by the academics' study. Out of the full sample of twenty, six tutors admitted that they already, or very nearly, had what they considered to be their ideal jobs and these tutors reported very high levels of job satisfaction, motivation and morale. Of the remaining tutors eleven, who reported generally high levels of job satisfaction, motivation and morale, perceived their work as incorporating many elements of their 'ideal job'. The small minority of three that were rather more − though not excessively so − dissatisfied, applying their relative perspective to the evaluation of their situation, felt that their work had lost many of those elements that had made it, for them, more 'ideal' than it currently was.

Yet, whilst I dismissed the notion of 'high morale' or 'low morale' institutions, it was clear from my findings that there is a very strong institutional dimension to both schoolteachers' and academics' job-related attitudes. Since it is within the contexts in which individuals work that the job-related needs that both underpin and reflect their job-related ideals are able to be met, the institution is immensely influential on levels of job satisfaction, morale and motivation. The nature of this influence is individualized, because job-related needs and ideals are diverse. It is a question not of a model of general motivational, or morale-friendly, institutional policies and ethos but of the degree of match between individuals and their institutions: what I have referred to elsewhere (Evans, 1998) as round pegs and square holes, or, as Vancouver and Schmitt (1991) describe it, 'person-organization fit'. In my comparative analysis I tried to identify more precisely the constituent features of a good match.

Uncompromising Contexts: the Basis of a Good Match
Most (seventeen of the twenty) of the academics' and some (nine) of the schoolteachers' cases represent, to varying degrees, good matches. Common to all of these cases was the individual's general acceptance of institutional policy and practice. This was a genuine acceptance, rather than what Lacey (1977) terms strategic compliance, but it did not preclude specific areas of contention; it was an overall, rather than a wholehearted and total, acceptance. Similarly, mismatches were represented by cases of individuals' overall dissension of institutional policy and practice.

The bases of acceptance or dissension of institutional policy and practice were a complex and dynamic interrelated combination of individuals' ideologies, values, knowledge, understanding, expectations and prioritizations, all of which are constituent elements of professionality, as I define it in Chapter 1. With reference to my research into schoolteachers' job-related attitudes, I have previously (Evans, 1998) identified as the basic determinant of the degree of individual-institution match the extent to which there is ideological compatibility between school leaders – in particular, headteachers or principals – and teachers. Leadership, then, I reasoned, is one of the most potent influences upon morale, job satisfaction and motivation. Indeed, my research uncovered many examples of schoolteachers' reports of the extent to which their job-related attitudes were influenced – positively and negatively – by their headteachers or principals.

Moreover, in uncovering this relationship between perceptions of leadership and teachers' attitudes to their jobs, I found that my research findings corroborated those of others (Ball, 1987; Hayes and Ross, 1989; Nias, 1980; 1989; Nias *et al.*, 1989; Rosenholtz, 1991; Veal, Clift and Holland, 1989). In particular, in one of the earliest studies of teacher morale – a questionnaire survey of nearly 1,800 American teachers – Chase (1953) became aware of this relationship: 'When teachers' expectations are fulfilled with regard to the leadership of administrators and supervisors, their morale soars; when their expectations are disappointed, morale takes a nose dive' (Chase, 1953, p. 1).

However, in the light of analysis of the findings of my study of academics, I now consider it an oversimplified and inadequate interpretation that morale, job satisfaction and motivation are significantly influenced by leadership. I do not reject my original identification of leadership as a significant influence on job-related attitudes; rather, my comparative analysis led me to qualify it. I present a fuller interpretation – informed by my comparative analysis – of precisely *why* it is so influential and of the nature of its influence.

Comparison of the job-related factors that were applicable to my two samples, schoolteachers and academics, highlighted leadership as a potentially significant one, since I was struck immediately by the disparity in relation to the extent to which leadership impacted upon the working lives of each of the two samples. This striking disparity served as an important catalyst for my comparative analysis. Amongst my sample of schoolteachers, which, in this respect, seems to be typical of the profession as a whole as it still is today, institutional leadership was a dominant feature of individuals' working lives. This was the case even where leaders were considered ineffective or inadequate. The nature of teachers' working lives within the social and administrative structure of the school is such that it is very leader-dependent. In the developed Western world at the current time – the turn of the millennium – frequent policy changes and reforms aimed at improving standards, and an emphasis on accountability, mean that effective teaching in schools and colleges cannot be done unilaterally. It now involves collegial co-operation and interdependence and institutional coherence of policy and practice, all of which require co-ordination on the part of one or more leaders. Leadership which is deficient because it fails to provide the necessary co-ordination therefore impacts as much upon teachers' working lives as does effective leadership. Amongst my sample of academics, however, leadership featured considerably less prominently in relation to individuals' working lives. The nature of these academics' work was such that most of it seemed to be leader-independent and able to be carried out with a high degree of autonomy. Perhaps one reason for this is that research constituted a large proportion of the academics' work, and this is an activity which may generally be carried out effectively independently of institutional or departmental leadership. Authoritarianism and hierarchism, which underpin the structure of institutional organization in the compulsory education sector, were not evident in the day-to-day business of academic life, as it was reported by my sample. Indeed, there were many references to the freedom of choice, autonomy and generally low accountability enjoyed by academics (see Evans, 2001b, p. 299 for illustrative quotations).

Of the schoolteachers whom I interviewed and observed, those who reported low levels of morale and job satisfaction and, in some cases, motivation attributed their negative attitudes to poor leadership and management in their schools. From the evidence outlined so far, therefore, it seemed reasonable to assume that leadership is an important factor that needs to be incorporated into consideration of what influences job-related attitudes amongst education professionals: negative attitudes are associated with contexts where leadership features prominently, positive attitudes are associated with contexts where there is much more leader-independence.

The issue turned out not to be so simple and straightforward. Firstly, school leadership did not necessarily have a detrimental effect on the job-related attitudes of my teachers; there were two examples of relative indifference on the part of teachers to their headteachers' leadership and management, as well as several examples of leadership that was attributed as fostering very positive job-related attitudes (two teachers made positive assessments of their current headteacher, whom they shared, and three teachers referred positively to former headteachers). Secondly, academics' working lives are not as leader-independent as they may appear. My comparative analysis was complicated by the existence of two levels of leadership that were applicable to the academics: departmental and institutional. Although departmental leadership appeared to impact only negligibly upon their day-to-day working lives (five departments were represented by my sample), the academics were essentially influenced by institutional leadership, since it determined the wider, pervasive ethos within which they operated and which they accepted, and which, in turn, was reflected in policy- and decision-making that impacted upon their work (the university in question had a distinct ethos reflecting a strong, explicit research culture). Thirdly – and this is, I suggest, one of the most significant revelations to arise from my comparative analysis – leadership is not, *fundamentally*, in itself, an attitudes-influencing factor. Rather, it is the medium through which are transmitted the values and ideologies represented by the contexts in which people work. My current definition of a work context is *the situation and circumstances, arising out of a combination and interrelationship of institutionally and externally imposed conditions, that constitute the environment and culture within which an individual carries out her/his job*. What influences job-related attitudes is the extent to which these contexts are acceptable to individuals, on the basis of the degree of congruence between their own values and ideologies and those that shape the work contexts. Leadership is *seen to be* an attitudes-influencing factor because it imposes considerable influence on these work contexts, either actively or, in the case of ineffective, laissez-faire leadership, by default.

The precise nature of the values and ideologies that underpin individuals' conceptions of what, for them, are 'ideal' jobs was another significant finding to be uncovered by my comparative analysis. In the cases of schoolteachers and academics, job-related ideals incorporated ethical, epistemological, affective, professional, economic and egocentric considerations to encompass views on six specific issues:

- equity and justice
- pedagogy or androgogy
- organizational efficiency
- interpersonal relations
- collegiality
- self-conception and self-image.

It is impossible to arrange these issues hierarchically because individuals differed in their prioritizations of them. Nevertheless, all six were incorporated into every conception of an 'ideal' job.

The basis of a good match is an 'uncompromising context': a work context that does not require individuals to compromise their ideologies as reflected by their views on the six issues listed above. An 'uncompromising context' is one that accommodates individuals' views on these six issues – particularly those that they consider most important. Within my two samples the nature of individuals' views on each of these issues was wide-ranging.

These six issues clearly matter to schoolteachers and academics. In general, a good match, therefore, is a work context that does not compromise the individual's professionality. What education professionals evidently want is to be able to practise, unhindered, within a context that is compatible with their needs, expectations, values and ideologies.

My comparative analysis revealed leadership to influence job-related attitudes not directly, as I previously believed, but in an indirect way, through its capacity for shaping work contexts that either match or are at odds with what individuals want in relation to equity and justice, pedagogy or androgogy, organizational efficiency, interpersonal relations, collegiality, and self-conception and self-image. It is this degree of match that fundamentally affects how people feel about their jobs and yet realization of this had eluded me until I undertook the comparative analysis. Whether they realize it or not, it is their work contexts – not their leaders – upon which people are essentially reliant, and analysis of the findings of a parallel study, encompassing a wider perspective than that afforded by examination of the schoolteacher study only, demonstrated this to be the case.

THE PROCESS OF COMPARATIVE ANALYSIS

How, then, do you set about undertaking a comparative analysis? In the section above I have outlined the process involved in developing my own thinking in relation to trying to identify the reason why two levels of morale, job satisfaction and motivation differed so much between two research samples. In addition, the account provided by Page, Samson and Crockett (1998) of the process whereby they identified, in turn, each of three different interpretations of why there was discrepancy between the responses to their research of their two sub-samples serves as an excellent description of a comparative analysis. The authors provide much detail of the reasoning and thought processes that prompted their successive revisions to their explanations, illustrating with great clarity how analytical researchers work. Similarly, Luttrell's (2000, pp. 508–15) description of her comparative analysis of two sets of data clearly explains the process that developed her knowledge and enhanced her understanding of the key issues emerging from her research:

> I quickly learned that the North Carolina women offered the same skeletal school story as the Philadelphia women did. They too cast school as a battleground and in us–them terms, but with two key variations on these themes. Paying close attention to these variations enabled me to develop a more nuanced analysis of the inseparability of race, class, gender, and a fuller appreciation for school context. (p. 510)

But it is one thing to read accounts of how a specific example of comparative analysis has contributed towards furthering knowledge and understanding; it is quite another thing to apply the process. In this section I provide guidelines to help you carry out your own comparative analysis.

The first stage in the process is to establish the degree of corroboration or inconsistency between the findings of the studies that you wish to compare. You will find it helpful to list the specific areas of consistency or inconsistency as I did in my own comparative analysis (Table 4.3; p. 83).

The key element of the comparative process is the uncovering of reasons why consistency and inconsistency in the findings from the different studies has occurred. The whole point of the exercise is to contribute to relevant knowledge bases; it is essentially an elucidatory quest, and the areas of inconsistency – and consistency – should be perceived as important clues. The skill of comparative analysis lies in recognizing the clues and using them to reveal answers and explanations which will eventually lead to the generation and development of theory. In comparative analyses the areas of inconsistency between findings constitute a puzzle that you, as the researcher undertaking the analysis, need to solve. Areas of corroboration, though, should be seen as important clues to help you because they provide the means of checking the feasibility of your developing analyses and formulation of ideas and theories. Often you may find yourself veering towards a specific explanation but consideration of the consistencies between findings will highlight flaws in the thinking that took you in that direction. Consistency between findings should not therefore be overlooked. It serves as a potential check against erroneous reasoning. Moreover, evidence drawn from consideration of areas of consistency is an important ingredient in the processes of reductionism and generalization that I identify in Chapter 9 as essential stages in the development of theory.

Uncovering reasons why inconsistency has occurred between two or more sets of research findings should start with examination of the research designs, which are the most obvious source of discrepancy. It is important to identify and examine areas of difference in relation specifically to differences in the research aim, objectives and research questions; differences between the samples; differences in the sampling processes; differences in the data collection, and differences in the data analysis. This is a stage of data display. Its purpose is to facilitate the process of making comparisons and uncovering reasons and explanations by making available the requisite information and having it to hand, in a form that is accessible.

From this point onwards your thinking should be like that of a detective trying to solve a crime by considering all possible explanations in turn and dismissing those that appear to lack feasibility. Every single distinction between the studies being compared needs to be listed and considered and its potential significance assessed. This is why it is important to have prepared and have to hand all of the information that may possibly be useful to you in solving the puzzle facing you. In the case of each distinction you should ask yourself, 'Is this likely to be – or *could* it be – an explanation of why the research findings differ?' If your answer is 'No', the distinction in question may be dismissed; otherwise, it should remain on what is developing into a shortlist of explanations. At this stage you should develop the skill of applying lateral thinking and of looking beyond the obvious in your search for explanations.

When this process is completed you will be left with a shortlist of reasons why two or more sets of research findings differ in at least one respect. This may be as far as you can go – often it is impossible to go beyond offering several possible solutions to the research puzzle – but, on occasions, you may feel that there is a strong enough case for retaining only one likely explanation. Whether you are left with one or several, though, you should have applied checking procedures to each explanation that you consider feasible. These are feasibility testing procedures which are as applicable to any research data analysis as they are to comparative analysis. They include *testing your thinking on someone else; research subject verification; identification of rival explanations* and *testing through future research.*

Testing Your Thinking on Someone Else

However experienced a researcher you are, it is always a good idea to present your explanation to others who have sufficient knowledge and understanding of educational research and/or the subject to which your explanation relates to be able to scrutinize and evaluate it, and who may offer helpful suggestions for revisions. If your explanation relates to a methodological issue, for example, it should be presented to other researchers whom you consider to be competent methodologists; if it relates to an aspect of teachers' thinking, you could test it on an audience of teachers. This kind of testing could be done informally, by approaching people privately, or it could be incorporated into the presentation of your ideas in a work-in-progress research seminar or conference paper.

Research Subject Verification

Where applicable, the thinking behind your explanation(s) may be tested on the subjects used in the studies being compared. This is most likely to occur where specific attitudes or behaviour of the research subjects forms a key issue within your explanation.

Identifying Rival Explanations
You should actively seek — rather than sit back and wait to encounter — rival explanations. This is the most risky — but rigorous — means of testing your thinking. You should challenge yourself to find an alternative, more feasible, explanation than the one you currently accept. Any such rival explanation should either be dismissed on grounds of reason or adopted in favour of the explanation that it challenged.

Testing through Future Research
Since there are always limitations with analysis that is applied retrospectively (that is, after the conclusion of a study), explanations derived by this means will always incorporate a degree of tentativeness. To reduce this, future research may serve as a means to test out such explanations. If the explanation is methodologically related, the research design of future studies can incorporate comparative procedures, using experimental and control mechanisms for testing it. If it is related to substantive issues within the topic of the research, the explanation may be tested through data collection. In future studies of educational leadership and management, for example, I will have the opportunity to test my explanation for the disparity between the job-related attitudes of my two research samples, presented above as an example of a comparative analysis. Since my explanation is that it is not, fundamentally, leadership that influences people's morale, job satisfaction and motivation, but the extent to which the contexts in which they work are perceived to be compromising or uncompromising, the data that I shall collect will focus on perceptions of compromising and uncompromising work contexts and on what I have identified as the six issues that matter to people in their work contexts.

To the analytical researcher the comparative analysis process is a repeating cycle of asking why inconsistencies have occurred between research findings; formulating explanations; testing the feasibility of these; rejecting, revising or reformulating explanations; testing the feasibility of these, and so on, until what remains is what is currently the most likely explanation. This explanation then constitutes an advancement in knowledge and understanding on those — the knowledge and understanding — resulting from the separate studies whose findings were compared. Herein lies the value of comparative analyses to educational research.

THE VALUE OF COMPARATIVE ANALYSIS

Comparative analysis is a mode of methodological enhancement. It has the potential to make a significant contribution to methodological and epistemological development and advancement. The nature and the potential of this contribution are evident in the case of my own comparative analysis, described in outline above. If I had not begun to examine the basis of the disparity between the findings relating to each of two of my research samples, schoolteachers and academics, it is unlikely that I would have embarked on the process of questioning the accuracy of my attribution of leadership as a key attitudes-influencing factor. I would not have developed further my 'fifth level of elucidation' to encompass identification of the precise common issues that underpin and determine the nature of the 'good match' principle, nor would I have refined my interpretation of why leadership appears to impact so significantly on morale, job satisfaction and motivation. The contribution that my revised findings make to the study of job-related attitudes amongst education professionals has arisen out of a comparative analysis that was a tool for delving deeper.

Here, then, is surely a lesson that may be applied to the development and promotion of reflective practice in educational research. In their article on reliability and validity, LeCompte and Goetz (1982) suggest that one way of reducing the threat of reaching spurious conclusions is to test conclusions against alternative explanations. Replication, too, has long been recognized as a means of testing and validating findings. With these two methods, though, the focus is generally on seeking verification, rather than highlighting and explaining differences. The comparative analyses that I have undertaken – one of which is described in this chapter and another in the next – had this latter purpose, and in addition they aimed, by examining disparity, to reveal underlying commonalities and generalizability.

Comparative analyses have much to offer as a tool that imposes methodological rigour. They potentially challenge the comfort that researchers derive from believing their conclusions to be accurate and their analyses complete. They present alternative evidence that needs considering, and they precipitate a re-think. They provide a mechanism for testing and verifying findings and refining research-generated theory. As such, they should be included within their repertoires of research practice by anyone who considers her/himself to be an analytical researcher. The next chapter provides the opportunity for developing comparative analysis skills.

A tale of two studies: a research puzzle to solve

In keeping with the pervasive message conveyed in this book, this chapter encourages extensive reflection and analysis in order to work out possible explanations for a puzzling occurrence. It follows on from Chapter 4's introduction of comparative analysis by exemplifying the way in which the general process of, and the guidelines for carrying out, comparative analysis may be put to use.

The chapter presents a research puzzle to solve by applying, as far as is possible, the comparative analysis process. This will be an imperfect application of the process because, as I point out in Chapter 4, effective comparative analysis is dependent upon access to and utilization of the original raw research data. In the case of the puzzle presented below, the raw research data consist of two full box files of transcripts of research interviews. I have successfully used this research puzzle as a means of allowing classes of graduate students to apply comparative analysis, having made available to them all of the original data. This provision is clearly not possible within a book. Nevertheless, I make available a selection of raw interview data, which I present at an appropriate point below.

My purpose in presenting a research puzzle to be solved is only partly that of providing a comparative analysis exercise. Another purpose is to introduce an issue that I have uncovered in the course of my own work and believe to be a potentially important, but overlooked, internal validity issue. Precisely what that issue is I do not reveal until later, since its discovery through the process of trying to solve the research puzzle below is one of the objectives of this chapter.

A TALE OF TWO STUDIES

The puzzle draws upon my early work as a researcher and involves two of the very first research projects in which I participated. I refer to these as the *Composite Study of Teacher Morale and Job Satisfaction* and the *Teaching as Work Project*. For brevity, I shorten these respectively to *the morale study* and *the TAWP study*.

Both studies were undertaken at roughly the same time. The morale study lasted from 1988 to 1993 and the TAWP study from 1990 to 1991. Both used samples of primary school teachers in England and Wales. The morale study used twenty-one Key Stage 1 and 2[1] teachers employed in four different schools, and the TAWP study sample comprised twenty-four Key Stage 1 teachers in twenty-two different schools. The main aim of the morale study was to identify and examine the factors that were influential on teacher morale and job satisfaction. The main aim of the TAWP study was to identify and examine the impact upon teachers' working lives of the implementation of the English and Welsh national curriculum, which began in 1989 in Key Stage 1 classes.

An outline overview of the findings from the two studies is that the morale study revealed teacher morale and job satisfaction to be influenced much more significantly by school-specific issues than by centrally initiated issues such as pay, conditions of service and educational reforms, including the implementation of the national curriculum, and the TAWP study revealed teachers' morale and job satisfaction to be strongly influenced by a specific centrally initiated factor: the impact on their working lives of the implementation of the national curriculum. This and other relevant information is presented in Table 5.1. See also Chapter 4 for further details on the research design of the morale study. The puzzle that needs solving is: Why was there such a difference between the findings of the two studies in relation to influences on teacher morale and job satisfaction?

Your task is to try to solve the puzzle. In order to do so, you will need to undertake – as best you can – a comparative analysis.

---

[1]   Key Stage 1: ages 4–7; Key Stage 2: ages 7–11.

Table 5.1: Outline information on the two studies

	Morale study	TAWP study
Purpose of research	To identify and examine the factors influencing teachers' levels of morale and job satisfaction.	To investigate the impact upon teachers' working lives of the implementation of the national curriculum.
Outline of research details	• research carried out by a single researcher working independently • sample of 21 Key Stage 1&2 teachers • data collected 1988–93 • semi-structured interviews used • 4 different schools represented	• research carried out by team of 4 • sample of 24 Key Stage 1 teachers • data collected 1990–91 • semi-structured interviews used • 22 different schools represented
Overview of main findings	• generally teachers' working lives had not been altered as a result of the implementation of the national curriculum • teacher morale and job satisfaction influenced primarily by school-specific factors • national curriculum has not significantly affected morale and job satisfaction, or stress levels, amongst the sample	• generally teachers' working lives had been considerably altered as a result of the implementation of the national curriculum • morale and job satisfaction had generally been adversely affected • stress had generally increased

SOLVING THE PUZZLE: A COMPARATIVE ANALYSIS

You may already have formed several ideas about the possible reasons for the discrepancy between the two sets of findings. If so, your comparative analysis may begin with your following up the issues that you consider important. Why was it that in the morale study the implementation of the national curriculum was not identified as a significant factor influencing morale or job satisfaction whereas in the TAWP study it was identified by most of the sample as influential on morale and job satisfaction, and in most of these cases its influence was reported to be negative? Indeed, the fact that it was not identified by the teachers in the first three of the four studies that made up the composite morale study prompted me to add a fourth, post-ERA (Education Reform Act), study. I reasoned that, at the time of the Rockville study, which was carried out 1988–9 (see Table 4.1), the full force of the implications for schools and teachers of the 1988 Education Reform Act, and, in particular, of national curriculum implementation and its testing, had not been felt. I therefore conducted a post-ERA follow-up study, involving follow-up interviews, with the purpose of ascertaining whether or not the importance on teachers' morale and satisfaction levels of school-specific issues was diminished by competing concerns about centrally initiated policy implementation. This study was restricted to teachers from Rockville County Primary School because they were the only ones of my interviewees who, at the time of their interviews, had not yet been affected by the demands of the national curriculum (see Table 4.1). (Teachers involved in the school climate and the 'extended' professionality case studies, which took place after the introduction in schools of the national curriculum, had been involved in its implementation.) Eight of the twelve Rockville teacher interviewees were re-interviewed in this post-ERA study. The findings of this fourth study, however, still revealed school-specific issues to be far more influential on morale and job satisfaction than the implementation of the national curriculum, which was scarcely mentioned by my teacher interviewees.

To present a clearer picture of the data from the morale and the TAWP studies I provide extracts from earlier publications and, where appropriate, from interview transcripts.

The TAWP study
The following are extended extracts from the report of the TAWP study, *Workloads, Achievement and Stress* (Campbell *et al.*, 1991):

> All the teachers ... reported that they were experiencing the work of teaching differently from before, in a way that was to do with the mental state in which they conducted their work. One of them, Ann, illustrated this state of mind by using a simile which we have called, following her, the 'running commentary' syndrome. There are two elements to this syndrome: a commitment to working very hard, doing one's best out of conscientiousness, linked to a lack of one's sense of achievement in their work, despite the effort, because there was always something else to be done ...

Well, what is frightening now is that we are being blinkered now into the national curriculum and so everything else is hanging on by its fingernails really. That's how I feel at the moment – the sheer amount of time required to cope with what you hope to achieve – it just seems to be expanding to fill the day and I am constantly getting to the state where I am noticing it far more now that I never complete what I hope to achieve. There is always, like, a carry-forward so that you never get the feeling at the end of a session or the end of a day, 'Great, I've done this that I hoped we would do', there is always something else ... I didn't use to feel that ... I used to get to the end of the day and think, 'Oh, great, we have done this'. So this has been a major change as far as I am concerned. (pp. 35–6)

The [running commentary] syndrome was experienced, though expressed differently, by every one of our teachers. (p. 37)

A finding common to nearly all our teachers [twenty of the twenty-four] was that the introduction of the national curriculum and assessment was making their classrooms less pleasant and enjoyable for them as teachers. (p. 37)

There was considerable variation in attitudes to teaching as a job and in the extent of satisfaction and dissatisfaction with teaching post-ERA. But such variation did not seem to be the case when they were talking about morale, which was universally ... perceived to be poor ... (p. 57)

A sense of low morale pervaded most [twenty-two out of the twenty-four] of the interviews, whether the teachers were talking about themselves, their colleagues in school, or the public perception of primary teaching as a job generally. The following extract is at one extreme. It is the view of Angie, a teacher who had decided to get out of teaching:

My commitment to the job, as you have probably read between the lines, has deteriorated ... I don't feel happy about it any more ... There seems to be this pressure on schools to show that they can do the national curriculum and that they are the best – they are going to be better than anyone else ... and the teachers are even doing it; they are competing against each other. My head [headteacher/principal] just expects so much work to be produced, and

this is all over the weekend, and every member of staff is saying, 'I dread six o'clock Sunday.' I thought, 'You dread *six o'clock* Sunday! – I'm spending *most* of Sunday working!'
...

A similar antipathy showed itself in Jane's view, despite her general approval for the national curriculum itself:

Yes, I think the national curriculum has improved things ... it has made it more interesting, if exhausting.

Interviewer: Do you resent the extra workload?
I do now, *very* much, and every year as it gets worse I resent it more ... I'm forty-five now and I really can't see myself keeping up this pace of work for more than another five or six years. I just don't think I could physically cope with it – because I always used to be tired during the holidays, you know, the first couple of days you're a bit tired, aren't you? – but now it takes two or three weeks! I mean, Christmas, I was really, really tired.

Interviewer: You don't envisage it getting any better? You don't think, 'Well, it's because it's new'?
No. I think the next couple of years will be even worse ... No, I can't see it improving in the near future for me at all.

Interviewer: Yes. Before the Education Reform Act – before the national curriculum – would you have seriously thought, 'Oh, good, I'm going to be retiring soon'?
No, I was quite happy, really. I just didn't contemplate doing any other job, but I have to say that I am consciously looking in the papers now to see what else there is that I'd like to do, because I feel so drained as a human being. I know that I can't go on at this pace indefinitely. (pp. 61–2)

It was not only the more senior teachers who saw morale as damagingly low ... Sheila, a young teacher, under twenty-five years of age ... provided a sequence of dialogue that captures the combination of lack of satisfaction, frustration, and lowered motivation that characterised most of our teachers' views. It is difficult to escape the overwhelming sense of her bitterness and disillusionment, explicitly attributed to the implementation of the Education Reform Act ...:

Interviewer: Right, can we go on to talk about the topics of morale, commitment and job satisfaction? Would you say that

your job satisfaction is greater or less than it was before the Education Reform Act and the national curriculum?
A lot less, because I feel I'm not getting the time actually with the children, which was why I went into teaching. I enjoyed being with children. I got a lot of satisfaction from talking to them, seeing them progressing in little ways like that, and now I feel that my time with them is so pressured that I tend to get very stressed and ratty with the children through no fault of their own because I feel these pressures to achieve so much in each session, whereas, before, you didn't have that. If a child started off doing an activity with you and it branched off to something completely different, that was fine, and that was rewarding, and you really got to know the children. But there is just not time for that now. I find myself quite often saying, 'Yes, yes – very nice, but let's carry on with this', and I hate it. I find that so wrong. So that's the major thing which has decreased my job satisfaction, really.

Interviewer: What about your morale and the morale of your colleagues? Has that altered over the past two years?
Yes, definitely! I've been at the school – I'm just beginning my third year – when I started in this school I was a probationer and the feeling has slowly gone more and more downhill. There's much more going into each other's classes – not so much for a chat of how the day went but of how awful everything is and how on earth can we get it all done? Just, generally, a very negative feeling which wasn't there when I first started. I think I feel that way, too – I mean, obviously, I started very enthusiastic and very committed, but more often now I'm finding myself frustrated, fed-up, and just thinking, 'What's the point?' ...

Interviewer: Is there anything in particular about the Education Reform Act that you could pinpoint as affecting morale or job satisfaction and commitment?
Personally, the lack of consultation. I feel it's all being done without me saying anything and I find that insulting because I'm a teacher; I'm at the sharp end of it and I'm not being asked what I think, and, 'Will this work or will this not work?' We're just being told to get on with it – do it – and that's been the thing that's really annoyed me the most, I think, and really made me feel, 'Why should I do it?' (pp. 65–7)

The Morale Study
The following is an extended extract, entitled 'The importance of contextual factors' from the book that reports the findings of the morale study, *Teacher Morale, Job Satisfaction and Motivation* (Evans, 1998, pp. 138–40):

> One of the key findings of my research was that job satisfaction, morale and motivation are predominantly contextually-determined. Interview evidence corroborated the impression which I had gained during the observation phases of the study, that the context of teachers' working lives represents the realities of the job and, as such, has a much greater impact upon job-related attitudes than do factors such as centrally-imposed policy or teachers' conditions of service, including pay. Only one of my interviewees, Jane, a mainscale Rockville teacher who had reached the top of the salary scale, was dissatisfied with teachers' pay. The same teacher also made reference to the wider issue of the demoralizing effect of teachers' low status in society. Only one other teacher, Kay, who held what was then an incentive allowance B, identified pay as a source of satisfaction. A few teachers even identified pay specifically as a relatively unimportant factor in relation to motivation:
>
> > I haven't looked at my payslip for the last twelve months ... and I don't know why − it's not a driving force any more. At one stage I used to long for pay day and look carefully at how much I'd got ... but it doesn't bother me any more. (Mark, Leyburn teacher)
>
> In all cases, it was school-specific factors that teachers identified as the most significant influences on their job satisfaction, morale and motivation. Issues such as the introduction of the national curriculum, which was intended as the main focus of the post-ERA follow-up study, the imposition of contractual hours and the five 'Baker days', designated for in-service training, were either relegated to subsidiary levels of importance in teachers' assessments of what affected their morale and/or job satisfaction, or were assessed within the context of their own school situations, and in relation to how these contexts shaped them. Pat, for example, in her 1992 follow-up interview, spoke of how the Rockville management was a constraint on her doing her job, including her implementation of the national curriculum:

You ask yourself, 'Why am I bothering? Why am I giving up time in the evenings ... time in the holidays, to do work which is not directly related to the class, to find that ... it's being ignored?' – or to find that you go to a management meeting with the head and he doesn't even know what a Core Study Unit is for history! He hasn't even bothered to read the document before he speaks to you! (Pat, Rockville teacher)

Particularly interesting, though, were some teachers' responses to my asking whether centrally-initiated factors affected their attitudes to the job. None of my post-ERA follow-up interviewees had actually identified ERA-imposed factors as being significantly influential on their own job satisfaction, morale and motivation levels when I posed open-ended questions about how they felt about their jobs. It was clear from their comments that any impact which the national curriculum, for example, had had on their working lives had been superseded by that of school-specific issues, such as management and staff relations. Yet, my asking them to talk specifically about the national curriculum prompted responses which seemed to be intended to conform with the popular belief that its introduction has demoralised and demotivated teachers. It was almost as if these teachers felt they would be 'letting the side down' if they failed to identify the introduction of the national curriculum as a negative influence on teachers' job-related attitudes. In doing so, however, they seldom spoke subjectively; rather, they conveyed the impression that they were passing on second-hand knowledge. They did not refer to specific colleagues whom they knew to have been demoralised by the demands of the national curriculum, nor did their evaluations include reference to their own experiences. More-over, when I probed deeper by asking if they could provide any subjective illustrations of how the introduction of the national curriculum had lowered their morale or job satisfaction, most were unable to offer any, and those examples that were related, such as that of Pat, presented above, only served to highlight the influence of negative school-specific factors. Rosemary's comments in her 1992 interview are illustrative of the generality with which complaints about the national curriculum were made. These are particularly interesting when considered alongside some of her other comments about her attitude to her work ... which convey a strong impression of a teacher who sustained high morale by adopting a positive response to change. She responded to my asking her to move onto consideration of the extent to which centrally-imposed factors, such as pay, conditions of service, and the introduction of the national curriculum, had influenced her morale and job satisfaction:

> I don't think pay really enters into it. If a pay rise comes along, everybody's happy. People can always use extra money, but ... er ... *I* think ... people would be happy with pay as it is – I don't think we've done too badly over these last few years, anyway; I think we've had *good* increases – a lot of other things have affected morale ... I think ... you know ... the coming of the national curriculum. The thinking behind it was good ... er ... and you can understand why it was done ... but, the *way* it was done ... the speed ... er ... was all wrong, and this is what gets teachers' backs up more than anything. There've been so *many* changes in such a short time ... not only *those* changes, but, they're bringing changes to *those* changes ... for instance, the maths and the science. The dust has hardly settled ... people are just coming to terms with the national curriculum in maths and science, and the attainment targets are changing. So, it means a lot of changing and planning of the curriculum in school ... and it's these *changes* that people are not happy with. ... It *is* frustrating, and you feel sorry for the coordinators who put a lot of work in, and they write the policies, and they link it to the national curriculum, and then ... it's all changed. And so, they've got to re-write and ... er ... make changes. The same with the record-keeping, and the assessment. Er ... and I think there's a lot of criticism at both government and at county level, in that they don't give enough guidance. (Rosemary, Rockville teacher, post-ERA study)

Similarly, Kay, who also reported high levels of job satisfaction, morale and motivation, highlighted, in a rather detached way, some of the frequently-identified problems that had accompanied the introduction of the national curriculum:

> *Interviewer: Do you have high morale?*
> At the moment, yes. I think it does come and go ... but, at

the moment, I'm thinking of next year, and what I'll be doing with my class ... er ... but, it does vary a lot ... I think, over the last few years, it's been very low with a lot of people, and outside influences affected that ... And I think, with the national curriculum ... people, at first, felt very threatened by it, and that made morale very, very low ... because you just felt that you'd been doing this job all these years and nobody was satisfied with you ... you know ... what more did they want? Everybody felt they were doing their best ... but, somehow, it just wasn't good enough. I think, now that we've looked into it a bit more we can cope with it, and most people feel *fairly* happy about ... at least doing *some* of it ... you know. (Kay, Sefton Road teacher, school climate study)

The following are illustrative excerpts from interview transcripts:

Well, I would say that my morale at the moment is lower than average ... because of all the stresses and strains of various things that've been going on.

Interviewer: Yes. Can you elaborate?

Yes ... mainly with the deputy [headteacher] ... not doing the job she was supposed to be doing ... the pressure on other staff ... everybody's feeling it and, of course, everybody's discussing it, which tends to bring morale down ... negative views on things ... I don't think she went round visiting classrooms as it was claimed she did ... We don't seem to know where she went – this was a question in everybody's minds – 'Where was she?' Now, I went, with Joanne [a teacher colleague], straight to Geoff [the headteacher] ... because I thought, 'What *is* Margaret [the deputy headteacher] supposed to be doing? Where is she?' He said, 'Well, she hasn't got a timetable, as such', and we said, 'Well, she *should* have' ... Sometimes she'd be in the staffroom – if you had to go in for first aid equipment you'd find her.

... But, I don't think Geoff has been strong enough. He should've put his foot down and said, 'Look, you're doing this. I want you to do *this* timetable', but, instead, he lets it come from Margaret herself, and I think it's the same with Alison [a senior teacher] ... you know, you get things like, 'liaising with so-and-so', or, 'liaising with the nursery school' – I mean, that's too vague. But he lets that pass. Now, you couldn't get away with that as a class teacher ... Some people are doing less than others, and getting more money for it. (Elaine, Rockville teacher, Rockville study).

... Margaret shouldn't have a job as deputy head ... Alison shouldn't – well, they shouldn't, really, for what they do and the amount of money they're paid. For the amount of money that they get paid, and the responsibilities – well, they should have class responsibilities *as well as* all those extra responsibilities ... as far as the conditions of service are concerned – but they *don't*! Whereas, we *do* ... and, I mean, that's not right! ... (Jane, Rockville teacher, Rockville study)

I mean, it's disgusting! I mean, she [Margaret] does have a timetable now, but it's *so* ambiguous and so flexible, it's just beyond ... beyond reason! ... Well, to say we've got all these managers, how can the school *be* so mismanaged – it's a farce! (Patricia, Rockville teacher, Rockville study)

I'm not happy at the school ... I didn't think it was desperate ... but, ... the other week ... she (Mrs Hillman) ... conducted a staff meeting in the usual style, just dropping her decision on us, and I thought, 'It's time to go.' (Mark, Leyburn teacher, 'extended' professionality case study)

I want a position which gives me more clout and more power ... an involvement in the management of the school ... to be an integral part of the decision-making machinery – which I'm not. (Mark, Leyburn teacher, 'extended' professionality case study)

Interviewer: Do you find the job satisfying enough? Does it stimulate you?
Well, yes, because, I think the way things are done at Rockville, I mean, having different year groups every two years, it certainly keeps you on your toes. And the changes that there've been whilst I've been there ... I mean, when I went there at first we'd a few Pakistani children, but there were no Bangladeshis, so there have been changes there ... and, I mean, there are changes that have come about in education itself ... er ... and changes in year groups and the children's different needs, and so on, I think keep you on your toes ... whereas, in a lot of other schools, in, perhaps, more affluent areas, with a good catchment area ... er ... the children's needs are not the same ... and I don't think there are the same changes within the school, and perhaps they don't even change classes. I mean, I know *some*

teachers who've been taking the same year group and the same type of ability for most of their careers. Now, to me, you get in a rut, and I think that's where a lot of the dissatisfaction creeps in. I think they tend to look outward for the root of the problems, rather than looking inward. (Rosemary, Rockville teacher, Rockville study)

I really like it here ... er ... but I know that you have to work a lot harder here than in a lot of places, and I don't know whether I'll always be prepared to put that work in ... I mean, at the moment, I'm happy here because ... I just like the feel of working here ... but I go home and I feel as if I'm under stress and I feel drained ... and, sometimes, I think, 'How long can I keep this up?' (Sarah, Sefton Road teacher, school climate study)

As I point out in Chapter 4, in using comparative analysis to shed light on the reasons why patterns have emerged across, or why discrepancies have occurred between, studies it is important to identify and examine areas of difference in relation to research design. These may include differences in the research aim, objectives and research questions; differences between the samples; differences in the sampling processes; differences in the data collection; and differences in the data analysis. Since you may wish to draw upon it in trying to solve the puzzle, information relating to such differences between the two studies in question is presented below, in outline.

Differences in the Research Aim, Objectives and Research Questions
These have already been identified, in part. My research questions in the morale study were:

- What factors do teachers perceive to influence each of their (a) morale, (b) job satisfaction, (c) motivation?
- To what extent is Herzberg's Motivation-Hygiene Theory (see Chapter 3) borne out in relation to my research sample?
- Is morale a group or an individual phenomenon?
- How are morale, job satisfaction and motivation interrelated?
- In what ways do teacher (a) morale, (b) job satisfaction, (c) motivation levels, as perceived by them, alter over time and what is the nature of any such change?
- How may levels of teacher morale, job satisfaction and motivation be raised?

The research questions in the TAWP study were:

- To what extent, and in what specific ways, do Key Stage 1 teachers perceive the implementation of the national curriculum to have impacted upon their working lives?
- What specific forms of implementation are evident, and to what extent, and in what ways, do these differ across the sample?
- What evidence is there of teacher development having resulted from the implementation of the national curriculum, and what is the specific nature of such development?
- What are teachers' evaluative views on the national curriculum: (a) in principle, (b) in its specific form?
- How do teachers evaluate the implementation process?
- To what extent, and in what specific ways, has the implementation of the national curriculum influenced teacher (a) morale, (b) job satisfaction, (c) motivation and (d) stress?
- Is the introduction of the national curriculum likely to have (a) a beneficial or (b) a detrimental effect on educational standards and what is the nature of such effects?

Differences between the Samples and in the Sampling Process
Details of the two samples are presented in Tables 5.2 and 5.3.

Table 5.2: Details of the teacher sample involved in the composite morale study

Pseudonym	Age at time of first interview	No. of times inter- viewed	Job status	School	Key Stage	Study(ies) in which involved
Elaine	35	1	Mainscale	Rockville	1/2	(i)
Rosemary	52	2	(i) A allowance-holder			
			(ii) deputy head	Rockville	1	(i), (iii), (iv)
Brenda	39	2	Mainscale	Rockville	2	(i), (iv)
Stephen	33	1	Mainscale	Rockville	2	(i)
Barbara	25	2	Mainscale	Rockville	1/2	(i), (iv)
Jane	40	2	Mainscale	Rockville	2	(i), (iv)
Pat	41	2	Mainscale	Rockville	1/2	(i), (iv)
Joanne	49	1	Mainscale	Rockville	2	(i)
Susan	30	2	Mainscale	Rockville	2	(i), (iii), (iv)
Jean	55	2	Mainscale	Rockville	1	(i), (iv)
Amanda	45	2	Mainscale	Rockville	2	(i), (iii), (iv)
Lesley	31	1	Mainscale	Rockville	1	(i)
Hilary	36	1	ESL mainscale	Rockville	1	(i)
Deborah	43	1	School secretary	Rockville	n/a	(i)
Helen	42	2	(i) B allowance-holder	(i) Woodleigh Lane	1	(iii)

			(ii) C allowance-holder	(ii) Ethersall Grange		
Kay	42	1	B allowance-holder	Sefton Road	2	(ii), (iii)
Sarah	28	1	Mainscale	Sefton Road	2	(ii)
Louise	40	1	Mainscale	Sefton Road	2	(ii)
Mark	32	1	Mainscale	Leyburn	2	(ii), (iii)
Fiona	41	1	Mainscale	Leyburn	2	(ii)
Ann	42	1	Mainscale	Leyburn	2	(ii)

Key to numbering of studies: (i) Rockville study; (ii) school climate study; (iii) 'extended' professionality case studies; (iv) post-ERA follow-up study (see Table 4.1)

Table 5.3: Details of the teacher sample involved in the TAWP study

Pseudonym	Year group taught	Status	No. in class	School catchment category
Ann	1&2	Mainscale	31+	MC
Betty	R	Mainscale	20+	WC
Christine	2	Mainscale	31+	Mixed
Denise	1	A allowance-holder	31+	Mixed
Ellen	2&3	Deputy head	26+	MC
Felicity	R&1	Mainscale	21+	WC
Grace	R	A allowance-holder	31+	MC
Helen	R	B allowance-holder	21+	WC
Irene	2	A allowance-holder	26+	MC
Jane	R&1&2	A allowance-holder	21+	MC
Kathy	R	Mainscale	26+	Mixed
Linda	2	C allowance-holder	26+	MC
Mary	2	A allowance-holder	21+	WC
Nina	1	B allowance-holder	31+	MC
Olive	2&3	Deputy head	31+	Mixed
Patrick	1	Mainscale	21+	MC
Rose	2	B allowance-holder	31+	WC
Sheila	R&1	A allowance-holder	21+	WC
Tricia	N&R	A allowance-holder	26+	Mixed
Ursula	R	B allowance-holder	21+	MC
Vivienne	1&2	A allowance-holder	31+	Mixed
Penny	R	A allowance-holder	31+	Mixed
Angie	1	Mainscale	26+	MC
Brenda	2	Mainscale	26+	WC

Key: R = reception (4–5 years); N = nursery (pre-school; 3–4 years); 1 = Year 1 (5–6 years); 2 = Year 2 (6–7 years); MC = mainly middle class; WC = mainly working class

Sampling in the morale study was effected by a process of personal introduction and recommendation that, to a limited extent, represented a form of snowball sampling. I initially selected

Rockville County Primary School for my research focus on the basis of its being referred to, anecdotally, as a 'low morale' school, in which there was, reputedly, much staff dissatisfaction. Access was facilitated by my being slightly acquainted with a few of the Rockville staff. Once in the school, during what I describe as a year's 'teaching-cum-observation' phase, I became better acquainted with the staff and was readily given permission to interview most of them in the next phase of the study. A very similar pattern occurred in my sampling on the other three studies in the composite study. It was a question of approaching individuals whom I considered, for various reasons, appropriate research subjects. The sample in its entirety represented teachers located in one small geographical area of England spanning two neighbouring towns and within one local education authority (LEA).

The sampling process in the TAWP study was different. The study had been funded by a teachers' union and the sample was selected from those of its members who responded positively to the Union's request for research participants. Selection was made on the basis of the entire sample's representing a cross-section of Key Stage 1 teachers in nineteen LEAs in England and Wales and incorporated consideration of factors such as geographical location, professional status, age, gender, years of experience and school details such as whether the school was a primary or an infant school, school size, and what type of catchment area it served, indicating the socio-economic status of its pupils.

Differences in the Data Collection

THE MORALE STUDY

In the morale study interviews constituted the main method of data collection, upon which my key findings are based. They were semi-structured, the schedule consisting of general topics towards which I wished to steer the interview conversations, within which were specific questions which were components of my research questions, but which were not necessarily always presented to interviewees in the same way. This was a study that I undertook independently and, since I was the sole researcher, all data were collected by me.

I typically began by asking teacher interviewees to describe, and then to account for, their own morale levels. In the cases of the studies in which I supplemented my interviewing by a form of what I loosely refer to as participant observation I asked all interviewees, irrespective of the level of personal morale reported, to comment upon specific incidents and circumstances which had occurred in the school, of which I had become aware through my informal observer role, and which, I was also aware, had given rise to some contention, disapproval and dissatisfaction amongst some teachers. I also asked interviewees to estimate the morale levels of their colleagues; both as individuals and, as far as it was felt possible to generalize, collectively. I asked, too, about conditions of service and non-school-specific issues. The interviews involved much tactful probing as I tried to elucidate the complexity underlying the reasons why individual reactions and responses to situations, circumstances and events differed, though my familiarity with the interviewees encouraged them to be open, honest and direct. It is impossible to provide a comprehensive list of questions employed in interviews of this kind because, although there was a core of broadly similarly worded questions which were included in all interviews, there were also many additional interviewee-specific questions, since this method of qualitative data collection incorporates an element of opportunism and spontaneity. The core questions included:

Can you try to describe your own morale at the moment? ... For example, is it really high, or really low, or rock bottom ... or whatever? What I'm looking for are factors which affect morale – either make it high or low – can you, sort of, elaborate?

Are you happy to stay at this school? Can you see yourself still being there in five years' time, or even ten years? Are you looking for another job? How desperate are you to leave? *Why* are you so desperate to leave? What do you particularly like about working there?

How does this school rate, compared with the other schools you've taught at? Are you happier there, or do you wish you were still at _____? What are your views on that? Is that a source of low morale, or of dissatisfaction to you? What, precisely, was it that bothered you about it?

What changes do you think need to be made at this school? If you were the headteacher how would you change things? What would be your priorities? Why? Would you retain the policy of _____?

Some people have said that _____/complained of _____. Have you found this to be the case, or does it not bother you?

Are you happy with teaching, as a career, in general? Are you glad you chose it? Do you ever feel like getting out of teaching? Why did you choose it, originally?

What do you like about the job? What gives you the most satisfaction? What makes a good day for you – describe a good day? ... and, a bad day?

Can you recall any incidents at any time during your career, which have had the effect of raising your morale, giving you a real lift? What about incidents which have demoralized you? Can you recall any?

Do you find the job satisfying enough – I mean, is it stimulating? Is it fulfilling? Does it challenge you? What aspects of the job do you find challenging? Are there any aspects of it that you could happily do without?

Are you satisfied with the salary that you receive?

What are your views on the introduction into teachers' conditions of service of the five Baker in-service training days? What are your views on the introduction of the national curriculum?

Presentation of a list such as this, however, only provides a very general indication of the approximate content, style and nature of the interviews. A great many more questions were asked than those in the above list, which identifies some of the main points of departure only – and for some teachers only – and is in danger of misrepresenting the interview content as over-simplified and lacking depth. Ideally, of course, to undertake a comparative analysis, all interview transcripts and field notes should be available to you. The above list, and the comparable one below relating to the TAWP study, are poor substitutes for these data. Interviews were geared to the individual interviewees and aimed at elucidating the background behind their perspectives and attitudes. Moreover, the sample of questions listed above has a tendency to suggest a sequence of interviewee responses and comments which reflect negative job-related attitudes, but sequences of more positively worded questions were used, when appropriate.

Interviews took place either (usually) at my home or at the interviewees' homes, or (occasionally) at school, and, with the exception of one, were tape-recorded. Duration of interviews ranged from thirty minutes to three hours, with an average duration of seventy-five minutes. All interviews were transcribed by me.

THE TAWP STUDY
This was conducted by a Warwick research team of four, three of whom carried out data collection: semi-structured interviews at a venue chosen by the interviewee. Each interviewee was interviewed on one occasion. Duration of interviews ranged from thirty to ninety minutes, with an average length of one hour. All interviews were taped.

The core interview topics and questions included in the schedule are listed below, although, as in the morale study, at the discretion of the interviewer different avenues were explored in response to individuals' comments:

> May we begin by talking about how the national curriculum has affected your working life?

> Has your working life deteriorated or improved as a result of having to implement the national curriculum, or has it remained pretty much the same? In what specific ways has it changed — can you provide examples?

> What is your view on the national curriculum as an idea, in principle? Do you approve of it? What do you specifically like and dislike about it? Do you feel it will help to raise standards — in what ways? Are your views on the national curriculum shared by your colleagues in your school?

> What would you say are the main sources of satisfaction for you at work? What are the sources of dissatisfaction? What causes you stress? Have your attitudes to your job been altered by the implementation of the national curriculum — in what ways? Has it been a source of stress? May we talk about your morale? Is it high or low? How has the national curriculum affected it? Has it increased your stress — in what specific ways?

> How is the national curriculum being implemented in your school as a whole? How seriously is your school's management taking it? Is management supportive of teachers who are having to implement it their classrooms?

Differences in the Data Analysis
The same process of analysis was applied to both studies: interview transcripts were examined for evidence related to the research questions and to additional, unanticipated, issues that emerged and were considered relevant to the main research aim. Several levels of

coding were applied to this evidence. The first level was typically that reflecting basic answers to the research questions, the second level delved deeper, identifying underlying reasons for patterns that emerged or for discrepancies. Subsequent levels involved increasingly in-depth analysis. The morale study involved several more levels of in-depth analysis – over a course of several years – than did the TAWP study, whose findings were published and widely publicized through the national media within a short time span. In the morale study data reduction was an incrementally reductive process, involving several levels of coding, focusing increasingly narrowly on categories of increasing specificity before the much broader overview analysis was applied which sought the fundamental source of de-contextualized commonality; what I refer to elsewhere (Evans, 1997c; 1998) as the 'lowest common factor'. First-level coding, for example, involved identifying evidence of levels of teachers' morale, motivation and job satisfaction and of factors which influenced these levels. Data display (Miles and Huberman, 1988) following on from this revealed a small number of general categories. Second-level coding, and several subsequent levels, then reduced data more narrowly into, for example, categories relating to more specific sources of job satisfaction, motivation and morale, such as working with children, interaction with colleagues, centrally initiated policy, school policy, school management etc. By this reductive process, alongside emerging conceptualization and re-conceptualization of job satisfaction and morale, described in Chapter 3, analysis eventually culminated in uncovering precisely what it was about the factors which were able to influence individuals' morale, job satisfaction levels and motivation, which did, in fact, allow them to influence them. Clearly, this also involved examining the individuals themselves.

Inter-coder reliability measures were applied to the analysis of the TAWP study, in which all four researchers were involved. In the morale study since I was working independently it was necessary to test the reliability of the categorization which was incorporated into my data analysis. This was done, following the method proposed by Atkins (1984, pp. 257–8), by using an independent judge, who categorized data from a sample of three interview transcripts. This revealed reliability of categorization.

POSSIBLE SOLUTIONS

Having been presented with as much information as it is feasible to provide within the confines of a single chapter, your task is now − as far as you are able − to apply a comparative analysis of the two studies in order to ascertain the reason why their respective findings were so different from each other. The two sets of findings have been presented and, in particular, the nature and degree of discrepancy between them has been highlighted. Following the guidelines and the example provided in Chapter 4 will lead you towards several possible solutions to the puzzle. To assist you in this I present below additional outline information, and also summarize information that has already been provided, relating to the commonalities and distinctions between the two studies.

The commonalities are the nature and composition of their respective samples and the timing of the data collection of the two studies, both of which were similar. In relation to the research findings, commonalities emerging from my analyses were that teachers in both samples reported that factors perceived as impediments to their capacity to teach − what they perceived as their efficiency as professionals − created dissatisfaction. What was perceived as irrationality of decision-making − at national and at institutional level − was identified as a source of dissatisfaction. Inefficiency was similarly identified as a source of dissatisfaction. Conversely, where teachers felt able to carry on working in ways that were familiar to them and which suited them, no dissatisfaction was reported.

Apart from the key distinction between the two sets of findings that forms the basis of the puzzle that is the focus of this chapter, a distinction between the two studies was the number of Key Stage 1 teachers in the samples. Although the sample compositions were similar in so far as they both comprised primary school teachers working in the UK, the TAWP sample was made up entirely of Key Stage 1 teachers, since these were the only primary school teachers who, at the time of the TAWP data collection, had experienced national curriculum implementation. The morale study sample, on the other hand, comprised more Key Stage 2 than Key Stage 1 teachers. Whilst most of this study's data collection was carried out when the implementation of the national curriculum had been extended to Key Stage 2 and had, therefore, been experienced by most of the sample, it could be argued that, by the time Key Stage 2 teachers faced it, national curriculum implementation was less problematic than it had been at the very beginning, when it was left in the hands of Key Stage 1 teachers. Key Stage 2 teachers therefore may have perceived the national curriculum and its implementation more positively since many of the initial difficulties associated with it had been ironed out or had been overcome by the pioneering Key Stage 1 teachers who passed on the lessons learned to their schools' management and to Key Stage 2 colleagues, with the effect that the latter were given an easier ride. However, this argument is weakened by the evidence from the morale study that even the Key Stage 1 teachers in this sample failed to identify the implementation as a significant influence on their morale, job satisfaction and motivation.

Another distinction is that the TAWP sample represented teachers from twenty-two different schools located in different parts of England and Wales whereas the morale study sample teachers represented only four schools. An obvious possible conclusion to draw from this is that the distinction between the findings of the two studies could be institutionally related, reflecting a distinction in school-specific approaches to national curriculum implementation. It could be the case that the four schools represented by the morale study sample happened to share a common type of implementation-related response to the national curriculum: either implementation was taken so seriously that it was effected with a degree of efficiency and expertise that made it comparatively effortless for the teachers concerned, or, conversely, it was taken on board with insufficient seriousness to allow it to impact upon teachers' work. The twenty-two schools represented by the TAWP sample, on the other hand, may all, coincidentally, have handled national curriculum implementation in ways that, to varying degrees, allowed the process to impact significantly upon teachers' work.

Whilst the comparative analysis process involves following up leads by examining all possible discrepancies that could offer an explanation for a key distinction between two or more studies, it is important, too, to assess the feasibility of each one as an explanation. Not only does the possible explanation presented above seem to rely far too heavily on circumstances reflecting a degree of coincidence that is difficult to credit, but it is also undermined by data from the studies. Data from the TAWP sample as a whole provided evidence of varying degrees of school-level implementation of the national curriculum, from which were identified four levels of implementation: the 'by the book', the 'common sense', the 'paying lip service' and the 'head-in-the-sand' approaches (Evans *et al.* (1994), pp. 100–6). The twenty-two TAWP schools were not uniform in their manner of national curriculum implementation; indeed, they were very diverse. Moreover, the four morale study schools were no less diverse in the level of implementation that they typically practised. Although the four labels were not applied to the morale study, the schools represented could be categorized as having each practised a different approach, so that all four implementation levels were represented within the study.

Another explanation is that, in my role as researcher, my familiarity with the morale study sample teachers encouraged them to be more candid and frank in interviews than the TAWP teachers were, and to disclose and discuss issues relating to school-level management and leadership that they considered to have impacted more significantly upon their working lives than had national curriculum implementation. This may, in part, account for the discrepancy between the two sets of research findings, but as a possible explanation it is also undermined by several cases of TAWP interviewees who, even though they did not know their interviewers, were as candid in their disclosure of issues related to school management and leadership as had been the morale study teachers. The following quotation is illustrative of the openness displayed by these teachers:

> We've got a male head and a male deputy, both of whom are feckless. The [Local Education] Authority is actually running an assessment meeting in a fortnight for all the heads of primary schools and he's not going! ... [H]e doesn't even know what we're doing in terms of this assessment ... it's frustrating – we're really working in a vacuum. (TAWP teacher)

Applying lateral thinking to the comparative analysis involves going beyond the obvious in the search for explanations. Some of the more obvious explanations are examined above, but the most obvious one is the uncomplicated explanation that stems from taking the data at face value, unquestioningly: that it is simply the case that the TAWP sample was made up predominantly of teachers upon whose working lives the implementation of the national curriculum impacted quite significantly, and that the morale study sample happens to comprise teachers who were comparatively unaffected by it. Yet before accepting this it is important to examine other, less obvious, explanations.

These, then, are just a few examples of possible explanations that need to be considered. None of them, though, seems as plausible a solution to the research puzzle as the one to which my own comparative analysis led me. I refer to this – currently, my preferred explanation – as the suggestibility issue.

THE SUGGESTIBILITY ISSUE

Whilst there are several possible reasons for the discrepancy in the TAWP and morale study findings, I believe it likely to have arisen predominantly – though not exclusively – out of suggestibility bias. The TAWP was introduced to research subjects as a study that sought teachers' perceptions of the extent to which, and the ways in which, national curriculum implementation had impacted upon their working lives and how this, in turn, had affected their attitudes. All interviewees were asked specifically about how their job satisfaction and morale were affected. Most reported lowered morale and decreased job satisfaction. The morale study, on the other hand, incorporated more open-ended inquiry about teachers' own morale and job satisfaction levels and invited suggestions of influential factors, before, as a final stage in the course of each interview, offering some for consideration. Under these circumstances it is perhaps unsurprising that those who were specifically asked, within the context of a study whose purpose was to investigate it, to talk about how the implementation of the national curriculum had affected their job-related attitudes typically responded that it had, indeed, detrimentally affected them. Moreover, since it was not part of the research agenda and, therefore, tended not to be raised by interviewers, the issue of what other factors also affect job-related attitudes was, for the most part, neglected by interviewees.

As a means of ascertaining what influences teacher morale and job satisfaction – which, to be fair, was not its main purpose – the TAWP was, therefore, inadequate and the data that it yielded relating to this issue are incomplete and, as a result, present an inaccurate and distorted picture of teachers' job-related attitudes. In this respect the morale study was more reliable. By incorporating much less suggestibility it provided data that challenge many assumptions and taken-for-granted notions, most of which are promulgated by the media and, in some cases, by politicians and trade unions, to the extent that they take on the status of accepted, unquestionable knowledge about what influences morale, job satisfaction and motivation. Through suggestibility that results from repeated exposure to highly publicized and plausible ideas – which are seldom publicly challenged or refuted – teachers may eventually and perhaps imperceptibly assimilate such ideas.

Essentially, I believe it is highly likely that, for example, if teachers are continually exposed to public perceptions that they are underpaid and that this is resulting in widespread demoralization within their profession, then asking them to comment upon pay-related issues and whether these affect their attitudes to their work will produce predictably confirmatory responses. Similarly, at a time when teachers' unions were protesting about, and media attention was focused on, the extra workloads imposed upon teachers by the implementation of the national curriculum – which was very much in the spotlight – it seems a reasonable explanation that suggestibility played a large part in determining the TAWP sample's responses to direct questions to which most of them had already been given the answers. In such a context, human nature being as it is, teachers are more likely to answer 'yes' than 'no' to questions such as 'Has the introduction of the national curriculum significantly affected your job?' and 'Has your morale been lowered by this?'.

I believe suggestibility to be a very significant but under-recognized specific internal validity threat that undermines the authenticity of much educational research. Suggestibility is an issue of which the analytical researcher needs to be aware and which s/he needs to tackle head-on. The next chapter examines the issue in more detail.

The suggestibility issue

Of all of the issues that are the foci of chapters in Part II of this book, suggestibility is the only one that — at the time of writing — remains at the conjecture stage. It is the only one that is untested by me, in the sense that it represents a strong hunch on my part but one that I am unable to support with firm evidence of its having occurred. Is the suggestibility issue, then, speculative only, or is it, indeed, the 'solution' to the puzzle of the tale of two studies presented in Chapter 5? Am I on the right track in believing it to be potentially the most significant issue in this case, or am I way off the mark?

The analytical researcher is not content to stop at the 'hunch' stage, nor does s/he find it acceptable to pass off speculation and conjecture as certainty. The plausibility of suggestibility's being a significant internal validity threat needs to be assessed. In the case of the two studies, we will never know with certainty what accounted for the discrepancy between the two sets of findings because, with the completion of the data collection of these studies, the opportunity to test the likelihood of suggestibility's being the key distinguishing factor has passed. But it is, nevertheless, imperative that the suggestibility issue be fully examined and investigated, and although studies that have been completed can no longer provide the opportunity for doing so, there are ways in which the potential effects of suggestibility — as I describe it in Chapter 5 — may be tested.

When an issue is at the speculative stage it is new; it is still developing, or being developed. By definition, it is embryonic. Because of this it throws up further, related issues that need examining. This is the case with what I refer to as suggestibility. Consideration of it raises all kinds of issues: conceptual issues; ontological issues; existentialist issues; issues relating to applicability and generalizability; avoidance procedural issues. This chapter examines such issues. It examines what, precisely, suggestibility is, what its implications are for educational research and ways in which researchers may deal with it.

EXAMINING SUGGESTIBILITY

At the end of Chapter 5 I introduced what I refer to as the suggestibility issue by presenting a descriptive example of how it may have occurred. Bias in research arising out of suggestibility – usually on the part of researchers – is not a new idea. It is a recognized threat to internal validity, which Keeves (1997a, p. 280) explains as being 'concerned with the credibility and authenticity of the findings arising from the manner in which a particular study was conducted'. Keats (1997, p. 309) outlines the nature of such bias:

> Bias can be present in the wording of questions and in the manner in which they are expressed. Questions that lead the respondent to be more likely to give one response than another are biased. Such questions may offer alternatives but omit some salient choices, or may subtly suggest that one answer is more acceptable than another ... In clinical research the interviewer may be working from a theoretical orientation that drives the questioning. Bias occurs if this orientation so limits the scope of questions that it reinforces what the interviewer wants to hear and neglects or misinterprets what does not fit within the expectations of the theory.

In the context of educational research I define suggestibility as *a feature that may be incorporated into research data collection, that represents a specific form of bias and a susceptibility to influence research subjects' perceptions towards greater corroboration of the researcher's or researchers' perceptions than would otherwise have occurred, by conveying to them something of the nature of what the researcher(s) anticipate(s) to emerge as specific causal relationships within the research findings.*

This definition highlights the specificity of the suggestibility with which I am concerned. It is confined to the data collection stage and precludes the various forms of researcher bias that may occur in data analysis and dissemination. The example of potential suggestibility that I identify in Chapter 5 is that of the TAWP. The very topic of this study – which was communicated to the research sample – is suggestible: an examination of the impact on teachers' working lives of the implementation of the national curriculum. This represents a very expectations-laden topic; it is highly suggestive that the national curriculum will, indeed, have impacted upon teachers' working lives and, in doing so, it prompts teachers to identify the nature of, rather than firstly to establish the existence of, any such impact. The morale study was, in this respect, much less suggestible because it was presented as a more open-ended investigative topic: an examination of teacher morale and job satisfaction and the factors that influence these.

Suggestibility is not confined to the introduction to the research subjects of the research focus, topic, purpose and objectives; it occurs also in a manner of which most researchers are aware: in the form of 'leading' interview questions and questionnaire items that prompt research subjects to respond in ways that confirm researchers' preconceptions and expectations. 'A genuinely open question', Wellington (2000, p. 79) reminds us, 'will invite opinions or views without either leading or prompting'. There are, of course, degrees, and different forms, of suggestibility in data collection and, since this book focuses on the development of advanced research skills, I do not address the issue of how, at a basic level, suggestibility-avoidance in framing questionnaire items and interview questions may be achieved. My concern is with more subtle, less generally recognizable, forms of suggestibility. The analytical researcher is not only aware of the dangers of suggestibility of various levels of subtlety within her/his own work but also is able to recognize this in other research and to assess its validity and, from this, its value and credibility as a contribution to the knowledge base in its field. Consider, for example, the questionnaire below: 'Items presented to the teachers to gain insight into their professional orientation' (source: Jongmans, Biemans and Beijaard, (1998), p. 298), which was used in a Dutch study to examine what the authors refer to as 'teachers' professional orientation' (Jongmans, Biemans and Beijaard, 1998, p. 295), after Hoyle (1975), and which seems to equate to what I refer to as 'professionality orientation' (see Chapter 1).

1 Cooperation with other teachers is necessary to carry out teaching tasks in an adequate way (cooperation with colleagues).
2 Continuous professional development is important for teachers (professional development).
3 School policy making is not the responsibility of the school management team only (involvement in policy making).
4 Non-teaching duties should be part of teachers' package of tasks (non-teaching duties).

5 Keeping up with their professional literature is very important for teachers (professional literature).

6 Individual teachers cannot decide on their own which teaching methods will be used in their lessons; on this point, agreements should be made at school level (teaching methods).

7 Discussing their way of teaching with colleagues is important for teachers (ways of teaching).

8 At school level, agreements should be made concerning the school climate (school climate).

9 Individual teachers should not decide on their own which subject matter they teach in their lessons; on this point, agreements should be made at school level (subject matter).

10 Teachers should incorporate new educational findings in their teaching activities (educational findings).

11 New educational theories are important, even for teachers with much experience (experienced teachers).

12 Comparing their own teaching activities with teaching methods shown to be effective in educational studies is important for teachers (teaching activities).

13 Teachers should not only be judged on the basis of the quality of their teaching activities (teacher assessment).

To an experienced and perceptive researcher the suggestibility incorporated into this study's data collection is very apparent. It represents what I refer to as the 'professional behaviour code' variant of suggestibility, which is predicated upon acceptance of a code of acceptable professional-related behaviour that is one of the features of professional culture, and to which most members of the profession in question – in this case, teachers – choose to adhere because failure to do so undermines the status of their membership of the professional group and threatens to distinguish them as deviant and to identify them as 'unprofessional'. The items in the questionnaire presented above relate to a specific aspect of teachers' professional behaviour code, recognized by all members of the profession – the requirement to develop professionally throughout one's career and to be receptive to, to keep abreast of and to incorporate into their work new ideas and theory. All members of the teaching profession know the 'acceptable' responses to the questionnaire items related to the professional behaviour code and may, in order to present favourable impressions of themselves, be tempted to select these. It is hardly surprising, then, that the findings of this study revealed the sample teachers to be of 'fairly extended professional orientation' (Jongmans *et al.* 1998, p. 299). The point is, though, that the 'acceptable' responses may not necessarily reflect teachers' genuine views and ideologies.

The problem that currently exists within educational research in relation to suggestibility is that we know very little about the more subtle forms of suggestibility that fall within my definition of the concept. All researchers are aware of the more obvious forms of researcher bias – of the need, for example, to avoid leading questions in research interviews and questionnaire items – but I believe that suggestibility undermines research validity in more extensive and sometimes almost imperceptible ways. 'Extended' professionals amongst the educational community, and, indeed, the wider social sciences research community – those who may be categorized as analytical researchers – are aware that avoiding leading questions represents only a token gesture in reducing researcher bias since leading questions constitute only the tip of the iceberg:

> Many important causal processes are hard to observe because of the imperfection of the research instruments. For example, much interview-based research only confirms the views of the participants and records how they justified the decisions in which they participated. Many social scientists believe the research process itself is 'theory-dependent' because researchers find the facts they are looking for. (John, 1998, p. 11)

Suggestibility – as I define it – is a methodological issue that needs examining in order to reveal more about its nature and the impact that it has on the research process. Although it is a recognized threat to validity I do believe that, generally, insufficient attention is paid to it. In the interests of methodological development, and in pursuit of the rigour that is often in very short supply in educational research, the issue needs testing.

TESTING THE SUGGESTIBILITY ISSUE

Until tests to ascertain its existentialist status are carried out, we will never know for certain whether suggestibility, in the narrow way that I interpret it, is indeed a problem in educational research. Then, if it *is* found to be a significant validity threat, we will need to know more about the forms that it takes and the extent of its influence if we are to incorporate into research designs measures for controlling it. Such is the nature of analytical research.

Before discussing how the suggestibility issue may be tested, it is worth looking once again at my definition of it on page 121. Since this clearly indicates data collection as the potential source of suggestibility, it is at this stage of the research process that any testing of the suggestibility issue must occur. In order to decide what testing mechanisms may be set up, we may use as an example the specific case of the TAWP research, described in Chapter 5, and consider how this study could have been conducted in order not to *control* the suggestibility issue but to investigate it; to ascertain the nature of it and the extent of its impact. Let us, then, use the TAWP research to formulate a suggestibility-issue-testing model.

If we wish to test whether something is occurring, and to what extent and in what form, we may often need to make comparisons by using an experimental and a control group. The TAWP research (see Chapter 5) used a sample of twenty-four teachers representing the different key variables that the research team considered potentially significant: age and length of service; type of school in relation to socio-economic status of pupils on roll; professional status/seniority and age range(s) taught. Semi-structured interviews were used to collect data, and a schedule ensured that, as far as is possible within the limitations imposed by using three interviewers, the entire sample was asked a common set of core questions. In a study designed to test the suggestibility issue the sample of twenty-four could have been split into two sub-samples of twelve, each representing the range of key variables reflected in the larger sample, and each of which would have been subjected to different treatment.

In order to decide in what precise ways the two sub-samples would be treated differently it is necessary to identify the specific suspected source of suggestibility. This may have been simply the researchers' communicating to the research subjects the topic and purpose of the research, or it may have been the combined influence of this and several 'leading', or 'suggestive', interview questions, or verbal or non-verbal interviewer responses to interviewees' comments. These are the kinds of issues that relate to the nature of suggestibility and which may be uncovered by testing. Clearly, though, designing a study to test for suggestibility effects by using control and experimental groups is not an easy task. The best we could hope to achieve is a strong indication of the likelihood of something's having occurred. Certainty is an unrealistic goal. Nevertheless, we are able to go further along the path that leads towards certainty than we were when we simply recognized the possibility that suggestibility may perhaps have occurred.

Using the TAWP as a specific example, a test of the extent and the nature of the impact of suggestibility upon research data could therefore have used two sub-samples, A and B, one of which would have been subjected to data collection that is not designed to counteract the suggestibility that I suspected to have permeated the research, and the other would have been subjected to data collection that was much more 'suggestibility-aware' and aimed at suggestibility avoidance. Sub-sample A, for example, would not have been told that the research was aimed at identifying the impact upon teachers' working lives of the implementation of the national curriculum. Instead, the study would have been introduced as one seeking evidence of teachers' perceptions and experiences of the national curriculum, and the interviews could have been much more interviewee-led than interviewer-led, with direct topic-defining questions kept in reserve for the later part of the interviews, to be introduced if their topics had not been covered by this stage. Sub-sample B would have been treated as was the sample used in the original TAWP: it would have been told the purpose of the research and asked the specific core interview questions listed in Chapter 5, p. 113. Data analysis would have included comparison of the two sets of data. This could have been qualitative in nature, incorporating impressionistic comparison, using inter-coder reliability measures, or it could have been more systematic and included significance testing, such as Chi-square, which compares expected with actual frequency, or, in cases of smaller samples, the Fisher test (see Siegel and Castellan, 1988, pp. 102–24).

This represents a basic model of a study whose purpose includes the testing of the suggestibility issue. It may be repeated with adaptations that are directed towards teasing out more precisely the nature of suggestibility – whether it occurs through the wording used in interview questions or questionnaire items, or simply through the vocabulary used by the researchers' communication of the research topic to research subjects; whether some research subjects are more 'suggestible' than others; whether some researchers, through unconsciously administered forms of verbal or non-verbal communication, are more 'suggestive' than others. It must surely, after all, be a very fine line that separates unresponsiveness from 'unsuggestiveness' on the part of a research interviewer.

Whether they wish to incorporate it into studies designed for testing the suggestibility issue or simply into their own research designs, researchers need to know how suggestibility avoidance may be effected. In the absence of reliable data from any study that has tested the issue, experientially informed conjecture and commonsense reasoning must form the basis of ideas. Such ideas are discussed in the next section.

DEALING WITH SUGGESTIBILITY IN RESEARCH

If there is a possibility that data distortion occurs through suggestibility conveyed through the communication of the research topic then one obvious way of avoiding it is to mislead research subjects about the purpose and scope of the study in cases where you consider there to be high risk of suggestibility. There are, of course, ethical considerations to weigh up carefully here, and I discuss these later. For the moment, though, let us, for the sake of argument, go along this path.

If you are to practise misleading in order to avoid threats to internal validity through suggestibility you need to become adept at distinguishing potentially suggestive from apparently innocuous research topic descriptors. Take a look at the list below and identify those that − simply through the choice of words used to describe them − you consider to pose the greatest suggestibility threats:

- a study of teachers' attitudes towards black students
- a study of the impact of performance management in UK schools on teacher morale and motivation
- a study of teenage girls' experiences of bullying at school
- a study of school leavers' career aspirations
- a study of the impact on teachers' workloads and job satisfaction of the introduction in the UK of AS level examination curricula
- a study of staffroom relations
- a study of ten-year-olds' understanding of place value
- a study of women teachers' experiences of sexual discrimination at work
- a study of the impact upon teacher development of in-service courses
- a study of teachers' attitudes towards special educational needs (SEN) pupils.

Clearly, in terms of the potential suggestibility of the data collection that would be used in these studies, it is impossible to distinguish some as posing a greater threat than others since we have no way of anticipating how suggestible would be interview questions posed or questionnaire items used. In terms of the topics themselves, though, some seem more susceptible to suggestibility than others. A study of women teachers' experiences of sexual discrimination at work, for example, seems the kind of topic that might suggest to some respondents or interviewees experiences of discrimination that they may not otherwise have identified. Suggestibility of this kind would be reflected in thought processes on the part of research subjects – which may or may not be communicated to researchers – that may be depicted along the lines of 'Well, I'd never though of it as discrimination before, but now that you come to mention it ...'. A study of the impact of performance management in schools on teacher morale and motivation; a study of teenage girls' experiences of bullying at school and a study of the impact on teachers' workloads and job satisfaction of the introduction of AS level examination curricula: these are similarly potentially suggestive – as are several other of the listed topics. Any topic is potentially suggestive, in fact, that has the potential to prompt the 'Well, I'd never really thought of it in that way before, but now that you come to mention it ...' kind of thinking on the part of the research subject; any topic that encourages the research subject to re-think her/his position, or to bring about a change of attitude, or to represent her/his thinking or viewpoint or stance differently from how s/he would present it if s/he did not feel pressured into trying to meet what s/he interprets as the expectations of the researcher.

More innocuous are topics that are not expectations-laden in the manner in which they are communicated. A study of school leavers' career aspirations probably falls into this category – although this, too, could be interpreted as incorporating some suggestibility in so far as it might suggest to school leavers who have no career aspirations that they ought to have them. A study of ten-year-olds' understanding of place value is similarly comparatively innocuous. If suggestibility does exist in the form that I have identified it then it does so in degrees, and it is impossible to avoid completely. Nevertheless, it may be reduced.

It may be reduced by a form of deception that presents the research topic to research subjects differently from how it is understood by the researchers. This may involve presenting it as a more general topic than the researchers intend it to be, but one which covers similar issues, or it may involve presenting it as quite a different topic. A study of (women) teachers' experiences of sexual discrimination at work, for example, could be obscured within what is presented to research subjects as a more general study of women teachers' perceptions of teaching as work, or of their attitudes towards teaching. More deceptively, it could be presented as any study that gives the researchers a cover – and the opportunity – to collect data pertinent to the issues in which they are interested without divulging the precise narrow focus that they have in mind. A study of the teaching profession in the twenty-first century, or of teachers' career patterns or of school organization or micro-politics are three possibilities. There are many more.

When he wanted to undertake an observational study of infants' schooling, Ronald King (1978) successfully approached the head-teacher of an infants' school for research access with the explanation that he was not sure what he was looking for or what the specific focus of his research would be; he simply wanted to undertake an exploratory study. In King's case this appears to have been a genuine explanation, but it could just as easily be used as a means of avoiding suggestibility. As an exercise, examine the list of ten research topics on p. 127 and consider how, for each one, you might present the research topic to potential research subjects in as 'non-suggestible' a way as possible. List such alternative research topic descriptors alongside their more suggestible partners and leave unchanged those that you consider comparatively innocuous. Below is my version:

a study of teachers' attitudes towards black students	a study of teacher–student communication
a study of the impact of performance management in UK schools on teacher morale and motivation	a study of management in schools and colleges
a study of teenage girls' experiences of bullying at school	a study of teenage girls' experiences of schooling
a study of school leavers' career aspirations	a study of what young people want out of life once they have left school
a study of the impact on teachers' workloads and job satisfaction of the introduction in the UK of AS level examination curricula	a study of the implementation in schools and colleges of AS level examination curricula

a study of staffroom relations	a study of staffroom culture
a study of ten-year-olds' understanding of place value	a study of ten-year-olds' understanding of place value
a study of women teachers' experiences of sexual discrimination at work	a study of women teachers' experiences of teaching as work
a study of the impact upon teacher development of in-service courses	a study of teachers' attitudes towards in-service courses
a study of teachers' attitudes towards SEN pupils	a study of teacher–pupil relations

But what of the ethics of this deception? Many people reading this will dismiss suggestibility avoidance of this kind as totally unacceptable. It does, after all, go against the principle of informed consent (Burgess, 1989), or, more precisely, 'fully informed consent', which Guba and Lincoln (1989, p. 122) identify as the issue of securing respondents' consent and acquainting them with the purpose and scope of the inquiry.

Opinions differ widely on this issue. On the one hand, the 'by-the-book', uncompromising, ethical line upholds the research subject's right to be fully informed about the purpose, aims, scope and nature of the research in which s/he freely agrees to participate:

> But many research and evaluation projects cut corners on these requirements, and, in graduate courses, students are often told forthrightly to tell respondents to their dissertation research 'as little as possible' regarding the aims of the study as our own experience in serving on dissertation committees clearly shows … Such a posture does little, if anything, to redress the problems created by crossing the informed consent requirement with the problem of allowable deception of research participants. Clearly, a person cannot, in fact, give her or his informed consent if duped regarding the true purposes of the research or evaluation or his or her role in it. (Guba and Lincoln, 1989, pp. 122–3)

> It is of course impossible in research to anticipate all the kinds of information which may be of interest, but those being researched would seem to have a right to know beforehand what in general terms the researchers would be looking for and for what purpose. (Pring, 2000a, p. 149)

On the other hand, many distinguished researchers – some of whom clearly fall into the category of 'extended' professionals and analytical researchers – condone deception; some, indeed, admit to having practised it themselves.

Burgess (1989, p. 65), for example, feels that his failure to provide research subjects with specific details of his research plans constitutes an infringement of the principle of informed consent:

> Certainly, in my study teachers had been informed that the research was taking place but it was not possible to specify exactly what data would be collected and how it would be used ... In this respect, it could be argued that individuals were not fully informed, consent had not been obtained and privacy was violated.

Bogdan and Taylor (1975, pp. 34–5), too, evidently condone the practice of being economical with the truth:

> people at different levels of an organisation generally make the assumption that he or she is there to learn about, or how to deal with, those at another level. For example, you may want to study the relationships between staff and inmates at a prison. The staff may think that you're interested in the inmates while the inmates will think that you're interested in the staff ... While it is inadvisable for the observer to intentionally create false impressions, there are certain advantages to allowing subjects to maintain such misunderstandings.
> *The rule, then, is to be honest, but vague or imprecise.*

For rather different reasons Riddell (1989, pp. 81–3) reports having deceived her research subjects:

> I was reasonably sure that if I placed too much emphasis on gender I would simply not be allowed into the school. I therefore decided that in my initial letter and subsequent meeting with Mr East, the headmaster of Greenhill, I would explain my research project in terms of an investigation into the operation of the option choice system in the school. I would certainly mention that gender and class were among the variables that I wanted to look at, but I would not dwell on the precise focus of the research any more than was necessary. Since the headmaster clearly had a view of educational research as neutral and objective, it would have been catastrophic to introduce myself as a feminist ... In this way, I was certainly not

adopting a covert role, but, on the other hand, it could be argued that I was not fully explaining the purpose of my research to my sponsors ... Sometimes I left the school quite convinced that I would be asked to leave the next day on the grounds that I had gained access under false pretences.

Similarly, Kelly (1989, pp. 101–2) writes of her decision to concentrate on the 'professional' aspects of her research project when negotiating access, rather than dwell on the wider, feminist ramifications:

> Whether this was the correct decision, from a tactical viewpoint, is debatable ... What is certain is that it did not conform to the high ideals of informed consent. We did not attempt to disguise the wider intent of the project, but neither did we go to great lengths to explain it ... The greater ethical good of attempting to broaden opportunities for children outweighs the lesser ethical dubiousness of playing down the overall aim of the project. I am not arguing that the principle of informed consent should be abandoned: only that it should be viewed in combination with other ethical considerations, rather than as an over-riding principle.

In many cases deception on the part of researchers is recognized as a measure taken to increase validity; to encourage research subjects to be more candid in relation to what they say and do and to guard against data distortion by research subjects' misrepresenting themselves in order to meet researchers' expectations or to present themselves in a good light. As Hammersley and Atkinson (1996, p. 265) point out:

> divulging some sorts of information might affect people's behaviour in ways that will invalidate the research. For instance, to tell teachers that one is interested in whether they normally talk as much to girls as to boys in the classroom could produce false results, since they may make an effort to equalize their intentions.

And Scott and Usher (1999, p. 130) justify their stance: 'the issue is not primarily about deception, but about validity. In some situations ... being open and honest would have fundamentally changed the situation.'

Your own stance on the issue of whether or not it is acceptable to mislead or deceive research subjects in such ways will reflect your general position on ethical issues in research. Hammersley and Atkinson (1996, pp. 276–7) identify 'four contrasting positions which have had an impact on thinking about ethical issues': the view that specific forms of research strategy are unacceptable; the view that what is and is not legitimate is a matter of judgement and is determined by the context; the view of 'ethical relativism', which 'implies that there is never a single determinate answer to the question of what is and is not legitimate behaviour on the part of the researcher. This is because judgements about the good and the bad are always dependent on commitment to a particular value perspective, and there is a plurality of values and cultures to which human beings can be committed'; and the view that ethical considerations have no relevance. The educational research community is divided in relation to these positions. Some researchers' views, it would appear, reflect the first position; other researchers who condone or practise deception in the interests of research validity or wider access – as we have seen from the quotations presented above – represent what could be any of the remaining positions, but are most likely to be the second or third.

I share the views expressed and implied by those researchers quoted above to whom deception is acceptable. There is little point in carrying out research whose findings are, to varying degrees, invalidated by data distortion that is a by-product of the full disclosure necessary for securing 'fully informed consent' (Guba and Lincoln, 1989, p. 122). Whilst fully accepting the impossibility of eradicating all threats to validity and reliability in research, I do believe that those who take their research seriously should do as much as is possible to reduce these threats, and if harmless deception of research subjects is one way in which this may be achieved then it is a path that should be followed in the interests of injecting more rigour into educational research, so that the knowledge base derived from research will have authenticity and, ultimately, policy and practice may be made more effective. This, after all, is surely what educational research is all about.

There is, however, a compromise solution for those who are torn between the ethical unacceptability of deceiving or misleading research subjects and a concern to increase research validity. This involves initial deception, which is maintained throughout data collection, followed by full disclosure in the form of confession-cum-apology-cum-explanation. Research subjects are told of the subterfuge and deceit, but the rationale for it is explained and, hopefully, accepted. This solution may not be appropriate for every situation. Riddell's comments, presented above (pp. 131–2), suggest that, in her case, full disclosure after the event might have provoked anger and antagonism rather than understanding. In many cases, though, those who have participated in or permitted research will respond with understanding at being told, 'Now that I'm in a position to be able to tell you what the real focus of my research is … ' or, 'I hope you appreciate why I felt I couldn't tell you this before, but … '.

Such was the response of one group of research subjects who participated in a study of high-school science teaching carried out by Page, Samson and Crockett (1998), although, in this case, the research subjects had not been deliberately deceived about the scope and focus of the research. The research team had been unable to provide them with specific details because they were unclear themselves about precisely what they were looking for. The response of one research subject to the information presented at the dissemination seminar confirmed that validity may indeed have been threatened if the researchers had been more explicit beforehand:

> Al counters Dick's implicit criticism that the project was vague, noting that he 'think[s] it's good we *didn't* know what you were looking for because, uh, we would taint your study. There's a tendency to teach to the observer, not to the class …' (Page, Samson and Crockett, 1998, p. 312)

In the absence of data from studies that test the suggestibility issue it is evidence of this kind that provides the strongest indication of its potential as a validity threat.

Recognizing the dangers of and dealing with suggestibility represent reflective practice in educational research because generally the issue is, in many respects, neglected. The more obvious, accepted forms of researcher bias are taken on board by most researchers but it is left to the analytical researchers to recognize, to test and to control the more subtle forms of suggestibility. I have discussed one approach to suggestibility avoidance but reflective practice involves more than trying to avoid it; it also involves being able to recognize when, despite your best efforts, suggestibility may have distorted your research data and, through the presentation and dissemination of your findings, disclosing to others your suspicions. Full disclosure of this kind is the mark of the analytical researcher. I discuss it in detail in the next chapter.

Telling it as it is

A colleague with whom I once taught was notorious amongst the staff peer group for presenting quite a different report of events from that of others who were with her during, and who witnessed, the same events. On one occasion I recall her relating to a full staffroom the sequence of events involved in having asked permission of the headteacher to arrive at school an hour later the following day in order to attend an emergency appointment at the dentist's. 'She [the headteacher] was very put out by it', this teacher reported. 'Well, if you *must* go, I suppose you'd better', the headteacher was reported to have replied, after considering for a while. My colleague continued, 'She was very surly — I suppose I'm out of her good books for a few weeks now.' Yet those of us who had witnessed the request to the headteacher found our colleague's version incomprehensible. It certainly did not tally with our consensual recollection. As we interpreted events, the request was given a prompt and courteous positive response, without a hint of surliness or resentment. The fact that our colleague presented her version confidently and openly in our presence and even, from time to time, turned to us for corroboration — 'Didn't she?'; 'Wasn't she?' — suggests that she intended neither to misrepresent nor to mislead — nor even to exaggerate — but was, in good faith, simply telling a different tale from the one that we would have told and that, to the best of her recollection, she was telling it as she genuinely perceived it to have been. Even accepting and allowing for the principle of multiple perspectives that may lead to differences in interpretation, it seemed that, since she repeatedly emerged as having distinct, deviant, perspectives, this teacher habitually told a different tale to that of others and we began to take whatever she told us with a pinch of salt.

What if the teacher in question were an educational researcher? What if she were undertaking a form of participant observation study, in which her perceptions and interpretations of people's actions and the motives behind them were to be reported and disseminated? How authentic would her research be? How credible would her findings be? Yet examples such as this — of what is generally interpreted as distortion of the facts, or misrepresentation — are evident, in various forms and to varying degrees, in educational research. One particular variant of what is interpreted as misrepresentation or distortion of data — of giving research findings a particular slant that undermines the authenticity of the research — has been categorized as partisanship and, as such, identified in the Tooley Report (Tooley with Darby, 1998) as one of the 'worrying tendencies' in educational research.

The issue of accuracy of representation and reporting of research data — of the need for what I refer to as 'telling it as it is' — is the theme of this chapter. 'Telling it as it is' is a complex issue, not only because of the philosophical and sociological issues surrounding the notion itself, but also because, as a problematic research issue, it is so varied in the forms it takes. I am aware of touching only the surface of the issue in this chapter. My purpose is to home in on the specific issues that I believe I have tackled competently or to have begun to get to grips with in my own work, and to pass on to readers the benefit of my thinking and experience in these areas.

'TELLING IT AS IT IS': ISSUES AND EXPLANATIONS

But, there is no 'telling it as it is' — or is there? Is it achievable for researchers? There are, of course, philosophical issues that are relevant here; issues such as whether there is such a thing as objective truth, or of value-free knowledge; whether positivism or relativism or realism or phenomenology is the most desirable position for educational researchers to adopt. I do not intend to examine the competing claims of different philosophical positions and their implications for educational research since this is not the focus of my book. Moreover, such examination has been carried out extremely competently by others who are better qualified than I to carry it out (see, for example, Pratt and Swann, 1999; Pring, 2000a; Scott, 2000). I echo the sentiments reflected in Pring's (2000a, p. 88) warning: 'Beware of "isms" — and of the distinctions which arise from their rigid application.'

What I mean, in the context of this chapter, by 'telling it as it is' is *the reporting of research findings with sufficient accuracy to reflect a close alignment with the versions of the reality that the data reflect, as are likely to be formulated by research subjects and by consensual outsider viewpoints, or, in the event of significant disagreement, or likely disagreement, between researcher and subject in relation to these issues, the incorporation within the presentation of findings of the details and nature of this disagreement.* Perhaps this rather long-winded definition incorporates acceptance of a stance towards what Pring (2000a, p. 87) calls 'robust realism'; perhaps it does not – in any case, I have committed myself to avoiding 'isms'. Of the five theories of truth identified and explained by Bridges (1999) this definition seems to fit best within the one referred to as 'truth as consensus – "P" is true if and only if there is agreement that p, universally or among a relevant population', and summed up by Bridges's citing of Guba (in Bridges, 1999, p. 20):

> But how can we find out how things really are, and how they really work? ... The best we can do is to come to some consensus (or as near to it as possible) that can be managed given the level of information and sophistication that we have. The construction to be 'believed' is that one which, in the opinion of those best able to make such a judgement, is the most informed and sophisticated.

Essentially, what I mean by 'telling it as it is' is reporting what is broadly accepted generally as a close representation of the reality that those who participated in the research or who are in the position of evaluating it do not have too many reservations about accepting as being reflected by the research data: reporting of findings that ring fairly true, or, if broad consensus is elusive, the reporting of the nature and extent of any significant disagreement. I believe this is the best we can hope for in terms of accuracy of representation, and I am not sure how far those, such as Martyn Hammersely, who have been labelled 'methodological purist' (Hammersley, 1998) would accept this, but I believe there are occasions when, as researchers – no matter how 'extended' as professionals we are – we have to accept a compromise position. Such a position is reflected in Wilson and Wilson's (1998, pp. 355–6) illustration of the difficulties of reconciling different conceptions of things:

> We may all express an interest in 'values' or 'moral education'. But then one person will see this largely as a matter of maintaining good order in society, ensuring that citizens perform their social duties and responsibilities; whereas another sees it as more concerned with the individual's sentiments and

emotions, with his/her personal relationships, perhaps even with the soul. Clearly any programme (and any research) in this area will vary enormously, depending on these two conceptions. And since 'values' and 'morality' (and 'education') are notoriously slippery terms, it may seem that there is no way of negotiating this in the light of pure reason: all we can do, perhaps, is to establish some kind of 'consensus' about the conceptions and hence about the programmes.

My definition of 'telling it as it is' incorporates consideration of the possibility of opinions and views being swayed by research reporting; to accept something does not depend upon its having hitherto been acknowledged or accepted, so the possibility of pioneering researchers successfully disseminating innovative theories and radical ideas is not closed off. The essential issue is the credibility of the interpretation being advanced; credibility through feasibility and potential as well as credibility through confirmation of existing knowledge. 'Telling it as it is' therefore means presenting a tale that, were the full details of the research process upon which it is based subjected to close scrutiny, would 'stand up in court'.

Explained in this way, I believe 'telling it as it is' is perfectly achievable for researchers. It does not preclude values-influenced interpretation; I accept the argument (Alvesson and Sköldberg, 2000; Carr, 2000; Kelly, 1989; Foster, 1989; Scott, 2000) that value-free research is unachievable: 'nature cannot be viewed as it really is ... but only as seen ... through some value window' (Guba and Lincoln, 1989, p. 65), or, as Kelly (1989, pp. 101–2) puts it: 'Many social scientists would now accept that there is no such thing as value-free, objective or neutral research. What is seen depends on the spectacles which are worn when looking.' However, to 'tell it as it is', as I have defined the term, involves a particular form of reflective research practice incorporating mechanisms to reduce as far as possible the effects of partisanship and the more general influence of researcher values. The analytical researcher does not ignore the effects of her/his values or dismiss their influence as unavoidable. Rather, s/he confronts them, acknowledges them and attempts to deal with them head-on by incorporating recognition of them into the research process and dissemination. Before presenting ideas and guidelines for 'telling it as it is', though, it is important to examine some of the problems with research that fails to do so.

FAILING TO 'TELL IT AS IT IS': EXAMPLES OF KEY PROBLEMATIC AREAS

Failing to 'tell it as it is' involves telling a research-based tale that is not broadly, consensually acceptable. Precisely where, in the research process, this failure has its origins varies. In some cases it occurs during data collection and analysis and in such cases it reflects deviance in relation to interpretation. This may be done in good faith or it may reflect deliberate distortion or manipulation of data. In other cases failure to 'tell it as it is' occurs at the reporting and dissemination stage only. Failure to 'tell it as it is' therefore represents a form of deviance, which may be intellectual or ethical deviance, or both.

Because there are degrees — as there are with most research methodological issues — of failing to 'tell it as it is' and because, coupled with this, it may take different forms, there are many permutations of the ways in which this particular methodological weakness may occur. In this chapter I focus on just two of its key features: presenting a blinkered view, and manipulation of data. Failing to 'tell it as it is' typically involves either or both of these features.

Presenting a Blinkered View

This generally reflects an unquestioning, uninvestigative and over-simplistic approach to data analysis. It involves the presentation of a one-sided, blinkered view that reflects only the researcher's perspective and interpretation and fails to incorporate consideration or recognition of alternative interpretations. This may sometimes reflect partisanship, but it may also reflect simply an insufficiently probing and questioning analysis. The latter may arise from constraints of time and resources or from cognitive limitations on the part of the researcher who is inexperienced in, or unaware of the importance of, delving deeper in the analysis process to search for explanations for patterns and for discrepancies and for alternative emergent theories and identifiable causal relationships.

Presenting a blinkered view is the same as presenting a narrow view that is limited in scope and that fails to take in all that is available to take in. It may arise out of preconceptions and fixed notions that the researcher may not necessarily recognize as such and that s/he is unable or unwilling to dismiss. It may reflect dogmatism, oversensitivity, or simply analytical myopia.

A blinkered view presents only one side of the story — one out of several competing versions. It represents a single perspective. Those familiar with his novels will be aware of the prominence Arnold Bennett affords multiple perspectives in the story he tells of the romance between Edwin Clayhanger and Hilda Lessways. Particularly striking in this work of fiction is the misinterpretation of motives ascribed by each character to the other. In *Clayhanger* (Bennett, 1910), the hero, Edwin, has convinced himself that Hilda Lessways is attracted to him: 'He thought, "She's taken a fancy to me!"' (p. 221). The following extract is one of the many examples that Bennett presents of Edwin's misinterpretation of Hilda's motives:

> Janet went out first. Hilda hesitated; and Edwin, having taken his hat from its hook in the cubicle, stood attending her at the aperture. He was sorry that he could not run upstairs for a walking-stick. At last she seemed to decide to leave, yet left with apparent reluctance. Edwin followed, giving a final glance at the boy, who was tying a parcel hurriedly. Mr Orgreave and his daughter were ten yards off, arm-in-arm. Edwin fell into step with Hilda Lessways. Janet looked round, and smiled and beckoned. 'I wonder,' said Edwin to himself, 'what the devil's going to happen now?' I'll take my oath she stayed behind on purpose! Well ...' This swaggering audacity was within. Without, even a skilled observer could have seen nothing but a faint, sheepish smile. And his heart was thumping again ...
>
> Suddenly she moved her head, glanced full at him for an instant, and glanced behind her. 'Where are they?' she inquired.
>
> 'The others? Aren't they in front? They must be somewhere about.'
>
> Unless she also had marked their deviation into the Cock Yard, why had she glanced behind her in asking where they were? She knew as well as he that they had started in front. He could only deduce that she had been as willing as himself to lose Mr Orgreave and Janet. (Bennett, 1910, pp. 234–6)

In *Hilda Lessways*, though, we are presented with Hilda's different perspective:

> Janet went out first with her gay father. Edwin Clayhanger waited respectfully for Hilda to pass. But just as she was about to step forth she caught sight of George Cannon coming along the opposite side of Wedgewood Street in the direction of Trafalgar Road; he was in close conversation with another man.

She kept within the shelter of the shop until the two had gone by. She did not want to meet George Cannon ... She thought, 'If he saw me, he'd come across and speak to me, and I might have to introduce him to all these people, and goodness knows what!' The contretemps caused her heart to beat. (Bennett, 1911, p. 201)

She was somewhat out of humour with him [Edwin]. He had begun with losing sight of Mr Orgreave and Janet – and of course it was hopeless to seek for them in those thronging streets around St Luke's Square. (Bennett, 1911, p. 203)

Once we have access to this other perspective – that of Hilda herself – we see clearly that Edwin's version is inaccurate; that is, his interpretation of Hilda's motives is inaccurate. From his blinkered, somewhat self-centred standpoint that is coloured by his conviction of Hilda's attraction to him, he had failed to take in all the evidence that was available to him if he had been sufficiently receptive to looking for it, and he had accepted as the only plausible explanation the one that sprang to his mind first of all, without considering alternatives. But he got it wrong.

The same error may – and often does – occur in the research process, but it is not easy for those evaluating the research to detect because raw data reflecting perspectives other than the researcher's are seldom made as accessible as is the fictional Hilda Lessway's perspective. It is, therefore, impossible to judge with certainty that a researcher has 'got it wrong'; indeed, to do so would be to make precisely the kind of error that one is seeking to expose. The most we can do is identify potential spurious conclusions and, in doing so, question the accuracy of research. Tooley (1999, p. 171) identifies examples of research that is questionable in this way, which he categorizes as manifestations of partisanship:

Some of the areas which exhibited the most dramatic evidence of partisanship were research in gender and sexuality, and race and ethnicity. Many researchers seemed unable to tackle these issues in a manner which enabled one to be sure that they had engaged critically with their evidence, or that their conclusions were based upon what was really occurring in the classrooms examined.

He then (Tooley, 1999, pp. 171–2) presents in full quotations from an article that he considers to exemplify this weakness and comments upon what he implies are the author's spurious observations. Reporting research on the schooling experiences of black primary school pupils, Tooley writes:

> He quotes from the school report comments of a primary schoolteacher, Mrs Scott ... He tells us that 'the influence of racist discources is more evident when Mrs Scott explains the origins of *Paul's* "disobedient" behaviour' ...
>
>> Paul [...] is progressing well but needs to be guided [...] His mother is very keen that he should do well. I have had to guide his behaviour in the last few months, quite a lot, and explain to him the differences between right and wrong [...] He tends to 'follow' instead of being an independent boy. This is a shame as he has a good brain of his own and should have his own ideas in future. Good at sport ...
>
> Again, an outside observer may puzzle long and hard as to how this passage shows any evidence of 'racist discourse'. Trying to read between the lines as much as possible, all I can ascertain is that Paul is an intelligent boy, who sometimes goes astray and needs parental or teacher guidance. And he is good at sport — perhaps this is where the racism lies? Indeed, Connolly [the author] thinks so:
>
>> Paul is also, according to Mrs Scott's report, 'good at sport'. This sporting and athletic image is, again, a common theme running through the teacher's views on African/Carribean boys ...
>
> But perhaps it is simply true — Paul *is* good at sport — rather than being evidence of 'racist discourse'? Connolly does not seem to countenance such a possibility.

A similar example is found in Riddell's report of her feminist research (1989, p. 87):

> After talking to one mother and father for nearly an hour and a half, I was trying to bring the interview to a close with what I thought was a fairly innocuous question. I asked:
>
>> Are you generally happy with the education Stephen's getting?
>
> Mr Gammage, a policeman, replied:
>
>> Well apart from this bloody irresponsible strike that's been going on ...

Instead of bringing the interview to a calm conclusion, this resulted in a half hour's denunciation of the entire teaching profession. Analyzing how I responded to male attempts to establish power in the interview, I found that I generally backed off from conflict, and often found it difficult to probe for more detailed answers when what they said was very brief. Although I did not probe the women's responses either, they certainly offered me a far more intimate view of themselves. Of the three fathers whom I interviewed by themselves, one blocked my questions completely and gave yes/no responses to everything, and another answered very briefly. The headmasters whom I interviewed also provided proficient examples of school politics in operation, spending a very long time avoiding my questions.

As a woman – and a feminist – I feel able to question with impunity that may well be denied a man the researcher's conclusion that these reported incidents demonstrate 'male attempts to establish power in the interview'. My immediate response to reading this and similar passages in Riddell's paper was to categorize them as evidence of partisanship and of the author's having a feminist chip on her shoulder. Certainly, that the researcher's experiences reflect male dominance – or attempts to dominate – is one possible interpretation, but it is by no means the only interpretation. Ascribing motives to others – particularly in the absence of their own accounts and explanations for them – is an extremely inexact science that, at best, may be described as conjecture and, at worst, as arrogant assumption. It is highly susceptible to misinterpretation that leads to the generation of spurious conclusions. We are treading on thin ice if we subsume our unsubstantiated interpretations of the motives behind the nature of their responses within our data. This involves stepping over the line – albeit a thin one – that separates the manner in which data are collected and provided and the data themselves; it blurs the distinction between process and product. Based on the evidence available in her paper, and bearing in mind that, like any paper, this is unable to provide us with the full picture, I formulated the impression that the author is too ready to ascribe sexist or stereotypical gender-related motives to her research subjects. Her male interviewees seem unable to put a foot right; if they are loquacious and responsive she evidently interprets their responses as domineering, and their reticence is evidently interpreted as attempts to sabotage the interview through non-cooperation. This reflects what I interpret as her blinkered viewpoint, and in a later section I examine ways in which she might have analysed and presented her data in a more balanced way. Riddell's analysis contrasts sharply with Luttrell's (2000, pp. 513–14) description of how what was effectively the removal of her blinkers allowed her to see and re-analyse her research data in a new light:

> Identifying my reluctance to deal with strong emotions and mixed feelings about mothers – what could be called counter-transference in my fieldwork relationships – marked a major breakthrough in my research process. I again returned to all the interview material, and through this recursive process I discovered a range of maternal images and mixed feelings that the women had expressed, but that I had minimized in my analysis of the links between structure, culture and agency.

Riddell's interpretation of her male interviewees' behaviour would be justifiable if she had applied appropriate controls to, or, at least, consideration of, other variables together with incorporation of consideration of evidence that supported or conflicted with her interpretation before systematically assessing rival explanations. She presents no evidence of having adopted such a rigorous approach to her analysis.

Yet I have to acknowledge another side to the arguments I have presented within my criticism of Riddell's analysis. In his outline explanation of consensus theory Bridges (1999, p. 606) warns:

> Philosophers have tended to be sceptical of consensus theory as an account of what it means for a belief to be true ...
>
> Researchers ought perhaps to share especially in this scepticism of consensus, since it is, arguably, their particular function as intellectual citizens to challenge the easy and self-perpetuating consensus that society creates for itself. At the very least they have to observe that what any group of people believe or agree to be true may rest on, for example, unexamined tradition, the hegemony of a dominant class, the suppression or self-censorship of dissenting opinion or collective hysteria – all the things that intellectuals and researchers have traditionally been expected to subvert.

Applying this consideration to my criticism of Riddell's work, I am forced to accept the possibility that, in presenting my interpretation of her analysis as the reflection of a blinkered viewpoint, and my own as reflecting the more consensual form of truth, I may have fallen into the trap, to which Bridges refers, of perpetuating a consensus that fails to question – because it fails to see – the hegemony of one or more specific societal groups. In a sense, moreover, I seem to be trapped in a 'Catch 22'-type situation; by contending that Riddell's viewpoint is blinkered does not my own viewpoint then risk becoming so?

Manipulation of Data

This involves telling it as you, the researcher, want it to appear. Manipulation of data differs from presenting a blinkered view because it represents deliberate distortion of data, rather than an incapacity to see beyond a single perspective. Manipulation of data is a conscious, considered act that is carried out with eyes wide open. It has several forms and a range of degrees of intensity. Since researchers do not own up to manipulation of data and since it is practically impossible to detect in published or oral research reports I am unable to provide examples of it. My evidence of its existence is entirely anecdotal. I do not claim that it is a widespread feature of educational research; it is impossible to ascertain, or even estimate, the scale with which it occurs, yet I know, from my own experience, that it does occur. I confess to having practised it myself during my 'restricted' professional period; I know of colleagues who have practised it, and am aware of several cases of it amongst graduate students.

Manipulation of data involves the selective use of data as part of the selective presentation of findings. This may range from, for example, using research interview quotations out of context, or omitting sections of them – the form of data manipulation that I confess to having practised on a couple of occasions – to data omission: ignoring and excluding from the analysis process consideration of outlier cases, or, indeed, any cases that the researcher wishes to ignore.

There is a range of possible motives for the different forms of data manipulation. Constraints of time or resources – or laziness, general sloppiness or boredom with the subject – may prompt a researcher to analyse fully and include in the presentation of findings only a proportion of the data, and yet make no mention of this omission when reporting the research. Partisanship, or simply the desire to present an interesting set of findings in order to appear competent or to gain publicity, may lead to the manipulation of data in order to tell a good story, make a political point or expose what is considered to be an injustice with a view to providing ammunition for changes to policy or practice. Data that do not fit into, and that undermine, an emergent pattern that the researcher has identified or a theoretical model that s/he is formulating may be excluded from the analysis, or distorted in order to fit into them. Researchers may use a research interview quotation out of context, or with a few words or sentences omitted and replaced with an ellipsis in order to illustrate, and therefore support, a point that they wish to make or a trend or tendency that they believe they picked up during the course of their research, but of which they have little or no illustrative evidence. Such was the form of, and motive underpinning, my own manipulation of data. Much manipulation of data, I suggest, is done for the sake of telling a good tale. But telling a good tale is not necessarily the same as 'telling it as it is'.

DEVELOPING THE CAPACITY TO 'TELL IT AS IT IS': SOME GUIDELINES

Since I am restricting my guidelines for 'telling it as it is' to a section of a single chapter, rather than filling a whole book with them, as I could very easily do, I will focus once again just on the two specific weaknesses identified above: presenting a blinkered view, and manipulation of data.

'Telling it as it is' involves tackling these weaknesses – being aware of them and keeping in mind throughout the research process their elements and how these may be counteracted. The capacity to 'tell it as it is' is dependent upon a solid research process as a basis, without which the credibility of your research findings and the authenticity of your research may be undermined.

Presenting an 'Unblinkered' View

If you want to avoid presenting a blinkered view you need to remove your blinkers. Your whole research process – and particularly the data analysis – must incorporate consideration of different perspectives; different explanations and interpretations. You need to start thinking laterally.

If you are relatively inexperienced, a good way to start broadening your range of perspectives is to use other people as sounding boards for your developing ideas and emerging theorizing. Encourage – even challenge – others to come up with feasible alternatives. The next stage is to develop this capacity for formulating alternative ideas and explanations independently, so that you challenge your own thinking. This forms part of the process of reflective practice in research and of developing more advanced skills. Start by brainstorming. Think of as many possible explanations for or interpretations of your research data as you can, without regard for their feasibility; list the unlikely along with the likely explanations. Then, afterwards, sift through your list rejecting those that, after some thought, appear very unlikely, and putting question marks alongside slightly more hopeful ones. At this stage you may wish to try ranking the explanations that remain on your list, although you may consider several to merit equal ranking.

There is no reason why, in refining your list, you should not enlist the help of willing colleagues, or friends and relatives (they do not need to be researchers or academics – 'lay' people may just as easily as academics offer valuable insights on many educational research topics, particularly those relating to human behaviour and attitudes), or research subjects, where appropriate. However, do not be lured into acceptance of research subjects' explanations and interpretations as the only 'valid' perspective. To do so would be to present a blinkered view; one that simply shifts the single perspective offered from that of the researcher to that of the research subjects. 'Telling it as it is' involves much more than accurately representing the views of research subjects, which could be achieved by presenting raw data alongside minimal analysis. Much of the skill of 'telling it as it is' is tied up in the depth, thoroughness and creativity of the analysis that you apply to your data and, as the researcher, you should be able to formulate ideas and explanations that incorporate considerably more insight and theoretical subject knowledge than are afforded research subjects (Wilson and Wilson, 1998). Taking off your blinkers involves embracing multiple perspectives, evaluating these and assimilating them as best you can into a version that represents 'telling it as it is'.

The process – outlined above – of widening your vision to incorporate multiple perspectives may be applied incrementally to research data. It may be applied first to small 'chunks' of data, such as a few comments relating to a narrow, specific topic, made by one or more research interviewees, or a few – or even a single – example(s) of manifestations of specific observed behaviour. The process may then be applied to increasingly large and collective 'chunks' of data. Eventually it may be applied to the data in their entirety, as a collective unit, in order to present a summative analysis that leads to what, at that time, you offer as the essence of the findings of your research – the key, embracing message that emerges, or the key theory that you develop. The phrase *at that time* is significant. It is important to be aware that removing one's blinkers is also temporally related. This means that during the time that you are engaged on a specific area of study you remain receptive to the need to reappraise your perspective and the messages conveyed through your findings.

The consideration and assimilation of different perspectives should not be confined to your analysis of data — it should permeate your thinking as a researcher throughout the entire research process. It should be applied to the planning of the research design; the formulation of research objectives and the framing of research questions, for example, as well as the literature search and the choice of data collection methods. Indeed, an extensive literature review, which should be on-going throughout the entire research process, will yield multiple perspectives and offer information that lead you to reconsider and perhaps revise the interpretations and explanations that you had formulated. The intellectual satisfaction and the credibility among your peers that being an analytical researcher offers you come at a price — the work involves much ripping up and re-writing. Reflective practice in educational research means multiple drafts.

There are two key questions that you should ask yourself repeatedly through the research process, at every point where you find yourself formulating an explanation or an idea to explain causal relations or why things occur, or why they are as they appear to be:

- What evidence is there that this is the case?
- What evidence is there that this is not the case?

You may find it helpful to make two lists, side-by-side, of answers to these two questions. More specific, 'sub'-questions may be addressed in order to answer them. The following examples may serve as a checklist, though the list is illustrative only — there are many more questions that could be added:

- Does anyone other than I think this is the case?
- Does my interpretation involve assumption on my part?
- Does my interpretation ascribe motives to research subjects? If so, is there any other possible explanation for their motives?
- Would the research subjects be likely to concur with — *do they* concur with — my interpretation?
- Am I in danger of having ascribed to research subjects attitudes, emotions, motives, etc., on the basis of how *I* would respond in such circumstances, rather than on the basis of evidence of how *they* have responded?

- Does my interpretation corroborate other research findings?
- Is my interpretation consistent with any theoretical stance or proposition?
- Is my interpretation original and novel?
- Does my interpretation challenge, or fail to support, other research findings or theory or literature evidence? If so, why is this — how would I explain the discrepancy if challenged?
- Does my interpretation reflect my political stance or views on issues on which I have strong feelings?
- Would I be happy for all of my raw data to be scrutinized by others?
- To what extent do my research data support the interpretation that I have formulated — what proportion of the data supports it?
- Does my interpretation incorporate consideration of any of my data that do not support it?
- Since formulating my interpretation have I sought out evidence to support or challenge it?

This list includes questions that overlap to some extent, but the thoroughness of inquiry and introspection that is likely to result in asking yourself the same basic question in slightly different ways or with slightly different slants is a useful exercise in developing more advanced research skills.

At this point it is worth applying some of these questions to examination of Riddell's (1989) research evidence and interpretation, presented above. I have suggested that Riddell does not appear to have given due consideration to the different variables involved in her research. Addressing some of the questions listed above would have contributed to her doing so. In the case of Riddell's research, taking off her blinkers would have involved her asking herself questions such as:

- What evidence is there that these interviewees are trying to establish power in the interviews?
- What is another explanation for their motives?
- If they are trying to establish power during the proceedings is it necessarily because they are men? (At this point she should have identified and isolated different variables and considered each specific one, asking herself questions such as: Are they trying to dominate because (a) they're men; (b) they're men and I'm a woman; (c) they're middle class; (d) irrespective of considerations of gender and social class, I am a less domineering individual than they; etc.)

- What literature evidence is there of how: (a) male headteacher interviewees respond to female interviewers; (b) male headteacher interviewees respond to male interviewers; (c) female headteacher interviewees respond to female interviewers; (d) female head-teacher interviewees respond to male interviewers? How does this evidence compare with my experiences?
- How might the research subjects themselves interpret and categorize their behaviour?

Making it specific and relevant to Riddell's case, try addressing each of the remaining questions presented in the checklist above in order to see if this exercise suggests different perspectives from that presented by Riddell. A useful follow-up exercise to this would be to formulate questions of your own to apply specifically to the example presented by Riddell's report of her research, and then to extend the checklist on pp. 148–9 by generalizing these questions and adding them to the list.

Avoiding Manipulation of Data

Reflective practice in educational research has no truck with data manipulation. Although they may consider their motives for practising it to be justified and worthy – for example, to provide supporting evidence for an undesirable trend that they wish to expose – researchers who practise it are, nevertheless, the fraudsters of the profession. In this section I offer guidelines for developing a specific advanced skill that counteracts and offers an alternative to data manipulation.

I refer to this specific skill as *full disclosure*. Any good, basic research methodology manual will emphasize the importance of providing in research reports full details of the research design and process. Even inexperienced researchers are aware of the basic requirement of identifying the main research aim and objectives; listing the research questions; presenting full details of the nature and size of the sample, the reason for and the process involved in selecting it; describing the data collection process and explaining the choice of methods; discussing issues of reliability and validity and identifying the methods aimed at reducing threats to them; providing full details of the analysis process; and identifying limitations of the study. Full disclosure goes way beyond this.

Full disclosure involves sharing with those to whom you are reporting your research the precise details of the circumstances surrounding developments pertaining to the research process and the research data. Usually – though not necessarily – these will be non-standard and unanticipated developments. Full disclosure involves discussing openly and presenting your thought processes and details of your decision-making, rather than drawing a veil over them. It involves presenting clearly the epistemological and methodological limitations of your work Specific examples of features of full disclosure include:

- owning up to being – or having been – baffled or puzzled
- relating the detailed and protracted sequence of events leading up to a discovery
- relating the circumstances of a problem or difficulty, your response to it and the measure of your success in overcoming it
- describing your trials and errors in a specific research process
- identifying data that do not fit emerging patterns or trends and suggesting and discussing possible explanations for this discrepancy
- presenting ideas that represent speculation, conjecture and conditional causal relationships
- clearly identifying and explaining the bases of your ideas – it is perfectly acceptable to base ideas on speculation, conjecture and assumption, provided that you identify them as such
- posing questions that you have formulated but to which you do not yet have the answers
- detailing your reasoning in relation to why specific explanations do not seem to hold water.

There are available some excellent examples, provided by the educational research community's 'extended' professionals, of full disclosure accounts of their work and their research experiences. An example is provided by myself in Chapter 4 of this book, pp. 84–9, where I present details of my thinking that arose out of my comparative analysis and that led me to question, and, eventually, modify, one of my earlier research-based conclusions. This is not, by any means, one of the best examples available, since I was constrained in the amount of detail I felt able to include in my account by the need to address other issues in the chapter within a self-imposed word limit. A much better example is Hammersley's (1993) 'cautionary tale' of what he describes as 'ethnographic deviance'. Here he describes the trials and errors of two colleagues and himself in relation to developing theory from ethnographic research findings. An extended quotation from Hammersley's article indicates the depth of information and the level of detail provided, the candour of the author, and the pervasive discursiveness that typify the most advanced forms of full disclosure:

> We started analysis of this data by broadly following the procedures recommended by Glaser and Strauss. We put our ideas about the effects of examinations into the background, in order to see what themes would emerge. Themes did emerge, but they were very diverse, opening up many possible research projects. We wondered how we should choose amongst them, and how far our initial concern with the effects of examinations should guide our choice. But we faced considerable difficulties. Few of the themes related in any direct way to one another, or to our initial concerns, and none of them stood out from the rest as offering the most promising way forward. On top of these practical problems, we also began to have some more general doubts about grounded theory. It seemed to place us in a position where we were torn between idiographic and nomothetic goals, in a way that prevented either of these being pursued satisfactorily. While its declared aim is to develop a theory, at the same time it commits the researcher to producing open-ended, detailed descriptions of the situations investigated. We came to the conclusion that these two aims are incompatible. Indeed, we began to wonder whether this incompatibility might be the reason for what we saw as the failure of ethnographic work to develop and test theory effectively.
>
> In response to these practical and theoretical problems, we began to turn more to analytic induction as a guiding strategy for our research ... But we soon realised that our project did not fit the model of analytic induction ... Yet we had started our research with a set of hypotheses about possible effects of examinations, and our task seemed to be to find out whether those effects did in fact occur. From the point of view of analytic deduction we had set off on the wrong foot. The implication seemed to be that we needed to look at our data and find something to explain, so that we could then generate hypotheses about it. We considered this, but were puzzled by it. Why was it necessary to start with something to be explained, rather than starting with an idea about something that could make a difference? (Hammersley, 1993, pp. 2–3)

The first part of Hammersley's article continues in this candid, discursive style, employing vocabulary that is appropriate for conveying the trial-and-error and investigative, experimental, and sometimes unresolved, nature of the experiences being described: 'it seemed to us that ...', 'from all this we deduced that ...', 'in this way we attempted to ...', 'so we began trying to ...', 'I also came to question ...', 'I seemed to be caught in a process of ...', and, in particular, 'my reflections seem to have unearthed more, and more difficult, problems' (Hammersley, 1993, pp. 2–5, passim).

A similar example – though one relating to quite a different topic – is Page, Samson and Crockett's (1998) account (to which I refer in Chapter 4) of reporting research findings back to research participants – high-school science teachers – through what they refer to as 'teacher seminars'. One of the article's main themes is the unexpected discrepancy between the nature of the responses of the two sub-samples to the research findings presented to each of them. Typical of advanced-level full disclosure is the detailed description of the analytical process used in order to uncover the reason for this discrepancy. In total, the authors present and describe the reasoning that led them to three successive interpretations of the reasons for the discrepancy. Once again, I draw upon extended quotations to illustrate the features of full disclosure:

> In this second interpretation, we see three factors differentiating the two introductions. First, while we entered the [research dissemination] seminars as researchers from the culture of the university, we did not bring immutable researcher or university roles or values to the seminars. Rather, like the teachers', our own participation was shaped by the local school contexts – that is, we had been partially socialized to the high schools during the long process of studying in them. As a result, we found ourselves seduced by the congeniality at Westridge and somewhat put off by the contentiousness at Endeavor. Our different reactions had arisen occasionally as topics in our team meetings. In the teacher seminars, the differentiated responses became even more pronounced and influential. For instance, as we found ourselves more and more beleaguered at Endeavor, we quit pushing hard at Westridge to get teachers to acknowledge critical issues in the data. In retrospect, we must have felt we had as much critique on our hands as we could handle. Our reactions were more complicated than this suggests, too, because we found that we were not only appreciative of the approval at Westridge but sometimes very vexed by teachers' insouciance, whereas we admired the fervor

with which Endeavor teachers scrutinized our presentation of the materials we presented, even as we also thought them defensive. (Page, Samson and Crockett, 1998, p. 324)

We on the research team eventually became dissatisfied with this second interpretation, too. Whereas it highlighted how we researchers contributed to the different responses at the two schools, it still cast teachers as rather passive or reactive participants. The teachers acted as they did, the analysis suggests, in response to our presentation of the research. Like the first analysis, this interpretation also failed to consider that the drama in the seminars was not just going on between researchers and teachers; teachers there were also watching and performing for each other.

Our first and second analyses exhibited the conventional wisdom about reporting research to practitioners – that is, researchers should take measures to shift their power and privileges so that teachers are empowered. The conventional wisdom, however, neglects the fact that teachers already have power. Researcher agenda notwithstanding, teachers can appropriate a research project and use it for their own local purposes. Pursuing this tack, we began a third interpretation that looked at the teacher seminars as solidarity-building rituals for the two science departments. (Page, Samson and Crockett, 1998, pp. 326–7)

The example of Page, Samson and Crockett's account highlights particularly clearly the distinction between the 'restricted' and the 'extended' professional's response to issues and circumstances that are initially puzzling and difficult to explain, because their case includes examples of processes and procedures that took the researchers off in what they later decided were the wrong directions and which, therefore, 'restricted' professionals typically would be tempted to cover up. The analytical researcher, though, exemplified by Hammersley and by the American team, is simply not content to let sleeping dogs lie in the way that the 'restricted' professional is. The analytical researcher is not satisfied until s/he has given extensive consideration to explaining something that s/he initially has difficulty understanding. The analytical researcher is aware that the greatest intellectual challenges provide the greatest source of intellectual satisfaction and professional development, and full disclosure allows the processes involved in meeting such challenges to be shared by, and perhaps supplemented and augmented by, others. Full disclosure is one of the most valuable contributions a researcher may make to epistemological and methodological development. Manipulation of data, on the other hand, contributes nothing — indeed, in its worst forms, through its deception, it impedes development.

Full disclosure refers not to the depth of analysis that researchers employ in trying to puzzle things out, but to their communication to others of the precise nature and extent of the puzzle and the process they have applied to its solution, together with their perceptions of the flaws and limitations within that process. Full disclosure involves researchers' communicating precisely where they are at the point of communicating, how they reached that point and where they plan to go from there.

If you are a relatively inexperienced researcher, do not feel intimidated by the incisive reasoning pervading the deep analysis that Hammersley and Page, Samson and Crockett applied to their respective puzzles. Candid reporting even of having reached dead-ends or of being at a loss to explain an inconsistency or discrepancy within your findings constitutes full disclosure. Moreover, as you commit yourself to practising this feature of reflective practice you will find that, very quickly, the pressure to explain and describe in detail to others the thought processes that underpin and determine your analysis will encourage you to extend and deepen that analysis and increase your capacity for doing so. The next chapter takes up this theme.

8

Tools of the trade: developing coding and categorization skills

When I was in my final year of primary school my mother bought a booklet containing advice to parents on how to maximize their children's chances of passing the 11+ examination. I can still remember her reading aloud to me the first piece of advice listed in the mathematics section, 'Make sure your child knows the multiplication tables. Without them he [sic] will be like a carpenter without wood.' There is a parallel to this advice that applies to qualitative research: make sure your categorization skills are up to scratch — without them you will be unable to develop into an analytical researcher.

Categories are important to the development of reflective practice in educational research because they serve as stepping stones that lead the researcher towards theory development; indeed, Glaser and Strauss (1967, p. 36) refer to categories as conceptual aspects or elements of theory. The analytical researcher who wishes to engage in in-depth analysis needs to uncover patterns and trends and search for explanations for them, and to identify and explain deviations from these patterns and trends. This involves a process of grouping, sorting and classifying: of formulating and identifying categories and placing phenomena into these categories.

The process of coding — sorting data, according to the commonalities that they share, into categories — is the organizational process that makes sense out of the relationship between data. The deeper the level of analysis, however, the more difficult the categorization process is. To the researcher who wants to reach for the depths in her/his analysis, categorization is probably the single most difficult and most challenging activity to be undertaken. This chapter offers guidelines for tackling this important part of the research process.

THE DIFFICULTIES OF CATEGORIZATION

The reason why effective categorization is so difficult and challenging is to be found in the nature and the features of categories. Merriam refers to Holsti's (in Merriam, 1988, p. 136) guidelines for category construction:

1 The categories should reflect the purpose of the research.
2 The categories should be exhaustive.
3 The categories should be mutually exclusive.
4 All categories should derive from a single classification principle.

What makes effective categorization so difficult are the two requirements that categories be both exhaustive and exclusive. Gillham (2000a, p. 60) explains: 'a requirement for the derivation of categories is that they should be *exhaustive*. But another requirement is that they should be *exclusive*, i.e. that the kind of statements that go into one category clearly belong there and couldn't really go anywhere else.'

Ensuring that your categories are exhaustive and exclusive is relatively easy if you are undertaking superficial analysis. Indeed, at a superficial level of analysis your greatest problem is likely to be deciding on what basis you are to code the data:

> Imagine a large gymnasium in which thousands of toys are spread out on the floor. You are given the task of sorting them into piles according to a scheme that you are to develop. You walk around the gym looking at the toys, picking them up, and examining them. There are many ways to form piles. They could be sorted according to size, color, country of origin, data manufactured, manufacturer, material they are made from, the type of play they encourage, the age group they suit, or whether they represent living things or inanimate objects. (Bogdan and Biklen, 1992, p. 165)

The same multiplicity of choice applies equally to research data as it does to the practical example of sorting toys in a gymnasium. Coding of data, though, is a process that may occur at multiple levels of depth and complexity, as Bogdan and Biklen (1992, p. 177) illustrate:

> Codes categorize information at different levels. Major codes are more general and sweeping, incorporating a wide range of activities, attitudes, and behaviors. Subcodes break these major codes into smaller categories. In a study of career women's

experiences of work and family life when they had children after thirty, the major code, 'child care', also included five subcodes: – history of, – finances, – negotiation of, – preferences, and, – responsibility for.

First-level coding – representing superficial analysis – is typically simple and straightforward. If you were researching children's preferences for literature, for example, first-level coding of data generated by observation in a school library or a classroom reading corner, or by conversations with children, may reveal that eight-year-olds prefer fiction to non-fiction, or it may reveal preferences for specific authors. Yet, delving deeper into the nature of and the reasons for children's preferences would involve several levels of coding and more complex and challenging categorization. For example, categorization might eventually focus on the key features of literature reflecting children's different preferences. Faced with data in the form of a long list of features that appeal to children, such as: *involves animal characters; involves a 'villain' character; reflects interests and hobbies; incorporates attractive, colourful illustrations; relates an adventure; involves fantasy; has a recent film/television version; involves an action-packed plot; is easy to read;* and *has a happy ending,* how would you code these data? What categories of reasons why books appeal to children would you formulate? You may consider categories such as interestingness; quality of presentation; comprehensibility; and familiarity. But are these categories mutually exclusive? Would you categorize *easy to read* as a comprehensibility issue or a quality of presentation issue? The fact that it could be either demonstrates something of the complexity of categorization that accompanies deeper level coding. Moreover, could comprehensibility and familiarity be considered to be sub-categories of interestingness? If so, then the categorization is flawed because the categories represent different levels of coding and, reflecting this, different levels of specificity. This kind of flaw is perhaps more effectively illustrated by consideration of how you might sort a selection of kitchen utensils into labelled drawers that reflect categories of different levels. Would you place teaspoons and tablespoons into the drawer labelled 'spoons' or the drawer labelled 'cutlery'?

DEVELOPING CATEGORIZATION SKILLS

One of the key facets of in-depth analysis is the reduction of data into effective categories. First-level coding will typically involve the compilation of lists from the raw data. Some researchers simply present such lists as their findings and these, together with discussion, constitute the research analysis and presentation of findings. This represents the lowest level of analysis.

Consider the following list of what are presented as characteristics of effective school leadership, compiled by one of my own research students. The list is introduced by the student: 'The characteristics of effective leadership, which the staff at the two schools mentioned, were much more than simply the articulation of a shared vision. They are listed as follows', and then presented:

- well-organized
- trustworthiness and honesty
- approachable
- positive attitudes
- interpersonal skills
- strong leadership qualities
- abilities to make decisions
- innovative
- knowledge of the staff and children
- knowledge of teaching and learning
- knowledge of the school
- vision
- supportive
- high expectations
- encouragement of team work
- a leading professional
- lead by setting an example
- development of the staff.

This list is flawed in several ways that I identify below. As it stands, it will not contribute towards the development of theory without further treatment. To move on to a deeper level of analysis the student who compiled it will need to refine and reduce it by sorting into categories. To develop into an analytical researcher – an 'extended' professional – you need to move beyond the level of simply presenting research findings as lists compiled from raw data. You need to delve deeper. This is impossible to do well without the requisite skills for effective categorization.

My current thinking leads me to identify four skills that researchers need to develop and practise if they are to formulate categories that are effective. These skills are *recognition and elimination of overlap; recognition and incorporation of outlier and atypical cases; application of appropriate levels of the basis of categorization,* and *presentation of categories.* Underpinning these skills is the need for requisite knowledge; that is, knowledge and understanding of the properties of categories. It is essential that researchers are aware that an effective category has the properties, identified above, of being both exclusive and exhaustive.

Recognition and Elimination of Overlap

If you are to formulate categories that are mutually exclusive you need to be able to recognize overlap, so that you may eliminate it. One of the biggest clues that suggests your categories may overlap is the number of categories. Bogdan and Biklen (1992, p. 177) advise: 'you may come up with a list of codes that is extremely long. Try to cut that down. If you have over fifty major categories, they probably overlap. While it is difficult to throw away data or categories, analysis is a process of data reduction.' My student's list of effective leadership characteristics, presented above, is typical in relation to length and degree of overlap of students' initial attempts at data analysis and categorization.

It is not always easy to spot overlap. Usually, the deeper the level of analysis applied to the categorization process the more subtle and difficult to spot are the examples of overlap, and it is not uncommon for very experienced, analytical researchers to overlook them. Yet the capacity to identify overlap within categorization will stand you in good stead because not only will it equip you to categorize your own data effectively, but it will also increase your capacity to criticize the work of others, in the same way that Thomas (1997, p. 81) criticizes another researcher's categorization of meanings of the word 'theory':

> For my purposes here, I shall query several of his categories, conflate others, and add one. The first and fifth uses he identifies – theory as a hunch and theory as a hypothesis – may be conflated as looser and tighter versions of the same notion. The third and seventh uses – theory as evolving explanation, and normative theory – may be conflated.

Rather than rely on your own observational skills, then, if you are inexperienced it is better, at first, to apply a systematic approach to the recognition of overlap within your own and others' categorization. I suggest two, complementary, approaches which I refer to as *systematic comparative pairing* and *putting things in drawers*. You may find it helpful to apply either of these approaches, or both.

SYSTEMATIC COMPARATIVE PAIRING

This involves systematically comparing each of your categories with each other, in turn, to examine whether or not they overlap. If, for example, you have generated six categories, A, B, C, D, E and F, you need to compare category A with each of categories B, C, D, E and F, in turn; category B with C, D, E and F, in turn; category C with D, E and F, and so on, until each category has been compared with each of the other five.

In the case of each pairing the comparison is a two-way process. Thus, for example, category A is compared with B and, in the same way, category B is compared with A. The comparison involves your asking the same question twice in relation to each pairing: 'is this category a sub-category of the other?', or, put another way, 'is this category subsumed within the other?', followed by a further question if the answer to both of the first two questions is 'no': 'could this category be considered to be essentially the same thing as the other?' To illustrate this process let us apply it to a simple and straightforward case – that of my student's list of characteristics of effective leadership, which represents a basic categorization reflecting low-level analysis. Even if the list is not intended to represent categorization, but simply a list of findings, it nevertheless requires refining and reducing further because it incorporates so much overlap, and the systematic process suggested above is as appropriate for this purpose as it is for refining categorization.

The first characteristic listed, *well-organized*, needs to be compared, in turn, with each of the others, and each comparison is intended to answer the questions specified above. Firstly, then, we need to ask, 'is *well-organized* subsumed within *trustworthiness and honesty*?', then, 'is *trustworthiness and honesty* subsumed within *well organized*?' Since, I suggest, the answer in both cases is 'no', we then need to ask whether *well-organized* is essentially the same as *trustworthy and honesty*. Since it is not, then it appears that there is no overlap between these two characteristics. Thus, the process needs to be continued until every item on the list has been compared. Without going to such lengths it is easy, in this case, to anticipate where overlap will be revealed. The characteristic *strong leadership qualities*, for example, seems to subsume all of the others listed. Another example is that *approachable* and, perhaps, *supportive*, and, possibly several other of the listed characteristics could be considered to be sub-categories of *interpersonal skills*. There is overlap, too, between *a leading professional* and *lead by setting an example*, and *knowledge of the staff and children* is clearly subsumed within *knowledge of the school*. Overlap in this case — that of a preliminary list drawn up by an inexperienced masters-level research student — is relatively easy to spot even before the systematic comparative pairing process is applied. Nevertheless, the process is invaluable as an aid to revealing less obvious examples of overlap.

PUTTING THINGS IN DRAWERS
This involves the pictorial representation of your categorization as a chest of drawers — one drawer for each category generated — labelled appropriately. The next stage is to apply the process of examining your units of data and 'putting them away' in whichever drawer they belong. The purpose of this process is to reveal whether or not specific data may feasibly be placed in more than one drawer. If it may, then the categorization is flawed and incorporates overlap. Effective categorization will be represented by drawers in only one of which any specific portion or unit of data — at whatever level of analysis you are working — belongs.

To illustrate this process I draw upon an example from my own research data of what, for the present, I consider to be effective categorization. In Chapter 4 I present the findings of a comparative analysis that I undertook, which identifies six categories of issues that matter to people in the contexts of their working lives: equity and justice; pedagogy or androgogy; organizational efficiency; interpersonal relations; collegiality; and self-conception and self-image. To apply the process of putting things in drawers to uncover any overlap that may be incorporated into the categorization, six drawers must be labelled as the six categories, as shown in Figure 8.1.

The next stage involves sorting the research data by placing them in the drawers. Overlap will be revealed by data that could feasibly belong in more than one drawer. To illustrate I draw upon only a small sample of data, presented in the form of quotations from research interviewees, taken from full interview transcripts. The quotations provide evidence of what specific issues matter to the interviewee. Categorizing this evidence involves placing it into whichever category of issues that matter to people — out of the six issues identified above as drawer labels — it belongs. As an exercise you may like to try putting these units of data into the drawers shown in Figure 8.1 before examining my suggested categorization of them.

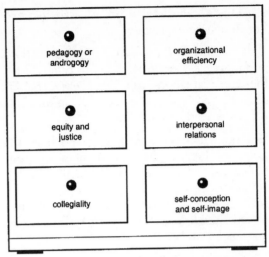

Figure 8.1: Issues that matter to people: an example of a pictorial representation of categorization

Quotation 1: Oh, he was very pedagogically aware! Oh, yes. He was Montessori trained ... he'd done a Montessori course ... And he had some *super* ideas – he did some lovely things with the kids ... He was very well-read ... and he cared very much about the children. (*primary school teacher speaking of the headteacher of a school where she once worked*)

Quotation 2: I mean ... part of it is ... I mean, this is the very, very lowest ... level, ... but I do resent the fact that he draws that salary ... for doing sod-all, ... and I resent that. That offends my sense of justice ... you know, when there are teachers who work a lot harder and get a lot less, and all that kind of issue. (*primary school teacher speaking of the headteacher of her school*)

Quotation 3: But, she was a very stringent person – not very gracious ... again, somebody who couldn't say, 'Please' and 'Thank you' ... and she could be a real ... tyrant – *very* unpleasant. She liked *me*, because I used to joke with her ... and I think she used to pick on weaker members of staff and make their lives very unpleasant – until they left. (*primary school teacher speaking of the headteacher of a school where she once worked*)

Quotation 4: You shouldn't have to do the amount of – you know ... timetables! All the stuff *I* do for the 2nd year course, really, it's a waste of academic expertise. I'm not trained as a secretary, or a book-keeper ... there's an awful waste of academic expertise and energy. (*university physics lecturer*)

Quotation 5: It was just ... the whole atmosphere in the school was *awful!* ... I mean, people were, sort of, in *this* camp, or *that* camp ... it was just the whole situation, really ... it was *awful!* Er ... it was, you know, sort of ... nasty, and not very nice. (*teacher speaking of the situation in the school where she worked*)

Quotation 6: And, having gone to Rockville [school] thinking that there was going to be a high level of interaction amongst my teaching colleagues, which was about professional expertise, increased competence, extending and developing your own ... er ... teaching performance ... what I *found* was ... the image I'd been given wasn't real ... I felt that ... er ... I lacked colleagues who saw it as a career or as a profession.

Quotation 7: There's nobody in that school with any vision – nobody with any educational philosophy – and that's what *really* frightens me to death ... Because, they think that you just go in and you teach, therefore children will learn. They don't seem to realize what a curriculum really is.

Quotation 8: I'm not prepared to jump through hoops any more in order to do what the University wants that's not how I see myself. I will publish what I want to publish and that's it. (*university lecturer*)

Figure 8.2 shows my suggestion for the placement of each of the eight quotations above. Presenting samples of data in this way to illustrate a point is far from ideal because it is, in a sense, contrived and false in so far as it fails to convey the complex and involved nature of the real process of data analysis. The eight quotations selected are all examples of data that I, with my knowledge of the full set of data and of the samples of teachers and academics used in the research, believe to be relatively straightforward and unambiguous and, therefore, easy to sort into the designated categories. Without this extensive background knowledge, though, sorting may be a little more difficult. Quotation 3, for example, I have categorized as a reflection of concern for the issue of interpersonal relations. Without knowledge of the full interview transcript, though, you may have placed this quote in the drawer labelled *equity and justice*. Similarly, quotation 4, which I placed in the *organizational efficiency* drawer, may, out of context, be interpreted as a *self-conception and self-image* issue. It is also important, as I point

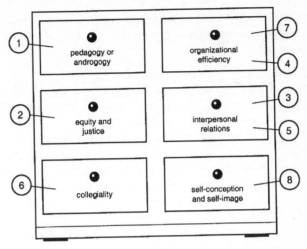

Figure 8.2: Sorting data into categories of issues that matter to people: an example of pictorial representation of categorization as labelled drawers

out more generally in Chapter 3, to clarify precisely what you mean by the labels used in your categorization and, though I do not present them here, I have formulated and presented elsewhere (Evans, 2001b) explanations of what I mean by each of the labels of my six categories of issues that matter to people, including, in particular, the distinction between two categories, *collegiality* and *interpersonal relations*, that at first glance may appear to overlap. Yet, while I raise this issue in order to clarify the basis of my confidence in my categorization, it leads on to the issue of ambiguity in data.

As I point out in Chapter 7, we are walking in a minefield of reliability and validity threats when we undertake research that involves examining people's attitudes, values systems, ideals, ideologies, understanding, motives – in fact, whenever we engage ourselves with trying to analyse what goes on inside people's heads. One of the greatest methodological hazards is that of imposing our own subjective standards on our analyses: of misinterpreting our research subjects because we are looking at their actions, speech and behaviour from our own perspectives instead of trying to see things from their perspectives. The more specific danger that may arise out of this in the categorization process is that of – on the basis of insufficient evidence – putting things into the drawers that *we* think they should go into, instead of putting them into the drawers where they really belong. This may occur in relation to data that are ambiguous. Take the following example:

> I actually feel that I can be part, again, of moving a school on ...
> of actually developing and growing in all sorts of ways – all of
> us, together.

Into which of the six drawers illustrated in Figure 8.1 would you put
this piece of data? The comment is that of a primary school teacher
anticipating her imminent change of post and transfer to a different
school. It is important not to lose sight of the basis of the
categorization that applies and the nature of the categories – issues
that matter to people. To categorize this piece of data, then, you
need to consider carefully what issue(s) of concern on the part of the
teacher it illustrates. This involves interpreting the teacher's key
focus. In the quotation four possible foci are evident: the teacher's
own professional development; improving the efficiency of the
school as an organization; improving the capacity of the school in
relation to pedagogy; and working productively with colleagues.
The quote could, therefore, conceivably be put into the *self-
conception and self-image*, or the *organizational efficiency*, or the
pedagogy and androgogy, or the *collegiality* drawer. The skill of
categorization at this level, reflecting in-depth, rather than superficial, analysis, lies in examining in context *all* of the evidence
available of precisely what it is that is the key issue here for this
teacher, and in making a reasoned decision on the basis of that
evidence. What constitutes that evidence will depend upon the
circumstances in which you find yourself undertaking your work. It
could, for example, be a full interview transcript, or it could be
evidence derived from observation, but what is essential is that you
look beyond the superficiality of the interview comment as it stands.
Although I have presented a single sentence spoken by a teacher in
order to illustrate the ambiguity of some data, in reality you would
not, of course, attempt to analyse a comment in isolation, out of
context.

The mechanism for applying in-depth analysis in this case is that
of trying to see things from the perspective of the teacher
concerned, so that you identify what is the issue for *her/him*, rather
than what would be the issue for *you*, if you were in her/his shoes.
(An excellent description of the application of this mechanism is
provided by Luttrell (2000, pp. 504–7) in her account of her
categorization of data from her study of working-class American
women's life stories.) This process involves stepping into the
minefield of reliability and validity threats, but it cannot be avoided;
it is a path that has to be taken if you are to advance at all in relation

to the kind of effective categorization that leads to theory development. If you tread carefully and proceed cautiously you have every chance of coming out of it unscathed.

The important point to emerge from this example is that it is conceivable that, for this teacher, the key issue is a complex interplay of *all four* of the categories identified above – that it is a combination of concern to contribute to the enhancement of her own professional development; collegiality in the school; organizational efficiency; and pedagogical capacity that is her focus – and that if this *were* the case it would not invalidate the categorization because it would not constitute overlap between categories. Explained in general terms, the point is that examples of combinations of, or multiple, categories within the data do not constitute evidence of overlap of categories. The test for overlap is whether or not the data may, through isolation or separation, in the smallest units available, be unambiguously placed into discrete categories and whether there is only one possible category into which each unit of data may be placed. The quotation presented above does not represent a single unit of data but an amalgam of units of data. Returning to a specific illustration of this rather complex point, imagine that you are physically sorting objects and placing them into the drawers in which they belong. Four of the drawers are labelled; *wooden boxes*; *spoons*; *knives*; *forks*. One of the objects to be sorted is a large, shallow, wooden box whose lid is closed. Your first inclination is to place this into the drawer labelled *wooden boxes*, but before doing so you decide to examine it more closely. On opening the lid you find that the wooden box is, in fact, a full canteen of cutlery containing knives, forks and spoons. Your immediate response to this discovery is one of frustration at the impossibility of placing the canteen of cutlery into any one of the labelled drawers. You consider two alternatives: the first is shutting the lid and putting the object in the drawer labelled *wooden boxes*; the second is re-labelling the drawers. Then you realize that the problem can be solved by emptying the box of its contents and then sorting everything into four appropriately labelled drawers. The problem had not been that the drawers were inappropriately labelled, but that you had failed to identify the separate elements of what made up the canteen of cutlery. There was, in fact, as closer examination revealed, no overlap – but there would have been if the drawers had been labelled: *canteen of cutlery*; *knives*; *forks*; *spoons*; *wooden boxes*.

Recognition and Incorporation of Outlier and Atypical Cases

Seldom do data fall neatly into tight categories at the first attempts at analysis. You will often find your emerging categorization undermined by what are referred to as 'outlier' cases – those that do not conform to any of the patterns that you have identified. As your analysis deepens and you move closer towards the development and generation of theory, such outlier or atypical cases will thwart your attempts at uncovering the generalizability that is a key element of theory. You may be tempted to abandon your theory development on the basis of its being flawed, or you may decide to compromise and identify outlier and atypical cases as exceptions to the rule.

The latter was evidently the response of Frederick Herzberg to what emerged as outlier cases in his work. According to Herzberg (1968) – whose research I examine in Chapter 3 – there are five specific features of work which motivate people, or which are capable of providing job satisfaction, and five specific features that are capable of de-motivating, or creating dissatisfaction (see Chapter 3). The essential point of Herzberg's theory is that what he identifies as hygiene factors are not capable of motivating or satisfying people, even though they may be sources of dissatisfaction: only the intrinsic factors – the five motivation factors – are able to do that.

The specific features that he identifies as either motivation or hygiene factors constitute Herzberg's categories of job-related factors that are capable of influencing – positively, in the case of five of them, and negatively in the case of the other five – people's attitudes to their work. This categorization is the key element of Herzberg's Two-Factor Theory. Yet, when he encounters outlier cases – data that do not conform to the categorization upon which he propounds his theory – Herzberg responds by dismissing as deviant the research subjects from whom the atypicality emanates:

> While the incidents in which job satisfaction were reported almost always contained the factors that related to the job task – the motivators – there were some individuals who reported receiving job satisfaction solely from hygiene factors, that is, from some aspect of the job environment ... The hygiene seekers are primarily attracted to things that usually serve only to prevent dissatisfaction, not to be a source of positive feelings. The hygiene seekers have not reached a stage of personality development at which the self-actualizing needs are active.

From this point of view, they are fixated at a less mature level of personal adjustment. (Herzberg, 1968, p. 80)

Instead of revising his categorization to incorporate the outlier or atypical cases, Herzberg simply suggests that they do not really count because they do not represent the 'mentally healthy' individuals who make up the bulk of his sample, and upon consideration of whose attitudes his theory is formulated:

> A hygiene ... is seeking positive happiness via the route of avoidance behavior, and thus his resultant chronic dissatisfaction is an illness of motivation. Chronic unhappiness, a motivation pattern that insures continual dissatisfaction, a failure to grow or to want to grow — these characteristics add up to a neurotic personality. (Herzberg, 1968, p. 81)

So — to clarify — what Herzberg appears to have been faced with in terms of research data is a predominance of research subjects who, as a sample, identified common issues and features that mattered to them in their work, and who identified the nature of the effect upon their attitudes of these issues and features. From these data he evidently formulated two main categories of factors that influence people's attitudes to their work: motivation factors and hygiene factors. Within each of these two main categories he formulated five sub-categories of specific job-related issues or features. In the case of the motivation factors these sub-categories were achievement; recognition (for achievement); the work itself; responsibility; and advancement. In the case of the hygiene factors the five sub-categories were salary; supervision; interpersonal relations; policy and administration; and working conditions. On the basis of the predominance represented by these data, Herzberg seems to have propounded a theory on the categorization that he formulated. But a predominance is not the same as unanimity, or universality. Alongside Herzberg's predominance of research subjects whose commonalitites gave rise to his categorization were evidently outlier cases who did not fit into the pattern. So, whilst his theory claims that people may derive job satisfaction only from achievement; recognition (for achievement); the work itself; responsibility; and advancement, he also uncovered evidence of people who reported deriving job satisfaction from factors which Herzberg's theory identifies as those from which it is impossible to derive job satisfaction. The factors identified by these outlier cases did not fit into Herzberg's categorization. Herzberg's five categories of motivation factors therefore are evidently not exhaustive. Therefore his categorization is flawed.

To be effective, categorization – particularly that upon which a theory is based – must incorporate consideration of outlier cases and atypicality; it must absorb them. Let us use the example of Herzberg's research findings to examine ways in which this may be achieved. Faced with examples of deviance, how should Herzberg have responded? Well, what he had effectively done was to 'sort' what he had, and in order to do this he chose to use two chests, each with five drawers. He put his own labels on the drawers and then began to sort, but, at the end of this process, he was left with items that did not fit into any of the drawers. He left these in a corner of the room, in a box labelled *miscellaneous*. What he should have done was to try to re-label the drawers in the chest dedicated to motivation factors so that all of the spare, miscellaneous items could be placed in drawers in which they belong. This might well have involved using a different chest, with more drawers. It might have involved taking some of the labels off the other chest – the one dedicated to factors that are capable of creating dissatisfaction, but not satisfaction – and putting them on the drawers in the motivation factors chest. It might even have involved getting rid of one chest and being content to use the remaining one, with newly labelled drawers, but whatever it involved the outcome should have been the disposal of the box labelled *miscellaneous*, and the neat sorting of all of the items so that none were left out of the drawers.

In more abstract terms, what Herzberg should have done is to re-examine the *level* of categorization represented by his categories. If he felt unable to merge what he had identified as two separate categories of factors that influence job-related attitudes – which, of course, he would have been reluctant to do because without this bipolarity his theory crumbles – because some of his research sample reported attitudes that were inconsistent with this merged categorization (that is, since most of his sample reported being unmotivated or being unable to be satisfied by those specific factors that Herzberg identifies as hygiene factors, he felt unable to include these factors as motivators), then he should have incorporated a higher level of reductionism into his categorization by generating less specific, but more widely applicable, categories. This, indeed, is a sound basic principle underpinning effective categorization: the greater the reduction of data, the greater the generality, the wider the applicability and the nearer universal applicability.

Application of Appropriate Levels of the Basis of Categorization
We have seen in the section above that there are multiple levels of categorization, reflecting different levels of reductionism. Another way of looking at this is to recognize the recursive nature of category specificity that gives rise to a kind of hierarchy of categories, sub-categories, sub-sub-categories and so on. This may be imagined as a set of Russian dolls that slot inside each other; one being contained within the next biggest one, which, in turn, is contained within the next biggest, and so on, until all of the dolls are encased, each one inside the next biggest, within the one that encompasses them all. The implications of this kind of level-determined structure for categories, though, as I point out in an earlier section, are that exclusivity is impossible to achieve within categorization that draws from different levels of the hierarchy with the effect that any one specific category is identified within the same categorization as one of its sub-categories. This would clearly result in overlap since there would be multiple categories into which specific data could be placed.

Developing the skill of recognizing categorization that incorporates different level categories is useful not only because it will make your own work more effective, but also because it will equip you to identify weaknesses in the categorizations of others. Elsewhere (Evans, 1997b; 1998) I have identified such a weakness in Herzberg's (1968) categorization. My own research has led me to suggest that Herzberg's five motivation factors – achievement; recognition (for achievement); the work itself; responsibility; and advancement represent a flawed, multi-level categorization. In-depth analysis clarifies the relationship between the first category, achievement, and each of the other four as hierarchical in so far as each of these four may be identified as either a reinforcer of, or a contributor to, achievement. The factors *the work itself* and *responsibility* are vehicles for achievement – means by which achievement may be experienced – and therefore they contribute towards it. Indeed, they could be considered to be elements of it. *Recognition (for achievement)* and *advancement* are mechanisms for reinforcing a sense of achievement. Moreover, it may be argued that *responsibility* is a facet of *the work itself* – which, in turn, seems to be rather an all-encompassing factor and that *advancement* may be interpreted as a sub-category of *recognition*. These flaws are perhaps best illustrated by considering into which category you would place job satisfaction derived from a recent promotion. What bases of her/his satisfaction might a recently promoted employee identify? It seems likely that such an example of job satisfaction would fall into the *advancement* category, but could it also be categorized as *recognition*, or *responsibility*, or *achievement*? All three are feasible.

There is another issue related to different levels of categories: the choice of which level to apply to your own categorization of data. Since categorization is a process of data reduction, how do you decide on the extent to which data should be reduced? On the one hand, the greater the reduction applied, the closer to theory generation you may get, but, on the other hand, the less the reduction, the closer to certainty you remain, and – at least initially – the further from speculation and conjecture. Yet, you cannot develop theory without going out on a limb and speculating. The problem of deciding on an appropriate level of category specificity to apply to one's research is one of which I have much personal experience. When asked, for example, what factors influence job satisfaction, morale and motivation I have often had to decide whether it is best to identify only one essential factor – the extent to which people perceive their job-related ideals to be being realized – or whether to identify several more specific factors – people's perceptions of their workplaces in relation to organizational efficiency; appropriateness of practice in relation to pedagogy or androgogy; quality of collegiality; quality of interpersonal relations; degree of equity and justice; and the acceptability of one's self-conception and self-image. Each represents a different level of data reduction, but which is the more useful?

The answer is 'it depends'. It depends on the purpose for which you intend your research findings, and, related to this, the audience at which you are directing them. For your own professional development as a researcher you should apply to your analysis increasing levels of reductionism, not only in order to take you towards the generality that is so important if you are to develop and generate theory, but also to enable you to understand the meaning behind the full spectrum of findings revealed by recursive analysis. Such a spectrum is revealed by researchers repeatedly seeking explanations for each set of findings as it emerges, stage-by-stage, until you feel that you can go no further and have reached the lowest common factor. As an analytical researcher you need access to the full spread of incrementally reduced data, from the very specific to what you believe to be the universally applicable. This 'full spread' represents the different layers of your findings. But as far as communicating and disseminating your findings are concerned, you may – depending on the circumstances – need to be more selective.

Taking reductionism to the extreme will leave you with a single category that represents the fundamental answer to the question(s) that your research addressed. This will be so general that it incorporates all cases of what, at a more shallow level of analysis, appeared atypical. Indeed, it will have been your search for an explanation to accommodate all cases — including apparently atypical ones - that led you to the single category. The problem is, though, that for practical purposes the findings revealed by such a level of reductionism are probably useless. Reductionism is all well and good, and applying it to your work is intellectually challenging and rewarding. But it is important to see it as a means to an end, rather than as an end in itself. If research is to be used to inform policy and practice, as I argue in the final chapter that it should be, then the more specificity it incorporates, the better. On the other hand, generality is essential to the development of theory. In the next chapter I address issues related to this tension.

Presentation of Categories
The key skill of presenting categories is that of explaining to others what each category is: what is included in it and the basis of its parameters. Conceptual clarity is essential; you should aim to present either a full and clear interpretation of what you mean when you refer to a category, or a definition of it. Without this clarity it will be difficult for others to evaluate your categorization. Your aim should be to explain your categories so clearly that they could be adopted by others in their own research. An example from my own work (Evans, 2002, pp. 131–2) is my explanation of what I refer to as two constituent change features of functional development, which I identify as a constituent element of teacher development:

> I currently perceive functional development as incorporating two constituent change features, or foci of change: *procedural* and *productive*. These respectively refer to teachers' develop-ment in relation to the procedures they utilise, and what and/or how much they 'produce' or 'do', at work. A teacher who, for example, changes her/his way(s) of carrying out some aspect — no matter how small — of her/his job would be manifesting procedural development, and one who starts to work longer hours and produce more resources — who begins to 'do' more — would be manifesting productive development.

Similarly, I explain equity and justice as a work-related issue that my research had revealed to be influential on education professionals' attitudes to their jobs:

> Situations and circumstances that were considered to be unfair were identified as sources of dissatisfaction by schoolteachers and academics. Precisely what constituted unfairness varied considerably from one individual to another, reflecting differences arising from professionality orientation, relative experience and realistic expectations. The range of perceived unfairness included situations and circumstances that: discriminated against the individual him/herself; discriminated against others; afforded unmerited advantages to others; and differentiated where it was felt there should be uniformity or commonality. (Evans, 2001b, p. 301)

The most difficult aspect of presenting categories, though, is labelling. The skill is to find a category name that is sufficiently all-encompassing to incorporate the full extent of what is included in the category, yet which excludes anything that falls outside of the category's parameters. Finding precisely the right name for a category – a name that conveys accurately its nature and constitution – is a task that I still find demanding on occasions, and it is one that students find extremely difficult. The more abstract the categories, the more difficult it generally is to find the right labels. It is not unusual for the labelling process to take weeks, or even months, involving repeated refinement. Often it is integral to the categorization process itself but occasionally it occurs after the categories have been conceived in the mind of the researcher and have remained suspended there for a while as nameless groupings whose nature and constituents are clear, but difficult to articulate. Seldom are suitable names found for all of the categories at once; often there will remain for some time one or two particularly tricky ones.

Names of categories are the mechanism for communicating one's understanding and conception of those categories. More often than not they provide the basis upon which categorization is evaluated by others – indeed, where definitions and explanations of categories are omitted, labels provide the *only* basis for evaluation. The words used to name categories need to be chosen with great care. They should incorporate, at best, definitional and, at least, descriptive precision.

The most prevalent weakness displayed in labelling attempted by inexperienced researchers is inconsistency in relation to nominal basis. This is illustrated by the list, formulated by one of my research students and presented above, of characteristics of effective school leadership. Here some categories are described using adjectives; others using nouns; some nouns are qualified by preceding adjectives, others are not; some items on the list are single words and others are short phrases. Effective presentation of categorization incorporates consistency in relation to the form that the label attached to each category takes.

If, as is most common among academics, you choose to present your labels as nouns, these need not necessarily be restricted to single words; adjectives – or even phrases incorporating relational nouns – are often required to qualify the main noun. This kind of labelling is illustrated by Carol Weiss's (1995, p. 143) five categories of characteristics of research that improve its usefulness to policy-makers (see p. 38). Sometimes, too, all of the categories in a set may draw upon a common noun to label them and are distinguished from each other by qualifying adjectives. Hargreaves and Goodson (1996, p. 4), for example, identify five categories: 'classical professionalism, flexible professionalism, practical professionalism, extended professionalism and complex professionalism'. A useful technique for ensuring consistency in relation to the nominal basis of your categorization is to try to use labels whose key nouns share a common suffix, such as: *-ism*; *-tion*; *-ness*; *-ment*; or *-ance*.

DEVELOPING CATEGORIZATION

Categorization, like its tool, reductionism, should not be considered an end in itself. It has a wider purpose: that of theory development. Categorization is a skill that exists across an extremely wide range of levels. It is the fundamental research skill which all researchers use – however inexperienced or incompetent they are. Yet it may also be developed to the extent that it leads directly – and opens up the door – to theory generation. In this sense it is like talking or writing; it may be practised at a crude, basic, underdeveloped level by infants or by uneducated or unpractised adults, and at the opposite extreme, in its most highly developed form, it may be manifest as an eloquent oration or as lucid, coherent, engaging prose. Reflective practice in educational research involves developing the skill of categorization to the most advanced levels, without which the development of theory will be unattainable. The next chapter examines ways in which this may be achieved.

9

Developing theory

Despite criticisms, outlined in Chapter 2, that educational researchers generally pay insufficient attention to the development of theory there is a distinct group within the research community of what Thomas (1997, p. 95) describes as 'committed theoriphiles' – people who, he suggests, value the 'cut-and-thrust of discourse in providing better ideas'. Such people represent 'extended' professionality in educational research. They are analytical researchers. The problem is, though, that they are under-represented, as Griffiths (1998, p. 34) observes:

> There are those of us who love theories and theorizing, who are willing to climb their heights, enjoying the exercise of grasping strange words and using them to reach new peaks of understanding. There are quite a lot of us, but, at least in the world of education, we are in a minority.

Clearly, theorizing must hold some attraction to this category of researchers. Indeed, Wolcott (1995, p. 183) observes that '[t]heory is something like physical exercise or taking Vitamin C: some people are hooked on it, even to excess'. From personal experience I can testify that the development of one's research findings into theory is an immensely satisfying activity, and my research into sources of job satisfaction among academics provides evidence that others – and, of course, not only those working in educational research – share this view (Evans and Abbott, 1998, pp. 101–2):

> The best days, when I've just, sort of, walked six inches off the ground ... er ... it's just realising something ... or discovering something that really does happen. (Ivan, physics tutor)

> I think ... that feeling of being 'on the edge' of something new, of finding something new ... is what satisfies me about the research ... I think it's exciting when ... if you're with a team of two or three people ... you've almost got some kind of

reinforcement that what you're doing is new, novel ... and is going to inform the debate. (Maggie, education tutor)

My research has been in two main areas ... and I do get a *huge* amount of satisfaction and excitement from working in those areas ... Intellectually, it's exciting to feel you're doing things which are new ... (Jenny, education tutor)

In Chapter 1, I identify researcher fulfilment as one of three strands underpinning the rationale for developing as an educational researcher, suggesting that the intellectual challenges posed by reflective research practice provide the pathway to this fulfilment. This chapter focuses on one specific manifestation of reflective practice that requires skills which are, in general, greatly underused by educational researchers: developing theory.

WHAT IS THEORY?

Problems of precisely the kind that I identify in Chapter 3, arising out of lack of conceptual clarity, underpin much of the theoretical under-development that pervades educational research. Thomas (1997, p. 77) highlights this issue:

Debate about theory is rarely accompanied by any discussion about its meaning. Any superficial examination (or, indeed, detailed examination) of educational literature discloses little consensus about the meaning of theory ... There is no bond between theory and the constellation of meanings it has acquired. The reader or listener, when encountering the word, is forced to guess what is signified by the word through the context in which it is applied.

But the problem of the reader or listener is different from that facing the reader who has to interpret the meaning of red in reading about a red rose or a red herring. There, context tells the reader or listener something unequivocal. Yet context helps little when we find 'theoretical' in educational discourse: a theoretical article has no a priori distinction from a theoretical view, a theoretical background, or a theoretical position ...

The essential problem, according to Thomas, is the lack of consensus:

'Theory' as a word must be one thing or another. It cannot – if it is to be used seriously to describe a particular kind of intellectual construction in education – have two or more meanings, unless the context in which it is used can universally and unequivocally distinguish those meanings. If we are to understand what 'pipe' means, the word must refer only to that class of objects normally thought of as pipes; it must not also refer to dogs, vacuum cleaners and trees. And if 'pipe' does happen to be inconvenient enough to refer ... to a musical wind instrument, to a tube, or to the note of a bird, I can be confident that the context – sentence, paragraph, or longer passage – will finish the job and furnish the right meaning. I cannot be so sure with 'theory'. For it is my contention that the context cannot distinguish the strong colors of meaning that alter with various uses of 'theory', since the users themselves are rarely aware of the meaning they intend (p. 79).

Pring (2000a, p. 76) makes a very similar observation:

it is rarely clear what people are against when they dismiss theory. It is important to distinguish between theory, in the sense of the assumptions which lie behind practice but which often go unacknowledged, and theory, in the sense of tightly organised systems of explanation.

The lack of consensus about what is meant by 'theory' has, I suggest, resulted in a complacency among researchers that stems from misunderstanding. I believe there are many researchers who consider themselves to have developed theory out of their findings but whom others would consider to have done nothing of the sort. The issue is one of different interpretations of what theory is and what it involves, which has given rise to different standards. The pursuit of theory is in principle generally recognized within the academic educational research community as a worthy – if not an essential – aim, and it is almost unheard of to encounter a researcher who confesses to disregarding it or failing to take it seriously. Despite this, it is also widely accepted that inadequate theoretical development occurs, and has occurred, from educational research (see, for example, Bridges, 1998; Griffiths, 1998; Hammersley, 1998; Ranson, 1998). It seems, then, that, while everyone laments the inadequacy, no one considers her/himself responsible for contributing to it. Is a large proportion of the educational research community therefore deluding itself? Well, the answer to this question depends, of course, on what is meant by 'theory'.

Robson (1993, p. 18) defines a theory as 'a general statement that summarizes and organizes knowledge by proposing a general relationship between events'. Wolcott (1995, p. 183) distinguishes between *'formal* theory' which he equates with 'what I call "capital 'T' Theory,"' or Grand Theory', and 'numerous other terms more modest in scope — *hypotheses, ideas, assumptions, hunches, notions* — that also capture the essence of the mindwork that is critical to fieldwork'. He applies this distinction to his expectations: 'I remain fascinated with the *potential* of theory, but in my own work and the work of my students, I have been more satisfied with, sometimes, a great *notion, hunch, idea,* or tentative *interpretation'* (p. 186). Yet, it is possible that others who do not make this distinction interpret the formulation of ideas, hunches and notions as engagement in the generation or development of theory. Indeed, Coffey and Atkinson (1996, p. 157) make the point:

> Theory can sound like something that is special, divorced from ordinary research skills, yet everyone can have ideas about the world about them ... We can all make interpretations. Whether we always grace such ideas with the grandiose label of theory, the important thing is to have ideas and to use them to explore and interpret the social world around us.

Since Coffey and Atkinson (1996, p. 156) also make the distinction between 'having ideas and using ideas' and 'the more daunting connotation of theory and theory construction', they evidently do not categorize the formulation of ideas and interpretations as theory generation. Nevertheless, their comments (p. 157), presented above, imply a less stringent application to the evaluation of others' work of an interpretation of what constitutes theory development than that of LeCompte and Preissle (1993, p. 118), who put forward their interpretation: 'Theories are statements about how things are connected. Their purpose is to explain why things happen as they do', and who, moreover, are disdainful of what they perceive as poor-quality research:

> In fact, many researchers eschew contact with theory altogether; they treat the process of developing a theoretical framework as little more than the collection of a few corroborative empirical studies into what could pass for a literature review and proceed directly to collect data. They leave a concern for theory to 'great men', but they do so at the peril of poor work. (LeCompte and Preissle, 1993, p. 118)

An illustration is provided by Hammersley, Scarth and Webb

(1985) of how the application of different interpretations of what constitutes theory creates multiple standards in relation to what is accepted as theoretical output. They refer, within the ethnographic research community, to one view of theory as 'constituting a picture of reality. On this view, studies complement one another in much the same way as pieces of a mosaic fit together' (p. 50). '[T]he relationship between the studies is that each provides a bit of the total picture ... Each study provides a description of one part of the city, education system or society. Added together, they give a panoramic view' (p. 51). Yet Hammersley, Scarth and Webb dismiss this interpretation of theory on the grounds that it is 'fundamentally misleading' (p. 52), and argue that 'the provision of a descriptive/ explanatory account of a particular setting or sequence of events is very different from the development and testing of a theory about some aspect of that setting or sequence' (pp. 52–4). 'The logic of developing and testing theory', they continue, ' is quite different from that of adding further pieces to the mosaic' (p. 54), and their bleak assessment of the theoretical output of one particular field of educational research implies a stringent application of evaluative standards that reflects a narrow interpretation of what counts as theory: 'There are very few examples of the systematic development and testing of theory in the sociology of education' (p. 54). Yet, despite the reservations of Hammersley, Scarth and Webb, there are, presumably, many ethnographic educational researchers who are perfectly satisfied that their contributions towards building up a mosaic picture of whatever specific area they are investigating counts as the development of theory. Herein lies the problem of misunderstanding within the research community that stems from the lack of conceptual clarity in relation to theory.

Ranson's (1998, pp. 50–1) criticism of educational research is based upon an interpretation of theory that is similar in its narrowness and degree of stringency to the implicit interpretations of LeCompte and Preissle (1993) and Hammersley, Scarth and Webb (1985):

> Only theory can provide the capacity to explain the issues – practical as well as policy – by constructing the propositions which analyse why such and such is the case. But theory contributes much more than this formal analysis implies: it introduces the ideas and concepts that locate the interpretive space for the analysis, and theory provides the critical challenge to practice by revealing the structures of power that underlie it.

Theory is the indispensable intellectual capital that connects the particular to its context while analysing, explaining and challenging the relationship between them. Theory, moreover, secures the lineages of action: 'savoir pour prévoir, prévoir pour pouvoir': a plausible interpretation of the past can more adequately guide the future. Theory tests the imagination, exposes the analytical rigour, ties ideas to practice. (Ranson, 1998, pp. 50–1)

Clearly, interpretations such as these are distinct from some of the wider, more all-encompassing ones identified by Thomas (1997, pp. 77–84) to illustrate the problematic effects of the uneven, inconsistent and eclectic conceptualization of theory pervading educational research – 'the multiple meanings of theory in educational discourse' (p. 80). He refers, for example (p. 79), to 'a widely held view ... that theory is anything that isn't practice' and which, he suggests, accepts as theory 'book learning and speculation'. 'If "theory" can mean any kind of intellectual endeavor', Thomas argues, 'then one would be forced to accept that any conjoining of words is a theoretical enterprise.' '[A]ny kind of structured reflection', too, Thomas points out (p. 80), is categorized by some as theory. He refers to Chambers's (in Thomas, 1997, p. 80) assertion that he can distinguish up to nine meanings of the word 'theory', but his (Thomas's) own re-categorization of these leads to the identification of four 'broad uses of theory in education': theory as the opposite of practice; theory as hypothesis; theory as developing explanation; and scientific theory (pp. 81–2). These four categories are further conflated by Thomas to form two separate continua: 'theory versus practice', and 'theory as plural versus theory as singular' (p. 82).

Yet the point that Thomas makes in this section of his paper is a valid one; expansive interpretations of what counts as theory have led to a prevalence of an 'anything goes' perspective on how researchers should be developing and applying their findings. This perspective is, to some extent, implied in Rajagopalan's (1998) response to Thomas's paper. The central argument – that it is impossible to rid ourselves of theory because theory pervades and permeates our lives – would seem to reflect an expansive interpretation of theory.

At the opposite extreme from the 'anything goes' perspective are perspectives such as those reflected in the interpretations of theory, presented above, of Hammersley, Scarth and Webb (1985),

LeCompte and Preissle (1993) and Ranson (1998) that incorporate recognition of the status of theory as a much higher order form of propositional knowledge – and derived from a more rigorous intellectual process – than ideas, hypotheses, notions, hunches and structured reflection. Since they incorporate interpretations of theory that accord it high status, these perspectives may be conflated into a single perspective that I will refer to as the 'elitist perspective' of theory. Within this elitist perspective specific forms or categories of theory are identified. These relate, variously, to the range and scale – and, by extension, status – of the theory, to its specific focus and to its epistemological basis: 'Theories vary in size, density, abstractness, completeness, and quality. They also come in various forms' (LeCompte and Preissle, 1993, p. 118).

Three distinct levels of theory are generally recognized, though there is disagreement in relation to how they are labelled. LeCompte and Preissle (1993, pp. 134–7) identify substantive theory, middle-range theory, and 'grand theory', or theoretical paradigms. Glaser and Strauss (1967, pp. 32–3) refer to 'the "minor working hypotheses" of everyday life', 'middle-range theory' and 'the "all-inclusive" grand theories'. Within 'middle-range theory' they identify two 'basic kinds of theory: substantive and formal':

> By substantive theory, we mean that developed for a substantive, or empirical, area of sociological inquiry, such as patient care, race relations, professional education, delinquency, or research organizations. By formal theory, we mean that developed for a formal, or conceptual, area of sociological inquiry, such as stigma, deviant behavior, formal organization, socialization, status congruency, authority and power, reward systems, or social mobility. (p. 32)

In addition, grounded theory, first identified by Glaser and Strauss (1967), is distinguished on the basis of the process by which it is generated, described by Strauss and Corbin (1990, p. 23):

> A grounded theory is one that is inductively derived from the study of the phenomenon it represents. That is, it is discovered, developed, and provisionally verified through systematic data collection and analysis of data pertaining to that phenomenon. Therefore, data collection, analysis, and theory stand in reciprocal relationship with each other. One does not begin with a theory, then prove it. Rather, one begins with an area of study and what is relevant to that area is allowed to emerge.

Within the elitist perspective several distinct features of theory are common to most interpretations of it: theory provides explanations of things; it is interpretative; it has generalizability; it has logical consistency; it incorporates structure; it facilitates prediction (Gillham, 2000b; LeCompte and Preissle, 1993; Merriam, 1988; Ranson, 1998; Strauss and Corbin, 1990; Wolcott, 1995). Pring's (2000a, pp. 124–5) comprehensive interpretation incorporates all of these, and goes beyond them:

> 'Theory' would seem to have the following features. It refers to a set of propositions which are stated with sufficient generality yet precision that they explain the 'behaviour' of a range of phenomena and predict what would happen in future. An understanding of those propositions includes an understanding of what would refute them – or at least what would count as evidence against their being true. The range of propositions would, in that way, be the result of a lot of argument, experiment and criticism. They would be what have survived the constant attempt to refute them. But they would always be provisional. A theory or set of interconnected and explanatory propositions would be suggestive of hypotheses which need to be tested out. Hence, a theoretical position is always open to further development through reflection, testing against experience and criticism. The more all embracing the theory (the larger its content) then, of course, the more useful it is. But that very usefulness makes it more vulnerable to criticism. And it may be the case that the variability of context of educational practices makes them less open to such large-scale explanatory accounts.

It is this interpretation of theory – located within the elitist perspective – that I adopt and apply to my use of the term hereafter, and to my examination of how theory may be developed by educational researchers. I use the term 'theorizing' to refer to the process of developing theory. Goetz and LeCompte (1984, p. 167) offer a more precise definition:

> Theorizing is the cognitive process of discovering or manipulating abstract categories and the relationships among these categories. It is the fundamental tool of any researcher and is used to develop or confirm explanations for how and why things happen as they do.

From the elitist perspective it is easy to acknowledge that – in answer to the question posed above – a large proportion of the educational research community is, indeed, deluding itself. I believe that much of what is passed off as – and perhaps genuinely believed to be – theory does, in fact, fall short of reaching the standards imposed by the elitists. It fails to incorporate the requisite features identified above and therefore lies outside the parameters of what counts as theory. This chapter focuses on the pursuit of theory as interpreted by elitists, which I believe to be consistent with reflective practice in educational research.

FROM RESEARCH FINDINGS TO THEORY

Alvesson and Sköldberg's (2000, p. 16) evaluation of the work of Glaser and Strauss (1967) is that they

> launched the rather liberating thesis that *anyone* can create their own theory, so long as they start from reality. Thus, not only geniuses, 'theoretical capitalists', can be creative in social science research. Even ordinary mortals can generate creative input as scientific entrepreneurs; they do not have to act as a verifying proletariat serving intellectual big business. Each one is the architect of her own theory. Certainly the theory should be tested, but this leads only to its modification, not its destruction, since a theory can only be replaced by another theory.

As an 'ordinary mortal', then, how do you set about transforming your research findings into theory? What does the process involve?

Several eminent researchers and methodologists have, in the course of their work, identified elements and aspects of the process of theorizing. 'Thinking about one's data – *theorizing*', Merriam (1988, pp. 140–1) writes, '– is a step toward developing a theory that explains some aspect of educational practice and allows one to draw inferences about future activity'. She adds (p. 141): 'Speculation ... is the key to developing theory in a qualitative study'. Coffey and Atkinson (1996, p. 139) also focus on ideas. They refer to 'ways of thinking with the data', which they explain: 'That means "going beyond" the data to develop ideas':

> Our task as qualitative researchers is to use ideas in order to develop interpretations that go beyond the limits of our own data and that go beyond how previous scholars have used those ideas. It is in that synthesis that new interpretations and new ideas emerge. The point is not to follow previous scholarship

slavishly but to adapt and transform it in the interpretation of one's own data. (Coffey and Atkinson, 1996, p. 158)

It is one thing, though, to be told glibly to develop ideas; it is quite another thing actually to be able to do so. Strauss and Corbin (1990, p. 42) refer to 'theoretical sensitivity' as 'the attribute of having insight, the ability to give meaning to data, the capacity to understand, and capability to separate the pertinent from that which isn't'. Becoming an analytical researcher involves developing theoretical sensitivity.

Wolcott (1995, p. 190) offers specific guidelines for developing your thinking in ways that have the potential to enhance your theoretical sensitivity:

> When formal theory seems to offer no helpful answer, the search for theory at a more modest level can be turned into a provocative question: What would be needed by way of theory to help me better organize and present my data and to recognize relevant aspects of my fieldwork experience?

And Coffey and Atkinson (1996, p. 157) emphasise the need to be proactive in the search for creativity, rather than sit and wait for inspiration:

> Good ideas might often be serendipitous, but serendipity can be encouraged by careful preparation ... Having ideas is not simply about waiting for an elusive and fickle muse. We should instead concentrate on making ideas and using ideas, emphasizing that these are part of the intellectual craft of research and scholarship.

Consistent with this view is Garratt's (1998) cautionary tale of the constraints imposed by pursuing a serendipitous approach to theory development.

Speculating, coming up with a hunch, hypothesizing – all of these are frequently identified as key stages, constituting the generation of ideas, in developing theory. To Glaser and Strauss (1967, p. 39) hypotheses represent a crucial initial stage:

> Whether the sociologist, as he [*sic*] jointly collects and analyses qualitative data, starts out in a confused state of noting almost everything he sees because it all seems significant, or whether he starts out with a more defined purpose, his work quickly leads to the generation of hypotheses. When he begins to hypothesize with the explicit purpose of generating theory, the

researcher is no longer a passive receiver of impressions but is drawn naturally into actively generating and verifying his hypotheses through comparison of groups.

From this initial step, they argue, the path to theory generation opens up:

In the beginning, one's hypotheses may seem unrelated, but as categories and properties emerge, develop in abstraction, and become related, their accumulating interrelations form an integrated central theoretical framework – *the core of the emerging theory.* (Glaser and Strauss, 1967, p. 40)

Merriam identifies a strikingly similar process (1998, p. 144):

The development of categories, properties, and tentative hypotheses through the constant comparative method ... is a process whereby the data gradually evolve into a core of emerging theory. This core is a theoretical framework that guides the further collection of data. Deriving a theory from the data involves both the integration and the refinement of categories, properties, and hypotheses.

However, whilst these observations and suggestions pinpoint the process involved in developing theory, if you have never really ventured so far you may need more specific, step-by-step guidelines to set you on the right track. I present these below.

From the Specific to the General: Guidelines for Theorizing
Developing theory does not necessarily have to involve the incorporation of universal applicability into explanations, but it should incorporate a sufficiently reductionist analysis of data to inject into them, as Pring (2000a) points out, generality and precision. There needs to be a move away from the specific. Reporting that teacher Ms X is dissatisfied and demoralized because she has been passed over for promotion, and that Mr Y's discontent with his job stems from his frustration at being unable to control his unruly class does not constitute theory; it is far too specific. It represents simple presentation of data. Reporting that Ms X and Mr Y manifested job dissatisfaction because they were experiencing frustrations that they felt incapable of overriding is still too specific to constitute theory, though it reflects a level of analysis that represents a step in the direction of theory development. However, reporting that one of the factors influencing the job satisfaction of

teachers – or a specific category of teachers – is the extent to which their actual work experiences confirm or undermine their ideal work-related self-conceptions does constitute theory because it reflects a level of analysis that has moved from the specific to the general.

Theory, remember, is a means of explaining something. If you are starting out on the path of theory development you need to remain focused throughout on the need to offer an explanation. This means that you must go beyond describing, although description may be used to illustrate theory. Your raw data represent the specific, and you should first look for explanations that relate to the specific before trying to translate these explanations into the general.

Let us start off with an exercise that draws upon an everyday example of human behaviour with which most people will be familiar: a trip to the supermarket. The process that I explain using the supermarket illustration is one of the most commonly used forms of theorizing: analytic induction, which Goetz and LeCompte (1984, pp. 179–80) explain:

> This strategy involves scanning the data for categories of phenomena and for relationships among such categories, developing working typologies and hypotheses upon an examination of initial cases, then modifying and refining them on the basis of subsequent cases ... Negative instances, or phenomena that do not fit the initial function, are consciously sought to expand, adapt, or restrict the original construct. In its most extreme application, analytic induction is intended to provide universal rather than probabilistic explanation: that is, all cases are to be explained – not merely some distribution of cases.

Analytic induction is not the only recognized theorizing process but I have chosen it as my model because it is the process that I most frequently use myself.

Try to identify the stages involved in the process of visiting the supermarket. If this were framed as a research question – for example, 'What forms of behaviour and specific actions are involved in a trip to the supermarket?' – you would first collect raw data in the form of evidence of what people do when they visit the supermarket, which is likely to involve either live observation of people or analysis of video data, or interviews. Since these data are not available, improvisation is necessary.

Firstly, draw upon your own experiences. Record everything that a trip to the supermarket typically involves for you, or, if you prefer, what your last trip involved. Record it as sequential stages, starting with your entry on to supermarket property, as with the following example:

drive to supermarket

find parking space

park car

lock car

check to see if you've got shopping list and money

walk to store

enter store

identify first item on shopping list

locate item in store ... etc.

Secondly, draw up a list identifying the stages that someone else's supermarket visit would typically involve. For this, use the example of someone whose typical supermarket trip differs from yours. This may be someone whose lifestyle is different from yours in certain respects. For example, if you drive a car you could choose someone who does not; or if you live alone you could choose someone who buys for a large family. This should be a realistic list, so it is probably better to draw upon real, rather than imaginary, examples.

Next, compare the lists by aligning parallel stages, as with these two examples:

drives to supermarket	catches bus to supermarket
finds parking space	alights from bus
parks car	
locks car	
checks to see if s/he's got shopping list and money	
walks to store	walks to store
enters store	enters store
obtains shopping trolley	picks up shopping basket
identifies an item on shopping list	walks along centre aisle
locates item in store	spots item that attracts her/his attention
places item in trolley	places item in basket

identifies another item on shopping list

locates item in store

repeats this sequence of identifying items, one at a time, and placing them in trolley, until all of the items listed have been sought and, if available, placed in trolley

recollects two items that s/he needs

locates items in store

places items in basket

wanders around store, looking for and examining reduced price items and special offers

locates a reduced item

calculates the reduction to ascertain if it is half of the original price, or less

rejects item because the reduction is less than half of original price

spots a half-price loaf of bread

places bread in basket

locates checkout with shortest queue

joins queue

transfers items from trolley to conveyer belt

obtains cardboard box

packs shopping into box

hands credit card to checkout assistant

goes to a checkout for baskets only

joins queue

places basket on designated shelf

obtains carrier bag

packs shopping in carrier bag

gives cash to checkout assistant

These two lists now serve as improvised data representing the visits to the supermarket of two research subjects. Although you would, of course, normally draw upon a larger sample, these two cases are adequate for illustrating and explaining the principles and the process of translating your analysis from the specific to the general. It is worth bearing in mind throughout, though, that a real research data analysis and theorizing activity would be complicated by the need to incorporate data from many more subjects.

The next stage is to search for similarities and differences between the two subjects. This is facilitated by the alignment of parallel stages. In the example that we are using one difference is the mode of shopping; one research subject does her/his shopping in a structured, planned manner and the other is opportunistic. Similarities include entering the store and joining queues.

The next task is the formulation of a third list: a list of the sequence of actions involved in a supermarket visit that is applicable to the entire research sample (which, in this case, is only two subjects). This represents the initial stage of moving from the specific to the general. Try formulating your own list before looking at the one that I present below.

The difficulties in this task occur in dealing with the differences between the two subjects; the similarities, or matches, are comparatively straightforward. The specific difficulty is that of marrying together the actions that are different and of representing them using appropriate terminology in order to incorporate them into a list that applies to both. This involves a process that I have referred to in Chapters 4 and 5 and elsewhere (Evans, 1997c; 1998) as searching for the lowest common factor, or lowest common factor analysis. Here categorization skills are required, and at this point it becomes clear how important categorization is to the process of developing theory. Essentially, searching for the lowest common factor involves putting into one drawer all – or, in this case, since only two research subjects are used, both – of the specific forms of behaviour, or actions, that represent parallel stages in the sequence of supermarket visit behaviour, and labelling that drawer accordingly. It is the labelling that poses the difficulty. Data reduction, as I describe and explain it in Chapter 8, is required here.

Below is my version of the third list, representing data reduction to the level of lowest common factor analysis:

journeys to supermarket

ends journey

approaches supermarket premises

enters supermarket

obtains shopping receptacle

locates desired items

places items in shopping receptacle

when all desired items have been procured proceeds to checkout

transfers items from receptacle to conveyer belt

procures receptacle for transporting shopping home

pays for shopping

Comparison of this list with each of those relating to the two research subjects reveals how, in order to incorporate applicability to both subjects, the specificity of the descriptions of the stages identified in these two lists has had to give way to language of generality. In order, for example, to place 'drive to supermarket', 'find parking space' and 'park car' in the same drawer as 'catch bus to supermarket' and 'alight from bus' the drawer has had to be labelled 'journey to supermarket', and in order to incorporate both 'obtains shopping trolley' and 'picks up shopping basket' I have had to use the more general, 'obtains shopping receptacle'. Specificity has been lost, too, in the sense of having reduced the number of stages incorporated into the process that the list describes. I was unable to find any way of categorizing together the several stages that made up the two rather different manners of each research subject of selecting items for purchase other than to reduce them to a single stage, 'locate desired items'. What is beginning to emerge is a potential theoretical model of human behaviour exhibited in supermarket visits.

The next stage is to test the width of applicability of the emergent model by a process known as *negative case selection* (Goetz and LeCompte, 1984, p. 175); effective theory development always involves testing. Karl Popper, the famous philosopher of science, contends that 'the criterion of the scientific status of a theory is its falsifiability, or refutability, or testability' (Popper, 1963, p. 37). He identified 'an asymmetry between verification and falsification: while no number of true singular observation statements can verify or prove the truth of a universal theory, one true singular observation statement can refute it' (Swann, 1999, p. 22). It is therefore important to address two questions: Is *all* of my research sample accommodated within this theoretical explanation? and: Can I find a real or hypothetical example of a case that does not fit within this theoretical explanation? If the model that you are formulating has sufficient width of applicability the answer to the first question will be *Yes* and the answer to the second question, *No*. If we apply these two questions to the model beginning to emerge from the list of the sequence of actions involved in a visit to the supermarket we find that the answer to both questions is *Yes*. It is quite easy to identify flaws in this list by thinking of several cases where some of the specific actions listed would not apply. For example, a person intending to purchase only one, or a few, items may not bother using a shopping trolley or a basket. This would preclude the need for several of the stages listed. The list at this stage, then, may be represented thus (*indicates limited applicability):

1 journeys to supermarket
2 ends journey
3 approaches supermarket premises
4 enters supermarket
5* obtains shopping receptacle
6 locates desired items
7* places items in shopping receptacle
8 when all desired items have been procured proceeds to checkout
9* transfers items from receptacle to conveyer belt
10* procures receptacle for transporting shopping home
11 pays for shopping

By this stage in the development of theory it is becoming clear that universal applicability is elusive. If we were to pursue universal applicability in the example being used we would need, as a first step, to discard stages 5, 7, 9 and 10 from our emerging model, which would then be reformulated:

1 journeys to supermarket
2 ends journey
3 approaches supermarket premises
4 enters supermarket
5 locates desired items
6 when all desired items have been procured proceeds to checkout
7 pays for shopping

Already this is reduced to being a much shorter sequence of actions than were its precedents – one in which descriptive specificity has been eliminated to the point that what remains is, by comparison, practically meaningless. Yet still there remain flaws in the list which, if removed, would shorten it even more.

Stage 6, for example, as it is worded, incorporates an assumption that the shopper will proceed to the checkout only after s/he has procured all of the items that s/he wanted to purchase. Yet this fails to accommodate cases where the shopper proceeds to the checkout even though some of the desired items were unavailable. This flaw could be rectified by adding the word 'available' before 'desired', but stage 6 would then still fail to accommodate all conceivable cases, such as that of the shopper who goes to the checkout having forgotten to procure certain 'desired' items. The use of the word 'desired' is extremely problematic if the principles of precision of choice of terminology — which I highlight in Chapter 3 as underpinning the conceptual clarity that is requisite of rigorous research — are adhered to. It is unclear whether, for example, 'all (available) desired items' implies all items in the supermarket that the shopper desires in the sense of 'would like to have', even though s/he could not afford to buy them all, or whether the term is restricted to reference to those items that s/he wishes to purchase on this occasion. Conceptual imprecision such as this could be eliminated by more careful choice of words and by the use of lengthier, but more precise, descriptors of the action involved, which could, in some cases, be split into two or more stage descriptors. A lengthier descriptor for stage 6, for example, could be split: stage 6 — procures all available items that s/he wishes to purchase on this shopping visit; stage 7 — proceeds to checkout.

Still, though, with revisions such as these, the list would remain flawed. For example, stages 5 and 7 respectively fail to incorporate consideration of the shopper who is unable to locate some of the 'desired' items, and also of the shopper who, for any of various reasons, does not pay for her/his shopping. These are flaws that could be eliminated by the use of more precise wording. The wording used to define the parameters of the applicability of the theoretical model, for example, could eliminate the flaw of failure to incorporate consideration of shoplifters. Identifying it as model of human behaviour exhibited in a supermarket visit is too imprecise and, as a result, fails to reflect the model that it is intended to label. The model applies only to supermarket customers who make purchases and its label needs to incorporate sufficient precision to convey that range of applicability.

What is becoming clear by now is that width of applicability comes at a price: the loss of specificity that incorporates meaningful illustration into the theory being developed. The wider the applicability you wish to incorporate within your model, the lower you need to search for a common factor, and universal applicability invariably leads you to the kind of generality that has very little practical use.

I have used the example of behaviour manifested by people on a shopping trip to the supermarket to explain the process that may be followed in order to formulate a theoretical model because it involves experiences with which most people are familiar. Yet, having used it for that purpose, it is now time to point out a flaw in the example as a basis of theory development, and to move on. The flaw is that the model formulated is descriptive rather than explicatory. This is because it relates only to observed behaviour. Theory, remember, explains things rather than describes them. In order to be explicatory our model would need to draw on data that go beyond observation and that seek meanings behind actions. This would involve data on people's motives, for example, or their attitudes. These data cannot be obtained by observation; questioning or talking to people would be needed. Different research questions would be addressed, too, such as:

- what prompts a shopper to select a specific item?
- what factors influence the mode of shopping on any one occasion?

The process of formulating theory would, however, be the same as that described above, relating to human behaviour manifested during a shopping trip at the supermarket; we would simply be applying it to different kinds of data. Yet the lowest common factor analysis may lead us, through the pursuit of universal – or, at least, very wide – applicability, to develop a theoretical perspective along the following lines: individuals' mode of supermarket shopping is determined by consideration of, and the need to accommodate, their current priorities. Whilst this may be theoretically accurate, it provides very little elucidation that may be put to practical use by, for example, retail managers. In order to provide this, elaboration in the form of more specific contextual illustration would be needed; for example, we could extend the theoretical observation above: individuals' mode of supermarket shopping is determined by consideration of, and the need to accommodate, their current priorities which, in turn, are determined by ... , and here we could list variables such as *personality, lifestyle, time available* and *main purpose of the shopping trip*. These variables, since they represent different levels of categories of variables (see Chapter 8), could then be categorized more effectively – and hierarchically. They could, for example, perhaps be sorted into 'fixed' variables, such as personality, and 'temporal' variables, such as time available, though this is only one of several possible categorizations and, moreover, it is not without problems; would you, for example, categorize 'lifestyle' as a 'fixed' or a 'temporal' variable?

One way round the problem of losing specificity through pursuit of the lowest common factor is to identify specific categories of shopping behaviour — typologies — identified through descriptive lists of their key features and given descriptive names. The problem with typologies, though, is that they identify only trends and common patterns. They represent a move away from constants and certainties. Moreover, it is difficult to formulate categories that are mutually exclusive. They serve as poor models because it is difficult to slot real people into only one of them; invariably, in the real world, people represent hybrid or combination typologies. In any case, unless they serve to explain something and predict what would happen in the future, typologies do not constitute theory. Two categories of typologies exist: atheoretical and theoretical typologies.

An alternative approach is to regain the specificity lost through the process of seeking the lowest common factor by using it — specificity — to illustrate and inject meaning into the generality within the theory that you have developed. I think of this as taking a U-turn along the path that leads from research findings to theory development. This path starts off with the collection and examination of raw data that are very specific. It then takes you, through a reductionist analytical process, towards the lowest common factor relating to the research data, from which may be extracted the generality that is needed to formulate theory. By this point you have left far behind the colourful illustrations that exemplify the principles and processes that form the basis of the theory that you have developed, but you have, thus far, proceeded in one direction in order to get where you wanted to be. Now, you need to go back in the opposite direction — back towards the contextual specificity from whence you first set out — in order to find illustrative examples of the theory that you have formulated and to provide elucidation that gives it meaning and usefulness to those who need to make sense of it and/or to apply it to policy or practice. In some cases this reversal of direction may, indeed, represent a U-turn, since it involves going over different ground. In other cases it may represent the retracing of your steps for a while and then, perhaps, branching off onto another path — a new one, but one which leads in the same direction.

I draw upon an example from my own work to illustrate the analytical processes described above. The first example is my

Table 9.1: Summary of four levels of elucidation of what influences teachers' job satisfaction, identified by Evans (1998)

Level	Bases	Examples of elucidation	Main weaknesses
1	conventional wisdom; commonsense reasoning	job satisfaction is influenced by pay and conditions of service	weak epistemological basis; assumes homogeneity amongst teachers
2	empirical research	job satisfaction influenced by age and seniority; leadership style; gender	inadequately developed analytical basis; identifies trends and typologies that fail to have universal applicability and that exclude many; generality is not matched with precision and accuracy
3	empirical research	job satisfaction influenced by degree of match between person and institution, or between person and leader	fails to incorporate consideration of lowest common factor analysis, therefore has limited explicatory capacity
4	empirical research; lowest common factor analysis; logical deduction and reasoning	job satisfaction influenced by congruence between individuals' values and those manifested in their workplace cultures; degree of expectations' fulfilment	lacks illustrative contextual specificity

contribution of a fifth level to what I have identified as 'levels of elucidation' of what influences teachers' job satisfaction (Evans, 1998, pp. 19–20; see also Chapter 4). I summarize the first four levels in Table 9.1.

The fourth level of elucidation is one of in-depth analysis and recognition of the need for conceptual clarity and precision. Recognizing the inaccuracies associated with crude generalization which ignores individualism, it focuses upon the lowest common factor in relation to determinants of job satisfaction amongst individuals. Analysis at this level seeks commonalties and generalization, but it seeks commonalities and generalization which are accurate in terms of their having wide – if not universal – applicability, because they are free from contextual specificity. This level has contributed much to elucidation not only of what job satisfaction is, but of what, fundamentally, are its determinants.

For practical purposes, however, despite its analytical and

conceptual sophistication, the elucidation provided by level four has, on its own, limited value. Information that, for example, teachers' job satisfaction is dependent upon their job-related needs, or expectations, being met is useful, but needs supplementing if it is to be applied meaningfully. My response to this consideration has been to contribute a fifth level of elucidation, which I felt was needed in order to provide that supplementary information. The analysis upon which this fifth level of understanding is based applied the lowest common factor analysis of level four to teaching-specific exemplars. This fifth level of elucidation, in a sense, combines the contextual specificity of level three with the generality, precision, width of applicability and explication of level four to present illustrations of the theory of what influences job satisfaction. The product, or output, of this may look the same as that of level three, but it is superior to it because it incorporates the theory that level three omits or fails to develop fully.

The path that I took in order to develop a fifth level of elucidation is described in outline below. Firstly, I examined very specific raw data, such as that revealing teachers' job satisfaction to be influenced by specific disagreements between them and colleagues, or by specific circumstances and incidents in the workplace, such as the perceived laziness and inefficiency of the deputy headteacher, or the hierarchical management structure. Secondly, I applied – over several levels of coding – the reductionist lowest common factor analysis that I explain above in my supermarket shopping example, in order to seek generality. This generality was – very briefly – that teachers' job satisfaction is determined by their perceived proximity to what they conceive of as their 'ideal job' – the extent to which their job-related ideals are perceived to be met – and that individual teachers' professionality orientation, relative perspectives and realistic expectations accounted for the diversity in relation to what specific issues affected job satisfaction. This exemplifies the fourth level of elucidation. Also representative of level four, I applied the process that I explain above in the supermarket shopping example to develop a model of the process whereby individuals experience job fulfilment (the stages illustrated in the model are explained fully elsewhere: Evans, 1998, pp. 13–18; Evans, 1999, pp. 78–84). This model is shown in Figure 9.1. Level five is then represented by my identification of more specific illustrative examples of the model, presented in various forms. One form is the exemplification of how the model of the job fulfilment process operates in relation to three strands of

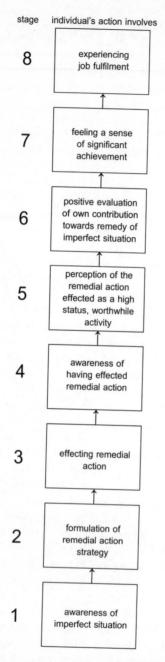

Figure 9.1: Model of the job fulfilment process in individuals

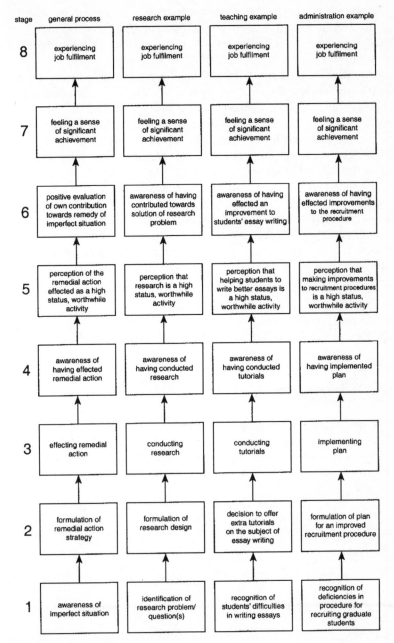

Figure 9.2: Illustration of the model of the job fulfilment process in individuals by application to examples of tutors' work

academics' work: teaching, research and administration. This is illustrated in Figure 9.2, in which each of the three examples of teaching, research and administration represents a different level of specificity.

Another form of more specific illustrative example of my model of the job fulfilment process is my identification of six specific issues that matter to people in their work contexts and that influence job fulfilment. This developed out of the comparative analysis described in Chapter 4. Both my identification of individuals' perceived proximity to what they conceive of as their ideal jobs and my identification of the six issues that matter to people in their workplace and which impact upon their job satisfaction constitute theory because they incorporate precision and generality, they allow predictions to be made about what would happen in the future, and they explain something: in this case, they explain how people derive job satisfaction. If you are uncertain about whether or not what you have developed as a result of your analysis counts as theory ask yourself:

- Does it explain something?
- What does it explain?
- Does it enable predictions to be made about the future?
- Is it general?
- Does it have universal applicability within the research population or sample to which I relate it?
- Is it precise?

It is important, too, to keep in mind Pring's (2000a) comments about theory, incorporated into his interpretation of it on p. 183, that a theoretical position may always be considered to be provisional in the sense that we should never close the door on the possibility of its being revised at a future date, and that it should always be tested against experience and criticism. The last chapter in this book focuses on one specific direction for the further development and extension of theory: pragmatization.

10

Beyond theory: relevance and usefulness through the pragmatization of research

Developing theory is all well and good, but the story doesn't end there — at least, it *shouldn't* end there. The whole rationale for undertaking research is to increase our knowledge, so that we can then apply that knowledge to making improvements to how we do things, for the purpose of increasing the effectiveness of the services that society provides, in order to improve the quality of people's lives. As Page (2000, p. 104) argues, research should 'be made to speak not only to theory and methodology, but also to practice and policy'. If we accept this rationale then it follows, of course, that the theory we develop from our research findings is not the last word.

The nature of the criticism levelled at educational research on the basis of its having insufficient impact upon policy and practice has been outlined in Chapter 2. This criticism is justified; the link between research-based theory, or (since, as I point out in Chapter 9, many researchers do not develop their findings into theory) research findings, and what goes on in the day-to-day business of educating people is weak, inconsistent, incoherent and generally inadequate, though I accept that there are exceptions to this trend. Pring (2000a, pp. 85–6) refers to 'the contrast between a theoretical perspective, through which people claim to have understood the social world, and the everyday discourse through which we normally talk about it', and warns:

> unless there can be a bridge between the common sense discourse and the more technical discourse, then the theory-based research will have little or no impact upon policy or practice ...
>
> The teacher, caught in the complex practical world of the

classroom, needs to see where the theoretical account latches on to his or her quite different universe of discourse. The theorist needs to show where theory corrects or improves the common sense beliefs that inform a teacher's practice.

This chapter addresses the key issue of the relevance and usefulness of educational research. It is a key issue because it constitutes the rationale for, and therefore gives meaning and purpose to, educational research. Informing policy and practice is what educational research is – or should be – all about. This chapter is about what I refer to as the *pragmatization* of educational research: the process that transforms research findings into something that is relevant and useful to teachers, policy-makers and others whose work involves them in the education sector.

THE PRAGMATIZATION OF RESEARCH: WHAT IT IS AND WHY IT IS NEEDED

The pragmatization of findings is a process that involves advanced skills and that represents reflective practice in educational research. I explain precisely what the process involves, and how to carry it out, in a later section. Here I clarify what I mean by the term.

The pragmatization of research is a systematic, planned process involving analysis, presentation and dissemination that is directed at transforming research findings into viable, specific ideas and recommendations for policy and practice. Of course, there is no shortage of suggestions for ways of bringing research findings to teachers (Hargreaves, 1996; Hargreaves, 1998) and to policy-makers (Kirst, 2000; Weiss, 1995). Most reflect the widely held, underlying belief that the main problem is one of poor communication: a problem explained by Griffiths (1998, p. 34):

> Teachers, advisers and policy-makers have pressing practical problems to solve. They all have implicit theories about their problems and reflect on them continuously, but such reflections are rarely couched in the language of high theory which is habitually used by those who are less practically engaged in the educational issues they address. Many theorists, like myself, enjoy theorizing and theory for its own sake, as well as for its practical results. We stand accused by teachers and policy-makers of mystifying the important questions that need to be answered. It should be possible, it is said, to learn more about practical issues like the educational achievement of ethnic

minorities, or the organization of schools, without being put off by the unnecessarily complicated terminology habitually used by researchers in universities.

Suggestions of ways of bringing research to teachers and policy-makers therefore incorporate ideas for ways in which researchers may make their findings more accessible to potential research users, such as writing at different levels of complexity and technicality, for different readerships (Kirst, 2000; Riddell, 1989); using more innovative writing, or 'new literary forms' (Coffey and Atkinson, 1996, p. 123); making oral presentations through seminars (Page, Samson and Crockett, 1998) and presenting research findings in the form of a play (Loughran, 1999, p. 5).

These ideas are fine as far as they go, and some specific examples of them have clearly been very successful in promoting and facilitating effective dissemination of research (Kirst, 2000), but taking research to policy-makers and practitioners on a wide scale – and getting them to use it in their work – involves more than presenting findings in straightforward, jargon-free language. One reason why this is the case is that poor communication is not the only problem. In a sense, the problem of poor communication is more complex than is implied by the suggested remedy that researchers need to direct some of their dissemination at a non-academic readership. It is complicated by the existence of a recognizable dichotomy within the educational research community, to which Ranson (1998, pp. 49–50) refers:

> While some colleagues define their vocation in terms of understanding and supporting the professional practice of teachers, others are committed to furthering knowledge of education within the social sciences. The field, it appears, is 'split between those wanting research to be relevant directly to practice and those wanting to make a theoretical and empirical contribution to knowledge'. This is an accurate account of the division which runs through many university departments of education.

The implications of this dichotomy are that the communication of research findings in user-accessible terminology and style is insufficiently widespread a practice to make a difference because not all educational researchers are sufficiently concerned about their research having an impact upon policy and practice to disseminate to non-academic readerships. The problem of poor communication is complicated also by the fact that much educational research focuses on issues that policy-makers and practitioners are unlikely to consider relevant and useful to their work, so that even if it were disseminated in user-friendly form it would hold little interest for them. Multi-level, or user-targeted, dissemination, then, whilst it is certainly a step in the right direction, is an over-simplistic response to demands for relevance and usefulness and, on its own, does not constitute pragmatization of research.

Poor communication is only the tip of the iceberg. The main, underlying problem is that too little research focuses on issues that matter to teachers and policy-makers. It is a problem (as I point out in Chapter 2) of different agendas, different priorities – different values, in some cases – and different interpretations of relevance and usefulness on the parts of researchers and potential research users. Pragmatization of research is a process that addresses this problem by tackling these differences.

I do not, by any means, suggest that *all* research should be directed at addressing issues that policy-makers or practitioners identify as important to them. This would stifle the developmental and transformational capacity of research; a capacity that is a valuable resource to the education sector. I have no wish to see educational research reduced to the status of a responsive service-provider, constrained within narrow epistemological parameters that mark out boundaries identified by myopic vision. Part of the role and responsibility of researchers involves enlightening people, revealing to them what they would not otherwise see, introducing them to and raising their awareness of new issues, and presenting them with information and ideas that set them thinking (Stein, Smith and Silver, 1999). A teacher may never have considered – let alone conceived of the idea of researching – the topic of children's self-esteem, for example, but, on being introduced to it through research findings, may nevertheless be fascinated by it and find it valuable to her/his work. Since practitioners and policy-makers may not know fully what issues are relevant and useful to them until research reveals them to be so, there is an obvious danger in having a research agenda that is entirely driven by them. I agree, too, with Tooley (1999, p. 178) that there does not need to be consensus in relation to a research agenda that pursues answers to an agreed set of questions: 'But why *should* there be a consensus? Surely, just as in other scientific research, progress depends on researchers moving forward on what *they perceive* to be the frontiers, being daring and entrepreneurial.' On the other hand, in relation to the fundamental rationale for undertaking educational research, there is little point in carrying out studies that do not, at the end of the day, manage to make even the smallest contribution to informing and developing policy and practice. My use of the phrase, 'at the end of the day' is deliberately chosen to emphasize that, even though informing and developing theory is a valid purpose of research, and that I consider it perfectly acceptable for some studies to reach only this stage, theory-related research output can be justified only if it is intended, ultimately, to make a contribution towards informing policy- and practice-related decisions.

I readily acknowledge that some educational research has had an impact on policy and practice. I go along with the idea that much research infiltrates policy and, through that, practice, by what is variously referred to as the 'percolation', the 'enlightenment' or the 'knowledge creep' process, which I examine in Chapter 2. The point is, though, that the educational research community, on the whole, is making too little effort – real and meaningful effort – to close the gap to which Page, Samson and Crockett (1998, p. 300) refer:

> Teachers are said to value practical, particular knowledge ... while researchers value theoretical abstractions, which they also have the resources to generate and disseminate. Given these cultural differences, teachers and researchers will struggle over knowledge about schooling without quite realizing why. They may find themselves dismissing rather than learning from the perspective of the other, with the result that the gap between educational research and practice remains unbridged, and the status quo unchanged.

What has so far been lacking on the part of researchers in general is a concerted effort to take research to practitioners and policy-makers.

One reason for this is that academic status is achieved by generating theory, rather than informing practice, and this, of course, accounts for the dichotomy referred to above. I emphasize that theory generation – as I point out in the preceding chapter – is a key function and purpose of research. It is an activity that I enjoy, and which I find enormously fulfilling on account of the intellectual challenges that it presents. But I see a greater purpose of educational research, to which theory is a contributor, and that is relevance and usefulness to policy and practice.

As far as the dichotomy within the educational research community is concerned, I have no objection to the principle of there being two differently focused groups. Generating theory is an essential function of educational research, and informing policy and practice is an essential function of educational research. Both functions therefore need to be carried out, as Edwards (2000, p. 300) points out: 'writing for other researchers is integral to the research process' and, 'the overlap between "academic" and "user" reviews of evidence should be substantial'. If both of these functions are best achieved by two groups, each tackling one function, to produce an end result that leaves no gap in provision, then there is no problem, and 'theorists' and 'pragmatists' may each remain such, functioning in a complementary – almost symbiotic – manner. But, in reality, what happens is that, because the two groups are uneven in size, their respective outputs are uneven; far more researchers focus on what may loosely – and erroneously, as I argue in Chapter 9 – be described as theory development than on applying their findings to informing and developing educational policy and practice. Moreover, the two groups do not seem to work in tandem, which would be achieved by the 'pragmatists' seeking out other researchers' theoretical findings in order to apply them to policy and practice, or, alternatively, by the 'theorists' feeding their findings to 'pragmatist' partners. Black (2000, p. 416) makes this point: 'researchers themselves do not collaborate to formulate coherent programmes aimed at influencing policy, and ... strong centres that might be a focus for such collaboration do not exist'. So there is no co-ordinated effort to 'treat' research-generated theory – the raw material for effective policy and practice – and any 'refinement' that does occur tends to do so incidentally, such as when researchers seek out other people's theoretical findings in order to support and develop their own into recommendations for policy and practice. Stopping at the theory development stage of research constitutes an important contribution to knowledge generation and is perfectly acceptable if others pick up where you leave off – at least on some occasions. In reality, though, this seldom happens.

What is needed, then, in order to develop educational research, is an increase in the extent to which theory is turned into specific, viable, recommendations and ideas that policy-makers and practitioners consider relevant and useful, that address the questions that they want answering, and that introduce them to issues of which they ought to be made aware. Achieving this is not dependent upon two identifiable groups of researchers, 'theorists' and 'pragmatists', working together more coherently. This has the potential to work in theory, but, realistically, it is a process that is unlikely to take off in a big way. More realizable, I believe, is the development of 'theoretical pragmatists', or, put another way, 'pragmatic theorists': researchers whose academic contribution incorporates a duality, involving their developing theory and then going the extra mile and 'pragmatizing' their theoretical findings. Such researchers do already exist, of course, but they are few and far between. The proliferation of such a group would represent a significant – and timely – development. If educational research is to move forward we need to see the emergence of such a specific category of analytical researchers. Moreover, these need to become a majority group, rather than a small, insignificant minority: a group that is committed to injecting relevance and usefulness into educational research findings and research-based theory.

The concepts *relevance* and *usefulness* are problematic, though. What do they mean, precisely, and who decides whether or not they have been achieved? Many researchers would claim that their research is relevant and useful, because by their own standards, and according to their own interpretation, it *is*. Yet teachers or policy-makers or, indeed, other researchers, may disagree with them. Here are parallels with the misunderstanding, to which I refer in Chapter 9, that allows many researchers to imagine themselves to be developing theory when, according to the elitist interpretation, they are doing nothing of the kind. The problem is that there does not appear to be an accepted, agreed definition or interpretation of, nor criteria for, relevance and usefulness, so there is no yardstick against which to measure claims of having achieved them. If the educational research community is serious about tackling the issue of relevance and usefulness, it needs, as a first step, to clarify what the terms mean and to identify criteria for achieving them.

Examining Relevance and Usefulness

Examination of the literature reveals a range of levels of specificity applied to what may be considered to be interpretations and explanations of what constitutes research that is relevant and useful to policy-makers and practitioners. Keeves's (1997b, p. 3) reference to research yielding 'results that have direct application' is vague, but, writing with McKenzie, he offers a more helpful interpretation of relevance and usefulness that is implicit in the identification of three categories of outcomes of educational research:

> In the first usage, knowledge is applied to a particular problem, and that knowledge may be derived from a particular

investigation or from a series of investigations. In the second usage, the knowledge available is cumulative knowledge and action is taken on the basis of cumulative knowledge. There is, however, a third and important form or outcome of educational research and development that involves the preparation of a tangible product for direct use in schools, classrooms, and homes and which incorporates the findings of educational research. (Keeves and McKenzie, 1997, p. 238)

Foster (1999, p. 393) interprets relevance in educational research as being related to areas of 'general debate and concern amongst policy makers and practitioners in education'. Most other interpretations of relevance and usefulness focus more narrowly on teachers' work. Whilst objecting to them for the narrowness of their emphases, Edwards (2000, pp. 306–7) refers to specific interpretations of criteria for usefulness that are concerned only with changing educational practice and impacting directly upon teaching and learning activities.

Pring's interpretation of relevance and usefulness does not appear to be quite so narrowly bound, but he nevertheless warns against educational research that is not distinctly educational, on the grounds that 'it may not be about what the "educators" need to know' (2000a, p. 8). He goes on to outline the cautionary tale of the recent closure of the School of Education at the University of Chicago, once regarded as one of the world's most prestigious educational studies centres, but which 'had disconnected its theoretical pursuits from the practice of school teaching whilst failing to produce the research which met the academic approval of the social scientists'. For Pring, relevance and usefulness in educational research are determined by its relation to 'the practice of educating' (p. 29), irrespective of the social science discipline in which the research is located:

> it may be that educationally relevant research may often be properly placed in the disciplines of psychology, sociology or philosophy. But it can only be relevant if it relates to the 'practice of education' – to the activities, engaged in on the whole by teachers, which have those characteristics which pick them out as *educational*. (Pring, 2000a, p. 9)

He suggests a more specific criterion for relevance and usefulness as the capacity of research for informing teachers' work:

> And what status can such research have unless it contributes to

a growing understanding of situations, howsoever provisional and subject to further growth through criticism, upon which teachers, as learners, can draw in their 'problem-solving' and to which they might contribute in the light of experience and criticism? The interconnection between practising and theorizing is such that to institutionalize their separation is to make the theory irrelevant to the practice and the practice impervious to theoretical considerations. Perhaps this is the lesson to be learnt from Chicago. (Pring, 2000a, p. 30)

Similar to this is Pratt's (1999, pp. 39–40) implicit interpretation of relevance and usefulness as the capacity of research to 'contribute to policy-making by its ability to problematize and inform issues faced by policy-makers and practitioners'. But what, precisely, do Pratt, Pring and others mean by 'informing' teachers' work or issues facing policy-makers and practitioners? What are the features of research that achieves this?

Clearly, disagreement over level of specificity and narrowness of focus precludes precise consensus on how relevance and usefulness should be interpreted, although there is evidence of a general, vague, shared acceptance that they should be interpreted as relating to impact on educational policy-making and practice. My own interpretation is wide. I share Edwards's (2000) concern that clearly identifiable research-led change to what goes on in schools and classrooms should not be the only criterion for relevance and usefulness. My interpretation incorporates what I identify as four *ex post facto* criteria. I interpret as relevant and useful research which meets one or more of these criteria, which relate to *elucidation, awareness-raising, professional development* and *transformation*.

ELUCIDATION

The research should shed light on one or more issue(s) and/or question(s) about which practitioners and/or policy-makers are uncertain, or to which they want answers. The key words are *shed light on*. It is important to recognize that research may make a valuable contribution towards increasing practitioners' and policy-makers' knowledge and understanding without necessarily providing what may be interpreted – however temporarily – as unequivocal or definitive answers.

AWARENESS-RAISING

The research should raise issues and/or questions which generate interest on the part of practitioners and/or policy-makers. In this capacity, research acts as a catalyst that serves to introduce ideas or issues and awaken interest or concern, rather than as a vehicle for responding to an agenda of familiar issues drawn up by practitioners and/or policy-makers. The awareness-raising function of research therefore extends such agendas by adding new items.

PROFESSIONAL DEVELOPMENT

The research should lead to development on the part of practitioners and/or policy-makers. Elsewhere I have identified two constituent elements, functional development and attitudinal development, of what I identify as teacher development (Evans, 2002) but which may equally be referred to more generally as professional development and applied to non-teaching educational policy-makers. This criterion for relevance and usefulness in research involves either or both of these elements of professional development and may therefore be met by the manifestation of procedural or productive change or of intellectual change, all of which are incorporated within my interpretation of teacher development (Evans, 2002). Research that stimulates practitioners' or policy-makers' reflection or analysis, for example, would meet this criterion for relevance and usefulness.

TRANSFORMATION

The research should lead to change in policy and/or practice. This criterion differs from that relating to professional development in so far as its focus is not on change as manifested by and relating to practitioners or policy-makers, but on change brought about by them. The transformation-related criterion, in other words, is focused on change *effected by*, rather than change *that affects*, practitioners and policy-makers.

Issues for Consideration

Clearly, these four criteria for relevance and usefulness are potentially interrelated and cumulatively dependent, so that, whilst it is quite possible that a piece of research may meet only one of the criteria, it is more likely that its meeting one will effect a chain reaction culminating in all four being met.

Pragmatization is a process aimed at giving research relevance and usefulness. It is not an alternative to developing theory – a 'poor relation' in academic status terms – but a supplement to it, and it demands equally high-level skills as are required for generating theory. It is essentially an analytical process aimed at breaking down what have come to be recognized as the barriers to policy-makers' and practitioners' utilizing research findings in their work. Most commonly these barriers are identified specifically as

- *inaccessibility* – typically research findings are presented predominantly in written form and in publications that few policy-makers and practitioners read; (even 'professional' journals and magazines have small practitioner readerships)
- *poor communication to potential users* – 'academic-speak' is the most commonly used form of communication, rendering the findings difficult to understand for those who do not speak the language
- *irrelevance to potential users' work* – the findings often do not interest policy-makers and practitioners since they are considered to have insufficient practical relevance
- *generality of policy- and practice-related findings* – if they do draw implications and recommendations for policy and practice out of their work, researchers typically present them as general issues or discussion topics, rather than as very specific guidelines to be followed, and the result of this generality is usually that no one has the time or inclination to develop the issues into workable ideas that can be implemented in schools and colleges.

Whilst it is aimed at overcoming all of these barriers, the process of pragmatization of research is a response, in particular, to the last: generality of policy- and practice-related findings.

The point at which most researchers evidently consider their task completed is typically when they have drawn out of their findings the key implications for policy and/or practice and, in some cases – though many researchers fail even to reach this stage – when they have formulated a set of recommendations. It is at this point that, more often than not, researchers 'hand over' their findings to the next agency that will, they believe, take on their findings and apply them to educational policy-making or directly to work in schools and colleges, and, because this agency will do the part of the work that involves converting research findings into working policy and practice – turning ideas on paper into tangible action – the recommendations that the researchers have formulated are usually vague and general. There is no reason for them to be otherwise, they reason, because someone else who really is much better qualified than they are – someone who, as a policy-maker or practitioner, really understands what is needed in terms of formulating specific ideas that are workable – is going to come along and make a much better job of turning research findings into policy and practice than they, as researchers, could ever manage; after all, their business as researchers is not to make policy, nor to tell practitioners how to do their jobs, but to gather data, identify trends and patterns, or discrepancies and diversity, and offer reasons why these exist, and, in some cases, develop this into a theoretical framework. Their job, they believe, is to answer 'why ...?', rather than 'how ...?' questions. This issue, in fact, is raised in the Hillage Report (Hillage *et al.*, 1998, p. 37, para. 4.1.2):

> Some of the interviewees from the funding bodies felt that many researchers were too busy with their other academic duties to be heavily involved in practitioner dissemination ... which was not a valued activity. Some also felt that they did not have the necessary skills. One argued that 'it is not their competence' and another said that:
>
> *'the best researchers can be appalling communicators'.*

So researchers' recommendations are typically restricted to awareness-raising along the following lines, which are illustrative: teachers need to be much more aware of the peer-group pressures facing adolescent girls and should devise alternative methods of lesson delivery that incorporate consideration of this; headteachers should be aware of their capacity for influencing staff morale and motivation and should adopt more motivational, interpersonal leadership styles; university lecturers should be aware of the assessment-driven nature of undergraduate students' motivation and should bear this in mind when designing courses. Seldom are recommendations sufficiently specific to constitute ideas that are at the stage of being able to be tried out and put into practice: step-by-step guides, or 'how to ...' advice, and 'things to avoid' and 'must do' lists, even though, in many cases, research data will have revealed much raw material for these.

But the problem is, no one else *does* come along and turn research findings into policy and practice, as the Hillage Report (Hillage *et al.*, 1998, p. 58, para 6.3) points out: 'The final element of our proposals addresses what we see as a further fundamental weakness in the system: the lack of people and processes to help distil and/or interpret research findings for a practitioner and/or policy-maker audience.' There is no 'next agency' that habitually and system-atically picks up the story from the point where the educational researchers left it, of how to raise standards or make improvements to the educational system. This process seems to lie in the domain of 'no man's – or woman's – land' and, as a result, it is seldom enacted. Indeed, Edwards (2000, p. 300) warns: 'researchers should bear in mind how their work may be selectively cited and interpreted, and not step aside after publishing it in esoteric journals as though their responsibilities are now fulfilled'.

There are, of course, exceptions. Research that manages to secure a high profile and that hits a chord with policy-makers – usually at national level – does get fed into the system, but, as Weiss (1995, p. 141) reminds us, this is 'a chancy business'. The Warwick study of the implementation of the English and Welsh national curriculum (Campbell *et al.*, 1991) that was influential on the Dearing Report (1993) that changed the scale and nature of the national curriculum is one such example; another is the research carried out by David Wray and his co-researchers into effective teaching of literacy, and which was influential on the UK's National Literacy Strategy (Wray, 1997; Wray *et al.*, 1998). But these examples represent a small minority of educational research studies. Most research produces findings that lie dormant because no one is prepared to take on the responsibility of translating them from academic-speak into practitioner-speak, and of converting answers to the 'why ...?' questions into answers to the kinds of 'how ...?' questions (Pratt, 1999, p. 40) that practitioners and policy-makers ask.

The main problem is that, even when they are presented comprehensibly, recommendations from research findings demand time and effort to turn them from the general to the specific; from what, in practitioners' terms, is the practically meaningless, to the useful. Because of the demands of the job they do, time and effort are not at the disposal of practitioners. If they are to have any chance of being put into practice, then, research recommendations need to be handed over to practitioners on a plate, ready to enact, and not as a list of issues, guiding principles or vague ideas over which practitioners must sweat and pore to convert them into workable strategies. It is this business of putting it on a plate for the easy consumption of practitioners – and policy-makers – that constitutes the process that I call the pragmatization of research findings.

THE PROCESS

The pragmatization process involves much more than multi-level dissemination or the selection of research topics that reflect policy-makers' and practitioners' key concerns and interests. It is a process that is applied within the wider research process, after the generation of findings, and incorporated into data analysis and dissemination. It is a process that I have successfully carried out and which I explain below, first, by referring to the illustrative example of a specific pragmatization of my own research.

Managing to Motivate: an Example of the Pragmatization of Research
Some years ago I carried out what I refer to as a composite study (comprising four separate, but related, small-scale studies) of teacher morale, job satisfaction and motivation: all three of which, within the occupational psychology field of study, are categorized as attitudes. I have referred to this study in earlier chapters. Full details of this study's research design and the presentation of its findings are presented elsewhere (Evans, 1998); here I provide only those details that are pertinent to my illustrating the pragmatization process.

My main research aim was to identify the factors that influence teachers' attitudes to their work; more specifically, their morale, job satisfaction and motivation. I used semi-structured interviews as the main method of data collection supplemented by participant observation and, in one of the studies, questionnaires. My sample comprised primary school teachers in four schools in the UK.

Analysis of my findings revealed the influences on teacher morale, job satisfaction and motivation to be considerably more complex, and more fascinating, than I had ever anticipated. The key issues to emerge from my first analysis are outlined in the briefest of detail below:

- A diverse range of morale, job satisfaction and motivation levels was evident amongst my sample of teachers, even, most strikingly, amongst teachers who shared common experiences, circumstances and situations, such as those who worked at the same school – morale was revealed as an individual, rather than a group, phenomenon.
- This diversity was underpinned by individuals' relative perspective on their jobs, their realistic expectations, and their professionality orientation (see Chapter 1).
- Morale, job satisfaction and motivation are influenced most strongly by factors emanating from the institution-specific contexts in which teachers work, rather than by centrally initiated factors.

- Since it is a key influence on institution-specific work contexts, leadership is a significant influence on morale, job satisfaction and motivation.
- Since job-related attitudes are individually determined, no one leadership style emerged as categorically positive or negative in its influence. Teachers varied in relation to the specific leadership behaviour that suited, or did not suit them – what motivated one teacher may demotivate another. Nevertheless, several specific features of generally motivational leadership were identified.

As I undertook the lengthy, and involved, business – spanning several years – of analysing my findings, reformulating conceptions and ideas, re-analysing and then, again, re-conceptualizing, and re-analysing yet again, and so on, I became increasingly aware that, even though I had neither planned nor anticipated it, what I had uncovered was a wealth of data that not only addressed the important question of what influences teacher morale, job satisfaction and motivation and that allowed me to develop theory, but that also seemed to have the potential for providing very specific answers to the question: how may teacher morale, job satisfaction and motivation be improved? My sample of teachers spoke very candidly about their leaders and managers; in particular, their headteachers. They identified very specifically how their leaders' behaviour affected – positively and negatively – their own attitudes to their jobs and, in doing so, they had delineated both motivational and demotivational leadership and provided me with a framework for the formulation of a specific guide to school leadership that motivates teachers by avoiding doing that which antagonizes and focusing on that which brings the best out of people. Here, I realized, were research findings that could be rendered relevant and useful: findings that could be used to answer a very important 'how …?' question.

The process whereby I rendered my research findings relevant and useful – the pragmatization process – involved what I have identified as several stages and which I present in a general form in a later section. Since, in this form, it is sometimes difficult both to explain and to understand, I first exemplify the process by describing it in outline, below, in relation to my composite study of teachers' attitudes.

THE PROCESS, STAGE-BY-STAGE
The first stage was the identification of the key issues to emerge

from the findings, presented above. The second stage was my selecting – for the purpose of pragmatization – a key issue upon which I wished to focus: the significance of leadership as an influence on teachers' attitudes to their work. Stage 3 involved my considering who, or what agencies, could potentially exercise any control over this key issue – in other words, if anyone could do anything about the issue of the significant influence that leadership has on teachers' attitudes, who was it? My response was to identify three groups or categories of people, which I decided to call 'controllers'. I do not claim that these are the only possible groups of potential 'controllers', nor that they have equal potential for control. These three groups were: teachers themselves (since they could perhaps exercise control by adopting direct action or palliative strategies for dealing with the influence of leadership); policy-makers who were concerned with the development of the leadership role (since they could influence the remit and range of responsibilities of specific leadership roles); and school and college leaders.

The next stage – stage 4 – was to consider the range of different 'paths' that were available for me to follow in the pragmatization of my research findings. I identified several. I could follow the line of the future development of leadership policy in the UK, for example. This would involve examining issues such as whether the hierarchical pyramidal model of authority, control and decision-making in schools and colleges was the best model for getting the best out of teachers, or whether an alternative needed to be found. Another 'path' to follow might be that of teachers' capacity for coping with their leaders. This could involve – among other things – investigating ways in which teachers could interact with their leaders in ways that benefited them more: identifying specific coping strategies, or re-examining teachers' rights in relation to authority. A third 'path' that I identified was that of leadership practice. This would focus on providing guidelines for 'morale-friendly' leadership.

Having identified several 'paths' to follow, the next stage – the fifth – was to choose one. I chose the leadership practice path because I felt that I had so much data that was directly relevant to it and, moreover, I felt that these data lent themselves particularly well to the formulation of very specific guidelines for school leaders – advice on what to do and what not to do if they wished to raise morale amongst their staff and motivate them. Hand-in-hand with my selection of the leadership practice 'path' went my selection of one of the specific groups of 'controllers' that I identified at stage 3 — school and college leaders. By this stage, then, I had a clear focus and knew where I wanted to go with my analysis. I was set on drawing out of my findings relevant and useful information about how school and college leaders could carry out their responsibilities in ways that promoted high morale and positive job-related attitudes amongst staff.

Stage 6 was a natural progression from this. It was, in this case, practically automatic, but I have identified it as a separate stage from the last one since, in other cases, it may not necessarily be so clear-cut and automatic a transition. It involved my considering who should be the target(s), that is, the intended recipient(s), of the relevant and useful information on how school and college leaders could best carry out their responsibilities. I decided that the most obvious target should be the group whom I considered to be the best placed to put this information to good use by applying it to their practice — school and college leaders.

Stages 7 and 8 were stages of, respectively, identifying information that I needed and then gathering it. This was not research-generated information but background information on current issues related to school and college management, without consideration of which any leadership practice-focused guidelines I might formulate might lack credibility and viability. I needed to know whether the ideas I would present would be workable, or whether they would be dismissed as half-baked because I had overlooked a key statutory area of responsibility, for example, or a regulation that precluded school and college leaders from incorporating the ideas into their practice. I needed to know how schools and colleges are typically managed. I was aware of needing to bring myself up to date with state-of-the-art educational leadership in general, and also of ascertaining whether the ideas that I was formulating were as applicable to the secondary and post-compulsory sectors of education (since I was targeting their leaders), with their typically large institutions and staffs, as they were to the primary sector with which I was most familiar. I did this by sounding out my ideas on representatives of leaders from these sectors, and by getting a 'feel' for the current educational leadership scene from professional journals and magazines and publications from the DfEE.

The next stages involved my applying my research findings to the consideration first at a general level (stage 9) and then at a specific level (stage 10) of how school and college leaders (since they represented the 'target' that I had identified from within the group of 'controllers' identified at stage 3 and selected at stage 5) might, through their leadership, effect a positive influence on teacher morale, job satisfaction and motivation. I decided that, at a general level, this could be achieved by their adopting improved leadership practice that incorporates consideration of the perspectives of the 'managed' or the 'led'. Stage 10 involved my identifying more specific ideas for improved leadership practice. These included ideas for motivational leadership practice that incorporates consideration of teachers' individuality through, for example, responding to teachers' professionality orientation; giving teachers a voice, and giving praise – all of which had emerged from my research as key issues in motivating teachers.

Having formulated first general and then specific ideas for improved leadership practice, the eleventh stage was to be prescriptive: to turn my specific ideas for motivational leadership into advisory information that was likely to be of practical use to anyone wanting to develop her/his leadership competence. Effectively, this involved anticipating what 'how ...?' questions school and college leaders might want answering in relation to motivating staff and raising their morale. Incorporating consideration of what I had decided earlier was the kind of information that school and college leaders needed to know, I generated specific research-based 'how to ...' suggestions that would be appropriate for school and college leaders to carry out.

Stage 12 involved my assessing how viable were the prescriptive guidelines and the 'how to ...' information that I had formulated at stage 11. It involved identifying potential limitations, problems and repercussions. I had to make sure, for example, that school leaders potentially had the right and the authority to carry out the activities that I prescribed, and whether such activities typically fell within their remit of responsibility. I did this by drawing on the background information that I had gathered at stage 8 and, once again, by sounding out what were, by this stage, specific prescriptive, 'how to ...' ideas, on school and college leaders.

Stages 13 and 14 were the dissemination-related stages. Firstly, at stage 13, I formulated my dissemination plan. I identified what were likely to be the best ways of disseminating my pragmatized research findings and to whom they would be best disseminated – that is, who was the most appropriate 'dissemination target'. In my own case, my dissemination target was the same as the group of professionals whom I had identified earlier as one of the groups of 'controllers' and as the 'target' for the pragmatized findings – school and college leaders. It is possible, though, that, more generally, the dissemination target may include additional groups. I decided that a 'how to ...' book, aimed at, and written in a style appropriate for, practitioners, would be one way of disseminating effectively, and also I thought that articles written for a professional magazine, *Primary School Manager*, might find their way on to the desks of a few school leaders. Another dissemination method that I felt was likely to be even more effective was oral dissemination, through seminars and conferences attended by school and college leaders, and also through my own teaching at the University of Warwick, on continuing professional development (CPD) courses and on postgraduate degree courses, such as the MA in Educational Management.

The final stage, stage 14, was the actual dissemination stage. I wrote my book, *Managing to Motivate* (Evans, 1999a), and my articles (Evans, 1997d; 1997e). I also presented a paper at a local education authority (LEA) primary deputy headteachers' conference, and I have presented – and still do present – my findings on several occasions through my teaching on Warwick University courses of various levels, including a CPD course for middle managers in further education (FE) and masters-level modules on leading and managing people in education. I have also incorporated my findings into distance-learning MA modules.

I have a little evidence of how successful the pragmatization of my research findings has been. Students attending the courses to which I refer above give very positive feedback, indicating that my research has met my criteria for relevance and usefulness related to elucidation and awareness-raising and also, in many cases, professional development, as well as, in some cases, transformation. Those attending masters-level courses have also read my book and incorporated consideration of its relevance and usefulness into their course feedback. Other readers of my book seldom send me feedback, but a few have and have indicated that it has succeeded in providing elucidation and awareness-raising. I have also received second-hand feedback in anecdotal form. For example, a colleague told me that his wife, a school governor, was interviewing a candidate for a primary deputy headship and asked the candidate: 'How would you take the staff with you? How would you motivate them?' 'Well, as it happens', replied the candidate, 'I've just been reading an excellent book by Linda Evans ...'. Clearly, for this reader, there was some relevance and usefulness to my research.

A MODEL OF THE GENERAL PRAGMATIZATION PROCESS

Having presented and described the process through an illustrative example, I now present a general model that may be used as a guide to pragmatizing research findings. This is outlined in Table 10.1 and explained briefly, stage by stage.

Table 10.1: A guide to pragmatizing research findings

Stage	Action required
1	Identify the key issue(s) to emerge from the findings
2	If applicable, select key issue(s) upon which to focus
3	Identify who or what could exercise control over the selected key issue(s) – the 'controller(s)'
4	Identify selection of 'paths' available to follow
5	If applicable, select a 'path' to follow, determined by selection of 'controller(s)'
6	Identify a 'target'
7	Identify information needed to increase viability and credibility of research recommendations and prescriptions
8	Gather information needed to increase viability and credibility of research recommendations and prescriptions
9	Identify how the 'controller' may exert amelioratively directed control at a general level
10	Identify how the 'controller' may exert amelioratively directed control at a specific level
11	Formulate specific prescriptive ideas to be executed by the 'target'
12	Assess the viability of prescriptive ideas; identify potential limitations, problems and repercussions
13	Identify vehicle(s) for dissemination and dissemination 'targets'
14	Present pragmatized findings, communicating prescriptive ideas and the rationales for them to dissemination 'target(s)' as appropriate

STAGE 1: IDENTIFICATION OF KEY ISSUES

This involves identifying all of the key issues to emerge from the research findings.

STAGE 2: SELECTION OF KEY ISSUES

If applicable, the second stage in the process involves selecting the key issue(s) upon which to focus. It is feasible to select related or overlapping issues since the next stages in the pragmatization process may be applied to them simultaneously. Where only one key issue emerges from the research findings, stage 2 is clearly redundant, but where you are faced with a choice – as you most likely will be – your choice should be based upon your judgement of which issues seem to have the most potential for relevance and usefulness, as I interpret them above.

STAGE 3: IDENTIFICATION OF CONTROLLER(S)
Having selected a key issue, or issues, upon which to focus, the next stage is to consider who, or, in some cases, what, could exercise control over this issue. What this means is identifying who or what – in the sense of what agency, rather than what circumstances – could be in a position to effect or, alternatively, to resist, change to the issue.

STAGE 4: IDENTIFICATION OF 'PATHS'
At this stage, having identified potential 'controllers' of the selected key issue(s), several 'paths' to follow in the pragmatization process are likely to have emerged. An alternative way of describing these is as different foci of the process; perhaps even as different themes. They will relate to the different 'controllers' identified at stage 3.

STAGE 5: 'CONTROLLER'-RELATED 'PATH' SELECTION
This stage involves deciding in which direction the pragmatization analysis is to proceed: what theme(s) you want to focus on. It is difficult to distinguish whether this stage involves the selection first of a 'path' and then, leading directly from that, of a 'controller', or vice versa, but I do not consider this to be a significant issue. Your choice may be influenced by your own interests, by the current political agenda and whatever issues are topical, or by what you consider to be the potential of your data. There is, of course, no reason why the pragmatization process cannot incorporate a focus on more than one 'controller' and 'path', but this makes it more complex than if only one theme is selected.

STAGE 6: 'TARGET' IDENTIFICATION
Having selected one or more 'controller'-related 'paths' the next stage is to identify a 'target'. The 'target' is an identifiable category or group of key players who hold positions as 'controllers'. (On rare occasions, such as when the research and the pragmatization process are both focused on a single case-study institution, or when a single influential policy-maker may be identified as the key 'controller', the 'target' may be a single individual, or a small number of identified individuals, such as a senior management team, or the staff of a subject department in a school.) Often the 'target' will be precisely who has been identified as the 'controller(s)', but it may also be a sub-group within the 'controller' group. Selection of the 'controller(s)' as the 'target', though, constitutes a separate stage from

that of identifying the 'controller(s)' because it involves going a step further. This further step involves identifying the group not merely as those who are able to exert control over the key situations and circumstances underpinning the key issue selected at stage 2, but also as those whom you are targeting as the subject of the data analysis, presentation and dissemination of findings that form the pragmatization of your research; those at whom you will principally direct your attempts to enlighten, raise awareness, develop, or transform, as a means of meeting the criteria for relevance and usefulness that I identify above. The Hillage Report (Hillage *et al.*, 1998, p. 58, para. 6.3) recommends the use of targets of this kind: 'researchers should be encouraged to identify the audiences for their research and the appropriate intermediaries and target them accordingly'. In a sense, then, identifying a specific group as a 'target' involves identifying it as an agent of the pragmatization of your research.

Identifying a 'target' usually involves making choices – choosing from among those identified at stage 3 as 'controllers'. It is important to emphasize that although the 'target' represents at least one group of identified 'controllers' it may also, on becoming the 'target', take on what you intend as a role for it of potentially exerting control over the other 'controllers'. Your choice of target may be influenced by the same factors that may influence your choice at stage 5. It may also be influenced by your assessment of the potential of different 'controllers' for facilitating the pragmatization of your research by allowing it to meet the criteria for relevance and usefulness. In other words, you may choose as your 'target' the group that you consider the most likely to respond positively to – or to enact – your research recommendations. This consideration, though, will, in turn, be influenced by the nature and scope of your research data. In my own case, for example, I felt that the bulk of my data lent itself particularly well to the kinds of recommendations for practice that could be targeted directly at school and college leaders, rather than be targeted at them indirectly, through recommendations for policy-makers whose interests lie in developing the leadership role.

STAGE 7: IDENTIFICATION OF CREDIBILITY INFORMATION
If you feel that there are gaps in your knowledge and understanding of the area of practice or policy that is the focus of your pragmatization, and that these gaps could undermine the viability and credibility of your recommendations and prescriptions, then this

stage involves your identifying the kind of general or specific information that you need to access.

STAGE 8: COLLECTION OF CREDIBILITY INFORMATION
Once you have identified the requisite information, this stage involves collecting it. It is worth remembering that, since the purpose of the entire pragmatization process is to present research evidence to practitioners and policy-makers, the most useful sources of information will be representatives of these groups and information that they use in their work, such as statutory orders and policy documents, rather than academic texts.

STAGE 9: IDENTIFICATION OF GENERAL IDEAS FOR 'CONTROLLER'-EXERTED IMPROVED PRACTICE/POLICY
This stage may be best tackled initially by brainstorming ideas for improved general policy and practice that the 'controller' is in a position to be able to effect. One approach is to identify what you would list as key issues relating to policy and practice recommendations if you were to include them in an academic journal article.

STAGE 10: IDENTIFICATION OF SPECIFIC IDEAS FOR 'CONTROLLER'-EXERTED IMPROVED PRACTICE/POLICY
Again, brainstorming ideas may be the best approach initially, using the list generated at stage 9 as your starting point, and recording the ideas as what is often referred to as a 'web' or a 'branch' diagram, with the key issues identified at stage 9 recorded in boxes, from each of which lines radiate out to lead to recorded specific ideas. The best starting point for this brainstorming exercise is to identify specific 'how ...?' questions leading directly from the ideas generated at stage 9 that you consider to be the questions to which your identified 'target' is likely to seek answers. Here your knowledge of current practice or policy issues will help you to determine the kinds of questions that are likely to be relevant. However, this stage should not be confined to identifying what the 'target' is likely to *want* to know; it should also include what you, drawing on your research data, feel the 'target' *ought* to know.

STAGE 11: FORMULATION OF SPECIFIC PRESCRIPTIVE IDEAS
Here you simply come up with specific answers to the 'how ...?' questions identified at stage 10 and turn these answers into 'how to ...' ideas. Each 'how ...?' question may generate several – or, indeed,

many – 'how to ...' ideas. It may be helpful to imagine a representative of your 'target' group asking you a specific 'how ...?' question in teaching session or a seminar. Consider what answer you would give and whether the questioner is likely to be satisfied with the answer or whether s/he is likely to consider it vague and 'wishy-washy'. Your aim is to formulate prescriptive ideas that would satisfy a pragmatically oriented questioner.

STAGE 12: ASSESSMENT OF THE VIABILITY OF PRESCRIPTIVE IDEAS
The best way, by far, of assessing the viability of your prescriptive ideas is to test them on representatives of your 'target' group. This is the stage when you may need to identify qualifications to some of your prescriptive ideas, or to identify potential limitations and/or repercussions. This reflects the complexity of the process of prescribing ideas for policy and practice in the social sciences, where human behaviour is a factor that injects uncertainty and unpredictability into the process. Often it is impossible to generalize, and the best that we can do is communicate in terms of likelihoods, probabilities or possibilities, identifying various options and alternative courses of action, rather than blueprints for success.

STAGE 13: FORMULATION OF THE DISSEMINATION PLAN
This involves your answering the questions, 'Who are my dissemination targets?' and 'What is the best way of disseminating my pragmatized research to them?' Your dissemination target will obviously be the target that you identified at stage 6, but it is possible that, by this stage, you are also able to identify additional 'targets': other people or agencies that you feel would be interested in your findings. In the case of my research into teacher morale, job satisfaction and motivation, for example, additional targets could have been teachers, who represent 'the led' or 'the managed', or leaders and managers in parallel professions and other public services.

Deciding on the best way(s) to disseminate to your 'target(s)' requires understanding of the nature of their work and their attitudes towards receiving information. You need to consider what are likely to be their preferred ways of receiving information, which will require knowing the kinds of demands that are placed on their time. Ask yourself, 'Are these people likely to gain information by reading, and, if so, what kinds of texts would they prefer?', 'How long should such texts be?', 'Where should "readable" information appear in order to attract – and retain – the attention of these people?' You may decide that web-based dissemination is an appropriate alternative or supplement to books or articles, for example, or you may decide that – if you can manage to procure it – newspaper, or even television, coverage is the best approach.

STAGE 14: DISSEMINATION OF PRAGMATIZED RESEARCH FINDINGS
This final stage involves executing the dissemination plan. It is important to remember that, no matter how successful you are at converting your research findings into appropriate answers to practitioners' and policy-makers' 'how . . .?' questions, if they are not then taken to these people in a form that grabs their interest and attention the research will not meet the criteria for relevance and usefulness. As the culmination of the pragmatization process, then, user-friendly dissemination is of the utmost importance.

Table 10.2 presents the stages involved in the general pragmatization process alongside the example of the specific application of the process that I describe above.

THE ANALYTICAL RESEARCHER AND PRAGMATIZATION

The analytical researcher is typically intellectually curious and applies this curiosity to her/his development of her/his research technique and practice. S/he is constantly questioning the appropriateness and the quality of her/his work and seeking ways of taking it forward. S/he develops, and in some cases pioneers, advanced skills. S/he represents the research profession's elite: the 'extended' professionals.

The pragmatization of research, as I have shown in this final chapter, is an analytical process requiring advanced research skills and which can be as intellectually challenging as the development of theory. Yet it needs to be practised much more widely than it has been if educational research is to make any headway in fending off the vociferous criticism levelled at it. As McIntyre (1998, p. 193) points out:

> The need now is for imaginative fresh thinking about research strategies which can throw useful light on effective teaching and learning ... It will not be easy, and it will depend on considerable research expertise; but unless we make real efforts to generate and implement such strategies, complaints ... will continue and will be justified.

Table 10.2: An example of the specific application of the guide to pragmatizing research findings: Linda Evans's research into teacher morale, job satisfaction and motivation

Stage	General description of action involved	Specific outcome of action required
1	Identification of the key issue(s) to emerge from the findings	Identification of the following key issues: (i) diversity of teachers' attitudinal responses to shared and similarly described circumstances and situations (ii) diversity underpinned by individuals' relative perspective, realistic expectations, professionality orientation (iii) influences on job-related attitudes are context-specific (iv) leadership is a key influence on individuals' work contexts and therefore on their morale, job satisfaction and motivation (v) six specific, contextually determined issues are common influences on job-related attitudes: • pedagogy • equity and justice • collegiality • interpersonal relations • organizational efficiency • self-conception and self-image
2	Selection of key issue(s) upon which to focus (if applicable)	Selection of the significance of leadership as an influence on the contexts in which teachers work
3	Identification of who or what could exercise control over the selected key issue(s) – the 'controller(s)'	Identification as possible 'controllers' of teachers; policy-makers; school/college leaders
4	Identification of selection of 'paths' available to follow	Identification of three possible paths: (i) leadership practice; (ii) leadership policy; (iii) teachers' capacity for coping with leadership
5	Selection of a 'path' to follow, determined by selection of 'controller(s)'	Selection of leadership practice
6	Identification of a 'target'	Identification of school/college leaders as 'target'
7	Identification of information needed to increase viability and credibility of research recommendations and prescriptions	Identification of background information on current practice and issues in school/college leadership

Table 10.2: continued

Stage	General description of action involved	Specific outcome of action required
8	Collection of information needed to increase viability and credibility of research recommendations and prescriptions	Collection of background information on current practice and issues in school/college leadership
9	Identification of how the 'controller' may exert amelioratively directed control at a general level	Formulation of ideas for improved leadership practice that incorporates consideration of the perspectives of the 'managed' or the 'led'
10	Identification of how the 'controller' may exert amelioratively directed control at a specific level	Formulation of ideas for motivational leadership practice that incorporates consideration of teachers' individuality through, for example: • responding to teachers' professionality orientation • giving teachers a voice • giving praise
11	Formulation of specific prescriptive ideas to be executed by the 'target'	Formulation of step-by-step guides for school leaders on how to incorporate into their practice the ideas referred to in 9 and 10, above.
12	Assessment of the viability of specific prescriptive ideas; identification of potential limitations, problems and repercussions	Identification of potential limitations arising out of: • school/college size • leaders' personality and disposition • competing pressures of management that conflict with motivational leadership
13	Identification of vehicle(s) for dissemination and dissemination 'target(s)'	Identification of the following forms of dissemination: (i) oral presentations to leaders and aspiring leaders (ii) book aimed at practitioner readership (iii) articles in professional magazines and journals
14	Presentation of pragmatized findings, communication of prescriptive ideas and the rationales for them, to dissemination 'target(s)' as appropriate	Execution of 13, above

Pragmatization is one such strategy. It is the means whereby educational research may manifest its relevance and usefulness.

For pragmatization to be afforded the status that it deserves, though – a high status that will preclude its being considered a second-rate 'unintellectual' pursuit – it must be taken seriously and taken on board by the 'extended' professionals: the analytical researchers. The educational research community needs many more examples of skilled theorists and methodologists – eminent, respected academics – who are also prepared to extend their repertoire of skills to include pragmatization.

At the end of the day, what use is educational research if it does not inform and impact upon what goes on in schools and colleges? Surely, then, pragmatization is the ultimate stage of reflective practice in educational research. The fundamental rationale for developing the educational research profession should be to improve the quality of research so that it may better serve the education sector. It is on this goal, then – the improvement of education – that analytical researchers should set their sights, and towards this purpose that they should direct the advanced skills that they develop.

References

Alvesson, M. and Sköldberg, K. (2000) *Reflexive Methodology: New Vistas for Qualitative Research*, London, Sage

Atkins, M. J. (1984) 'Practitioner as researcher: some techniques for analysing semi-structured data in small-scale research', *British Journal of Educational Studies*, 32 (3), pp. 251–61

Atkinson, T. and Claxton, G. (eds) (2000) *The Intuitive Practitioner*, Buckingham, Open University Press

Back, L. (2001) 'A write off', *Guardian Education*, 24 April, p. 12

Baehr, M. E. and Renck, R., (1959) 'The definition and measurement of employee morale', *Administrative Science Quarterly*, 3, pp. 157–84

Bailey, R. (1999) 'The abdication of reason: postmodern attacks upon science and reason', in J. Swann and J. Pratt (eds) *Improving Education: Realist Approaches to Method and Research*, London, Cassell, pp. 30–8

Ball, S. J. (1987) *The Micro-politics of the School*, London, Routledge

Ball, S. J. (1997) 'Participant observation', in J. P. Keeves (ed.) *Educational Research, Methodology, and Measurement: An International Handbook* (2nd edition), Oxford, Pergamon, pp. 310–14

Bennett, A. (1910) *Clayhanger*, London, Methuen

Bennett, A. (1911) *Hilda Lessways*, London, Methuen

Beveridge, M. (1998) 'Improving the quality of educational research', in J. Rudduck and D. McIntyre (eds) *Challenges for Educational Research*, London, Paul Chapman, pp. 93–113

Black, P. (2000) 'Research and the development of educational assessment', *Oxford Review of Education*, 26 (3&4), pp. 407–19

Blunkett, D. (2000) *Influence or Irrelevance: Can Social Science Improve Government?* (London, DfEE) reprinted in *Research Intelligence*, 71 (March 2000), pp. 12–21

Bogdan, R. C. and Biklen, S. K. (1992) *Qualitative Research for Education: An Introduction to Theory and Methods*, Needham Heights, MA, Allyn and Bacon (2nd edition)

Bogdan, R. C. and Taylor, S. J. (1975) *Introduction to Qualitative Research Methods*, New York, John Wiley and Sons

Bottery, M. and Wright, N. (1996) 'Cooperating in their own deprofessionalisation? On the need to recognise the "public" and "ecological" roles of the teaching profession', *British Journal of Educational Studies*, 44 (1), pp. 82–98

Boyd, W. L. (2000) 'Editorial: what counts as educational research?', *British Journal of educational Studies*, 48 (4), pp. 347–51

Bridges, D. (1998) 'Research, dissent and the reinstatement of theory', in J. Rudduck and D. McIntyre (eds) *Challenges for Educational Research*, London, Paul Chapman, pp. 82–6

Bridges, D. (1999) 'Educational research: pursuit of truth or flight into fancy?', *British Educational Research Journal*, 25 (5), pp. 597–616

Brown, M. (1998) 'Educational researchers in universities: the condition of the workforce', *British Educational Research Journal*, 24 (2), pp. 125–39

Burgess, R. G. (1989) 'Grey areas: ethical dilemmas in educational ethnography', in R. G. Burgess (ed.) *The Ethics of Educational Research*, Lewes, Falmer, pp. 60–76

Campbell, R. J., Evans, L., Neill, S. and Packwood, A. (1991) *Workloads, Achievement and Stress: Two Follow-up Studies of Teacher Time In Key Stage 1*, Warwick, Policy Analysis Unit, University of Warwick

Carr, W. (2000) 'Partisanship in educational research', *Oxford Review of Education*, 26 (3&4), pp. 437–49

Chase, F. S. (1953) 'Professional leadership and teacher morale', *Administrator's Notebook*, 1 (8), pp. 1–4

Coffey, A. and Atkinson, P. (1996) *Making Sense of Qualitative Data*, Thousand Oaks, CA, Sage

Crace, J. (2001) 'Unreal world', *The Guardian Education*, 27 March, pp. 12–13

Darling-Hammond, L. (ed.) (1994) *Professional Development Schools: Schools for Developing a Profession*, New York, Teachers College Press

Davies, P. (2000) 'The relevance of systematic reviews to educational policy and practice', *Oxford Review of Education*, 26 (3&4), pp. 365–78

Day, C. (1999) *Developing Teachers: The Challenges of Lifelong Learning*, London, Falmer

Dearing, R. (1993) *The National Curriculum and its Assessment: An Interim Report*, London, NCC and SEAC

de Landsheere, G. (1997) 'History of educational research', in J. P. Keeves (ed.) *Educational Research, Methodology, and Measurement: An International Handbook* (2nd edition), Oxford, Pergamon, pp. 8–16

DfEE (1998) *Teachers Meeting the Challenge of Change*, London, DfEE

DfEE (2000a) *Performance Management in Schools: Performance Management Framework*, London, DfEE

DfEE (2000b) *Threshold Assessment: Guidance on Completing the Application Form*, London, DfEE

Donnelly, C. (2000) 'In pursuit of school ethos', *British Journal of Educational Studies*, 48 (2), pp. 134–54

Edwards, T. (2000) ' "All the evidence shows...": reasonable expectations of educational research', *Oxford Review of Education*, 26 (3&4), pp. 299–311

Eraut, M. (2000) 'The intuitive practitioner: a critical overview', in T. Atkinson and G. Claxton (eds) *The Intuitive Practitioner*, Buckingham, Open University Press, pp. 255–68

Evans, L. (1991) 'Teaching the national currriculum in Narnia', *Education 3–13*, 9 (3), pp. 50–5

Evans, L. (1992a) 'Robbing Peter to pay Paul', *Education 3–13*, 20 (1), pp. 48–53

Evans, L. (1992b) 'Teacher morale: an individual perspective', *Educational Studies*, 18 (2), pp. 161–71

Evans, L. (1997a) 'A voice crying in the wilderness? The problems and constraints facing "extended" professionals in the English primary education sector', *Teachers and Teaching: Theory and Practice*, 3 (1), pp. 61–83

Evans, L. (1997b) 'Addressing problems of conceptualisation and construct validity in researching teachers' job satisfaction', *Educational Research*, 39 (3), pp. 319–31

Evans, L. (1997c) 'Understanding teacher morale and job satisfaction', *Teaching and Teacher Education: An International Journal of Research and Study*, 13 (8), pp. 831–45

Evans, L. (1997d) 'Managing to motivate: some pointers for primary headteachers', *Primary School Manager*, July/Aug., pp. 16–18

Evans, L. (1997e) 'Leading from the front', *The Guardian Education*, 11 February, p. 6

Evans, L. (1998) *Teacher Morale, Job Satisfaction and Motivation*, London, Paul Chapman

Evans, L. (1999) *Managing to Motivate: A Guide For School Leaders*, London, Cassell

Evans, L. (2001a) 'Developing teachers in a performance culture: is performance-related pay the answer?', in D. Gleeson and C. Husbands (eds) *The Performing School*, London, RoutledgeFalmer, pp. 101–17

Evans, L. (2001b) 'Delving deeper into morale, job satisfaction and motivation among education professionals: re-examining the leadership dimension', *Educational Management and Administration*, 29 (3), pp. 291–306

Evans, L. (2002) 'What is teacher development?', *Oxford Review of Education*, 28 (1), pp. 123–37

Evans, L. and Abbott, I. (1998) *Teaching and Learning in Higher Education*, London, Cassell

Evans, L., Abbott, I., Goodyear, R. and Pritchard, A. (1995) *Hammer and Tongue: The Training of Technology Teachers*, London, The Association of Teachers and Lecturers

Evans, M., Lomax, P., and Morgan, H. (2000) 'Closing the Circle: action research partnership towards better learning and teaching in schools', *Cambridge Journal of Education*, 30 (3), pp. 405–19

Evans, L., Packwood, A., Neill, S., and Campbell, R. J. (1994) *The Meaning of Infant Teachers' Work*, London, Routledge

Farrugia, C. (1986) 'Career-choice and sources of occupational satisfaction and frustration among teachers in Malta', *Comparative Education*, 22 (3), pp. 221–31

Flew, A. (1954) 'The justification of punishment', *Philosophy*, pp. 291–307

Foster, P. (1989) 'Change and adjustment in a further education college', in R. G. Burgess (ed.) *The Ethics of Educational Research*, Lewes, Falmer, pp. 188–204

Foster, P. (1999) ' "Never mind the quality, feel the impact": a methodological assessment of teacher research sponsored by the Teacher Training Agency', *British Journal of Educational Studies*, 47 (4), pp. 380–98

Freeman, P. L. (1986) 'Don't talk to me about lexical meta-analysis of criterion-referenced clustering and lap-dissolve spatial transformations: a consideration of the role of practising teachers in educational research', *British Educational Research Journal*, 12 (2), pp. 197–206

Freidson, E. (1994) *Professionalism Reborn: Theory, Prophecy and Policy*, Cambridge, Polity Press, in association with Blackwell Publishers

Fullan, M. (1991) *The New Meaning of Educational Change*, London, Cassell

Fullan, M. and Hargreaves, A. (1992) 'Teacher development and educational change', in M. Fullan and A. Hargreaves (eds) *Teacher Development and Educational Change*, London, Falmer, pp. 1–9

Garratt, D. (1998) ' "Régime of truth" as a serendipitous event: an essay concerning the relationship between research data and the generation of ideas', *British Educational Research Journal*, 24 (2), pp. 217–35

Gillham, B. (2000a) *The Research Interview*, London, Continuum

Gillham, B. (2000b) *Case Study Research Methods*, London, Continuum

Gipps, C. (1998) 'Some significant developments?', in J. Rudduck and D. McIntyre (eds) *Challenges for Educational Research*, London, Paul Chapman, pp. 69–76

Glaser, B. G. and Strauss, A. L. (1967) *The Discovery of Grounded Theory*, Hawthorne, NY, Aldine (10th printing, 1979)

Goetz, J. P. and LeCompte, M. D. (1984) *Ethnography and Qualitative Design in Educational Research*, London, Academic Press

Gray, J. (1998) 'An episode in the development of educational research', in J. Rudduck and D. McIntyre (eds) *Challenges for Educational Research*, London, Paul Chapman, pp. 17–46

Griffiths, M. (1998) *Educational Research for Social Justice*, Buckingham, Open University Press

Guba, E. and Lincoln, Y. (1989) *Fourth Generation Evaluation*, London, Sage

Guion, R. M. (1958), 'Industrial morale: the problem of terminology', *Personnel Psychology*, 11, pp. 59–64

Hammersley, M. (1993) 'The ethnographer as reflective practitioner: a cautionary tale', revised version of paper presented at the Annual Conference of the British Educational Research Association, University of Stirling, 1992

Hammersley, M. (1998) 'The profession of a "Methodological Purist"?', in G. Walford (ed.) *Doing Research about Education*, London, Falmer, pp. 139–53

Hammersley, M. (2000) 'The relevance of qualitative research', *Oxford Review of Education*, 26 (3&4), pp. 393–405

Hammersley, M. and Atkinson, P. (1996) *Ethnography: Principles in Practice*, London, Routledge (2nd edition)

Hammersley, M., Scarth, J. and Webb, S. (1985) 'Developing and testing theory: the case of research on pupil learning and examinations', in R. G. Burgess (ed.) *Issues in Educational Research*, Lewes, Falmer, pp. 48–66

Hargreaves, A. (1996) 'Transforming knowledge: blurring the boundaries between research, policy and practice', *Educational Evaluation and Policy Analysis*, 18 (2), pp. 161–78

Hargreaves, A. and Fullan, M. (1998) *What's Worth Fighting for in Education?*, Buckingham, Open University Press, in association with the Ontario Public Schools Association

Hargreaves, A. and Goodson, I. (1996) 'Teachers' professional lives: aspirations and actualities', in I. Goodson and A. Hargreaves (eds), *Teachers' Professional Lives*, London, Falmer, pp. 1–27

Hargreaves, D. H. (1994) 'The new professionalism: the synthesis of professional and institutional development', *Teaching and Teacher Education*, 10 (4), pp. 423–38

Hargreaves, D. H. (1998) 'A new partnership of stakeholders and a national strategy for research in education', in J. Rudduck and D. McIntyre (eds) *Challenges for Educational Research*, London, Paul Chapman, pp. 114–35

Hayes, L. F. and Ross, D. D. (1989) 'Trust versus control: the impact of school leadership on teacher reflection', *International Journal of Qualitative Studies in Education*, 2 (4), pp. 335–50

Helsby, G. (1999) *Changing Teachers' Work*, Buckingham, Open University Press

Helsby, G. and McCulloch, G. (1996) 'Teacher professionalism and curriculum control', in I. Goodson and A. Hargreaves (eds) *Teachers' Professional Lives*, London, Falmer, pp. 56–74

Herzberg, F. (1968) *Work and the Nature of Man*, London: Staples Press

Hillage, J., Pearson, R., Anderson, A., and Tamkin, P. (1998) *Excellence in Research on Schools*, London, DfEE

Hoffman, J. V. (1999) 'What do reading teacher educators want from reading research? A call from the hall', *Issues in Education: Contributions from Educational Psychology*, 5 (1), pp. 77–83

Hoyle, E. (1975), 'Professionality, professionalism and control in teaching', in V. Houghton, R. McHugh and C. Morgan (eds), *Management in Education: The Management of Organisations and Individuals*, London: Ward Lock Educational in association with Open University Press, pp. 314–20

Husén, T. (1997) 'Educational research and policy-making' in J. P. Keeves (ed.) *Educational Research, Methodology, and Measurement: An International Handbook* (2nd edition), Oxford, Pergamon, pp. 251–7

John, P. (1998) *Analysing Public Policy*, London, Pinter

Jongmans, K., Biemans, H., and Beijaard, D. (1998) 'Teachers' professional orientation and their involvement in school policy making', *Educational Management and Administration*, 26 (3), pp. 293–304

Keats, D. M. (1997) 'Interviewing for clinical research', in J. P. Keeves (ed.) *Educational Research, Methodology, and Measurement: An International Handbook* (2nd edition), Oxford, Pergamon, pp. 306–10

Keeves, J. P. (1997a) 'Introduction: methods and processes in educational research', in J. P. Keeves (ed.) *Educational Research, Methodology, and Measurement: An International Handbook* (2nd edition), Oxford, Pergamon, pp. 277–85

Keeves, J. P. (1997b) 'Introduction: towards a unified view of educational research', in J. P. Keeves (ed.) *Educational Research, Methodology, and Measurement: An International Handbook* (2nd edition), Oxford, Pergamon, pp. 1–7

Keeves, J. P. and McKenzie, P. A. (1997) 'Research in education: nature, needs, and priorities', in J. P. Keeves (ed.) *Educational Research, Methodology, and Measurement: An International Handbook* (2nd edition), Oxford, Pergamon, pp. 236–43

Keeves, J. P. and Sowden, S. (1997) 'Descriptive data, analysis of', in J. P. Keeves (ed.) *Educational Research, Methodology, and Measurement: An International Handbook* (2nd edition), Oxford, Pergamon, pp. 296–306

Kelly, A. (1989) 'Education or indoctrination? The ethics of school-based action research', in R. G. Burgess (ed.) *The Ethics of Educational Research*, Lewes, Falmer, pp. 100–13

Kennedy, M. (1999) 'A test of some common contentions about educational research', *American Educational Research Journal*, 36 (3), pp. 511–41

King, R. (1978) *All Things Bright and Beautiful? A Sociological Study of Infants' Classrooms*, New York and Chichester, Wiley

Kirst, M. W. (2000) 'Bridging education research and education policymaking', *Oxford Review of Education*, 26 (3&4), pp. 379–91

Lacey, C. (1977) *The Socialisation of Teachers*, London: Methuen

Lampert, M. (2000) 'Knowing teaching: the intersection of research on teaching and qualitative research', *Harvard Educational Review*, 70 (1), pp. 86–99

LeCompte, M. D. and Goetz, J. P. (1982) 'Problems of reliability and validity in ethnographic research', *Review of Educational Research*, 52 (1), pp. 31–60

LeCompte, M. D. and Preissle, J. (1993) *Ethnography and Qualitative Design in Educational Research*, San Diego, CA, Academic Press

Levin, J. R. and O'Donnell, A. M. (1999) 'What to do about educational research's credibility gaps?', *Issues in Education: Contributions from Educational Psychology*, 5 (2), pp. 177–229

Locke, E. (1969) 'What is job satisfaction?', *Organizational Behavior and Human Performance*, 4, pp. 309–36

Loughran, J. (1999) 'Researching teaching for understanding', in J. Loughran (ed.) *Researching Teaching*, London, Falmer, pp. 1–9

Luttrell, W. (2000) ' "Good enough" methods for ethnographic research', *Harvard Educational Review*, 70 (4), pp. 499–523

McIntyre, D. (1997) 'The profession of educational research', *British Educational Research Journal*, 23 (2), pp. 127–40

McIntyre, D. (1998) 'The usefulness of educational research: an agenda for consideration and action', in J. Rudduck and D. McIntyre (eds) *Challenges for Educational Research*, London, Paul Chapman, pp. 188–206

Maslow, A. H. (1954) *Motivation and Personality*, New York: Harper and Row

Merriam, S. B. (1988) *Case Study Research in Education: A Qualitative Approach*, San Francisco, Jossey-Bass

Miles, M. B. and Huberman, A. M. (1988) 'Drawing valid meaning from qualitative data: toward a shared craft', in D. M. Fetterman (ed.) *Qualitative Approaches to Evaluation in Education*, London and New York, Praeger, pp. 222–44

Miles, M. B. and Huberman, A. M. (1994) *Qualitative Data Analysis: An Expanded Sourcebook* (2nd edition), Thousand Oaks, CA, Sage

Mortimore, P. (2000) 'Does educational research matter?', *British Educational Research Journal*, 26 (1), pp. 5–24

Mortimore, P., Sammons, P., Stoll, L., Lewis, D., and Ecob, R. (1986) *The Junior School Project: Main Report, Part C*, London, Inner London Education Authority, Research and Statistics Branch

Mumford, E. (1972) *Job Satisfaction: A Study of Computer Specialists*, London, Longman

Nias, J. (1980) 'Leadership styles and job satisfaction in primary schools', in T. Bush, R. Glatter, J. Goodey, and C. Riches (eds) *Approaches to School Management*, London: Harper and Row, pp. 255–73.

Nias (1981) 'Teacher satisfaction and dissatisfaction: Herzberg's "two-factor" hypothesis revisited', *British Journal of Sociology of Education*, 2 (3), pp. 235–46

Nias, J. (1985) 'Reference groups in primary teaching: talking, listening and identity', in S. J. Ball and I. F. Goodson (eds) *Teachers' Lives and Careers*, Lewes, Falmer Press

Nias, J. (1989) *Primary Teachers Talking: A Study of Teaching as Work*, London, Routledge

Nias, J. and Groundwater-Smith, S. (eds) (1988) *The Enquiring Teacher: Supporting and Sustaining Teacher Research*, London, Falmer

Nias, J., Southworth, G., and Yeomans, R. (1989) *Staff Relationships in the Primary School: A Study of Organisational Cultures*, London, Cassell

Nisbet, J. (1997) 'Policy-oriented Research', in J. P. Keeves (ed.) *Educational Research, Methodology, and Measurement: An International Handbook* (2nd edition), Oxford, Pergamon, pp. 211–17

Oshagbemi, T. (1996) 'Job satisfaction of UK academics', *Educational Management and Administration*, 24 (4), pp. 389–400

Page, R. N. (2000) 'Future directions in qualitative research', *Harvard Educational Review*, 70 (1), pp. 100–8

Page, R. B., Samson, Y. J., and Crockett, M. D. (1998) 'Reporting ethnography to informants', *Harvard Educational Review*, 68 (3), pp. 299–334

Pendry, A. and Husbands, C. (2000) 'Research and practice in history teacher education', *Cambridge Journal of Education*, 30 (3), pp. 321–34

Pollard, A. and Tann, S. (1993) *Reflective Practice in the Primary School*, (2nd edition), London, Cassell

Popper, K. R. (1963) *Conjectures and Refutations: The Growth of Scientific Knowledge*, London, Routledge and Kegan Paul

Pratt, J. and Swann, J. (1999), 'The crisis of method', in J. Swann and J. Pratt (eds) *Improving Education: Realist Approaches to Method and Research*, London, Cassell, pp. 3–11

Pressley, M. and Allington, R. (1999) 'What should reading instructional research be the research of?', *Issues in Education: Contributions from Educational Psychology*, 5 (1), pp. 1–35

Pring, R. (2000a) *Philosophy of Educational Research*, London, Continuum

Pring, R. (2000b) 'Editorial: educational research', *British Journal of Educational Studies*, 48 (1), pp. 1–9

Pring, R. (2000c) 'Editorial conclusion: a philosophical perspective', *Oxford Review of Education*, 26 (3&4), pp. 495–501

Rajagopalan, K. (1998) 'On the theoretical trappings of the thesis of anti-theory; or, why the idea of theory may not, after all, be that bad: a response to Gary Thomas', *Harvard Educational Review*, 68 (3), pp. 335–52

Ranson, S. (1998) 'The future of educational research: learning at the centre', in J. Rudduck and D. McIntyre (eds) *Challenges for Educational Research*, London, Paul Chapman, pp. 47–66

Redefer, F. L. (1959), 'Factors that affect teacher morale', *The Nation's Schools*, 63 (2), pp. 59–62

Reeve, R. A. and Walberg, H. J. (1997) 'Secondary data analysis', in J. P. Keeves (ed.) *Educational Research, Methodology, and Measurement: An International Handbook* (2nd edition), Oxford, Pergamon, pp. 439–44

Riddell, S. (1989) 'Exploiting the exploited? The ethics of feminist educational research', in R. G. Burgess (ed.) *The Ethics of Educational Research*, Lewes, Falmer, pp. 77–99

Robertson, S. L. (1996) 'Teachers' work, restructuring and postfordism:

constructing the new "professionalism", in I. Goodson and A. Hargreaves (eds) *Teachers' Professional Lives*, London, Falmer, pp. 28–55

Robson, C. (1993) *Real World Research: A Resource for Social Scientists and Practitioner Researchers*, Oxford, Blackwell

Rosenholtz, S. (1991) *Teachers' Workplace: The Social Organization of Schools*, New York, Teachers College Press

Sachs, J. (1997) 'Reclaiming the agenda of teacher professionalism: an Australian experience', *Journal of Education for Teaching*, 23 (3), pp. 263–75

Sachs, J. (1999) 'Rethinking the practice of teacher professionalism', in C. Day, A. Fernandez, T. Hague and J. Møller (eds) *The Life and Work of Teachers*, London, Falmer, pp. 76–89

Saha, L. J., Biddle, B. J., and Anderson, D. S. (1995) 'Attitudes towards educational research knowledge and policy making among American and Australian school principals', *International Journal of Educational Research*, 23 (2), pp. 113–26

Salmons, Y. (2000) 'One teacher trainer's perspective on a sample of academic educational research papers', *Educational Studies*, 26 (2), pp. 229–45

Schön, D. A. (1995) *The Reflective Practitioner*, Aldershot, Arena

Scott, D. (2000) *Realism and Educational Research: New Perspectives and Possibilities*, London, Routledge/Falmer

Scott, D. and Usher, R. (1999) *Researching Education: Data, Methods and Theory in Educational Enquiry*, London, Continuum

Siegel, S. and Castellan, N. J. (1988) *Nonparametric Statistics*, New York, McGraw-Hill

Smith, K. R. (1976), 'Morale: a refinement of Stogdill's model', *Journal of Education Administration*, 14 (1), pp. 87–93

Stein, M. K., Smith, M. S., and Silver, E. A. (1999) 'The development of professional developers: learning to assist teachers in new settings in new ways', *Harvard Educational Review*, 69 (3), pp. 237–69

Strauss, A. and Corbin, J. (1990) *Basics of Qualitative Research*, Newbury Park, CA, Sage

Swann, J. (1999) 'Pursuing truth: a science of education', in J. Swann and J. Pratt (eds) *Improving Education: Realist Approaches to Method and Research*, London, Cassell, pp. 15–29

Sylva, K. (2000) 'Editorial', *Oxford Review of Education*, 26 (3&4), pp. 293–7

Talbert, Joan E. and McLaughlin, Milbrey W. (1996) 'Teacher professionalism in local school contexts', in I. Goodson and A. Hargreaves (eds) *Teachers' Professional Lives*, London, Falmer, pp. 127–53

Taylor, S. J. and Bogdan, R. (1984) *Introduction to Qualitative Research Methods: The Search for Meanings*, New York, John Wiley (2nd edition)

Thomas, G. (1997) 'What's the use of theory?', *Harvard Educational Review*, 67 (1), pp. 75–104

Timpane, P. M. (1997) 'Politics of educational research', in J. P. Keeves (ed.) *Educational Research, Methodology, and Measurement: An International Handbook* (2nd edition), Oxford, Pergamon, pp. 261–3

Tooley, J. (1999) 'The Popperian approach to raising standards in educational research', in J. Swann and J. Pratt (eds) *Improving Education: Realist Approaches to Method and Research*, London, Cassell, pp. 168–80

Tooley, J. with Darby, J. (1998) *Educational Research: A Critique – A Survey of Published Educational Research*, London, OFSTED

Troman, G. (1996) 'The rise of the new professionals? The restructuring of primary teachers' work and professionalism', *British Journal of Sociology of Education*, 17 (4), pp. 473–87

Trow, M. (1997) 'Policy analysis', in J. P. Keeves (ed.) *Educational Research, Methodology, and Measurement: An International Handbook* (2nd edition), Oxford, Pergamon, pp. 205–11

Vancouver, J. B. and Schmitt, N. W. (1991) 'An exploratory examination of person-organization fit: organizational goal congruence', *Personnel Psychology*, 44 (2), pp. 333–52

Veal, M. L., Clift, R., and Holland, P. (1989) 'School contexts that encourage reflection: teacher perceptions', *International Journal of Qualitative Studies in Education*, 2 (4) 315–33

Wellington, J. (2000) *Educational Research: Contemporary Issues and Practical Concerns*, London, Continuum

Weinert, F. E. (1997) 'Translating research into practice', in J. P. Keeves (ed.) *Educational Research, Methodology, and Measurement: An International Handbook* (2nd edition), Oxford, Pergamon, pp. 263–8

Weiss, C. (1995) 'The haphazard connection: social science and public policy', *International Journal of Educational Research*, 23 (2), pp. 137–50

Whitty, G. (2001) 'Teacher professionalism in new times', in D. Gleeson and C. Husbands (eds), *The Performing School: Managing Teaching and Learning in a Performance Culture*, London, RoutledgeFalmer, pp. 159–73

Williams, G., (1986), *Improving School Morale*, Sheffield City Polytechnic, PAVIC Publications

Williams, K. W. and Lane, T. J. (1975), 'Construct validation of a staff morale questionnaire', *Journal of Educational Administration*, 13 (2), pp. 90–7

Wilson, J. and Wilson, N. (1998) 'The subject-matter of educational research', *British Journal of Educational Research*, 24 (3), pp. 355–63

Wolcott, H. F. (1995) *The Art of Fieldwork*, Walnut Creek, CA, Alta Mira Press

Wray, D. (1997), 'Research into the teaching of reading: a 25 year debate', in K.Watson, C. Modgil and S. Modgil (eds) *Educational Dilemmas: Debate and Diversity Quality in Education*, London, Cassell, pp. 141–65

Wray, D., Medwell, J., Poulson, L., and Fox, R. (1998) *Effective Teachers of Literacy: A Report of a Research Project Commissioned by the Teacher Training Agency*, Exeter, University of Exeter

Young, I. P. and Davis, B. (1983) 'The applicability of Herzberg's Dual Factor Theory(ies) for public school superintendants', *Journal of Research and Development in Education*, 16 (4), pp. 59–66

Index